CURRENT ISSUES AND TRENDS IN EDUCATION

SECOND EDITION

CURRENT ISSUES AND TRENDS IN EDUCATION

JERRY ALDRIDGE

University of Alabama at Birmingham

RENITTA GOLDMAN

University of Alabama at Birmingham

Boston   New York   San Francisco
Mexico City   Montreal   Toronto   London   Madrid   Munich   Paris
Hong Kong   Singapore   Tokyo   Cape Town   Sydney

Executive Editor: Stephen D. Dragin
Series Editorial Assistant: Katie Heimsoth
Marketing Manager: Tara Kelly
Composition and Prepress Buyer: Linda Cox
Manufacturing Buyer: Linda Morris
Manufacturing Manager: Megan Cochran
Cover Coordinator: Elena Sidorova
Editorial-Production Coordinator: Mary Beth Finch
Editorial-Production Service: Publishers' Design and Production Services, Inc.
Electronic Composition: Publishers' Design and Production Services, Inc.

For related titles and support materials, visit our online catalog at www.ablongman.com.

Between the time Website information is gathered and then published, it is not unusual for some sites to have closed. Also, the transcription of URLs can result in unintended typographical errors. The publisher would appreciate notification where these errors occur so that they may be corrected in subsequent editions.

Library of Congress Cataloging-in-Publication Data
    Aldridge, Jerry.
        Current issues and trends in education / Jerry Aldridge, Renitta Goldman—2nd ed.
        p. cm.
    Includes bibliographical references and index.
    ISBN 0-205-48620-7 (alk. paper)
        1. Education—United States. 2. Education—Aims and objectives—United States.
    I. Goldman, Renitta L. II. Title.

LA217.2.A42 2006
370.973—dc22   2006046016

Printed in the United States of America

10 11 12 13 14 15 16 V0CR 16 15 14 13 12

CONTENTS

PART III CHANGING VIEWS OF ASSESSMENT AND INSTRUCTION

CHAPTER EIGHT

Social Promotion, Retention, and Alternative Possibilities   135

Janice N. Cotton

**PART IV   ISSUES IN ACCOMMODATING INDIVIDUAL
AND FAMILY DIFFERENCES**

CHAPTER NINE

**Teaching in Inclusive Settings: The Challenge and the
Opportunity to Engage in Inclusive Strategies   148**

PREFACE

Five years ago the first edition of *Current Issues and Trends in Education* made its way into classrooms in departments, schools, and colleges of education. At that time the No Child Left Behind Act had just been signed into law by George W. Bush, and September 11th had just changed the way we view the world, including (in some ways) how we teach and the purposes of education. In fact, the final changes for the first edition were mailed from the World Trade Towers in New York City on August 9, 2001. Yes, many profound changes have occurred since the first edition and these changes are reflected in the organization, content, and presentation of this second edition.

ORGANIZATION OF THE TEXT

This textbook provides an introduction to current issues in education. It is divided into four sections: political, economic, and historical issues and trends; evolving notions of human development and learning; changing views of instruction; and issues in accommodating differences. The titles of many of the chapters in the second edition have remained the same. This is true for most of Section One—Political, Economic, and Historical Trends in Education. Of course much of the content of section one has changed drastically because of political changes, demographic shifts, and dynamic issues related to the rights of children.

The second section, Evolving Notions of Human Development and Learning, which begins with Chapter 4, still includes the chapter on theoretical shifts in our understanding of children. However, parts of the chapter on brain research have been collapsed into Chapter 4, and a new chapter on changing curriculum practices has been added. Previously, this was part of the chapter on theoretical shifts; however, since the No Child Left Behind Act was enacted, this has moved to the forefront of current trends in education.

Changing Views of Assessment and Instruction, the third section, begins with Chapter 6, a new chapter devoted solely to the issues related to the No Child Left Behind Act. Chapter 7, Developmentally Appropriate Practice, deals with looming problems about using developmentally appropriate practice in the increasing push for accountability as measured by standardized tests, and the more direct instruction and transmission curricula that reportedly produce these. Social Promotion, Retention, and Alternative Possibilities completes section three as a growing issue in light of high school graduation exams and state testing scores now required to pass certain grade levels in some states.

Section Four, Issues in Accommodating Individual and Family Differences, involves the most changes for the second edition. Chapter 9, Teaching in Inclusive Settings, has been updated to consider conflicts between the Individual with Disabilities Education Act and the No Child Left Behind (NCLB) Act. Although the Individuals with Disabilities Act requires accommodations and modifications for children with disabilities, NCLB limits accommodations for testing and accountability. Multicultural Education and the Cultural Curriculum, Chapter 10, has been expanded to present more current vignettes and cases related to real-world problem solving. Gender issues are included in this chapter as well. In the first edition, it was a separate chapter; however, it is a vital part of diversity and we believe this topic should be included in Chapter 10. Chapter 11 is a new chapter, Working with Families, which was a badly needed addition. Working with diverse families was considered salient enough to make it an entire chapter.

Chapter 12 is also a much-needed additional chapter since the publication of the first edition. This chapter on discipline and classroom management describes issues and trends related to everything from rewards and punishment to sanctions by reciprocity.

Finally, this resource closes with an epilogue entitled "What's Next? Future Issues and Trends in Education," in which we discuss both the controversies and the prospects the future holds for education. Of course, we do not have a crystal ball, but collectively we have taught for more than 60 years and believe that we have seen the pendulum swings, surprises, leaps, and retreats. We hope you are intrigued, skeptical, inspired, and devastated by educational possibilities of the future.

ACKNOWLEDGMENTS

We were fortunate to have Steve Dragin as the editor for the second edition as well as the first. His continued support and encouragement made the task of preparing the second edition easier. Meaghan Minnick, our editorial assistant, was always available to answer questions and provide information requested with almost lightning speed. No book would be possible without the thoughtful suggestions of the reviewers. These include Kathleen A. Dolgos, Kutztown University of Pennsylvania; Kathy Hawks, Concord College; and Norma J. H. Patterson, Grand Canyon University.

Many thanks go to our families and friends. Jerry dedicates this book in memory of his father, J. Titus Aldridge, and in honor of his mother, Winnie Aldridge, who is still independent, vital, and active at 95 years of age. He also thanks the following family and friends for their support and encouragement: Cecil Michael Baker, Ricky Aman, Jessica and Bruce Capp, Susan Durant, Shaun Wiler, Maryann Pearson, Norman and Rebecca Sudduth, Trish Crawford, Anne

Watson Bauer, Patricia Kuby, Kay Emfinger, Milly Cowles, and Rozlani Embi. Also, a very special thanks and dedication go to Mirna and Moises.

Renitta sends much love to Jay, Suki, and Gili, who value her unconditionally; to family and friends; and to all others who tell the truth when it counts.

CURRENT ISSUES AND
TRENDS IN EDUCATION

CHAPTER 1

POLITICS AND EDUCATION

If I were a rich man, I wouldn't give any money to Learning.
I would amend the Constitution, and Congress will do it if you
suggest it to 'em. Have 'em pass a Constitutional
Amendment, prohibiting anybody from learning anything.
And if it works as good as the Prohibition once did, why, in
five years we would have the smartest race of people on earth.
—Will Rogers

Power and knowledge are inseparable (Giroux, 1993). In terms of education, politics plays a major role in the relationships between power and knowledge. Because power is always deployed strategically to advance a particular project, we can look at education as a political endeavor, fashioned by those in power.

ARE OUR POLITICIANS UP TO THE JOB?

Thomas Friedman, Pulitzer prize–winning columnist for the *New York Times* wrote from Singapore about the crisis of Hurricane Katrina. He compares the United States with Singapore in a state of crisis. "Singapore believes so strongly that you have to get the *best qualified and least corruptible* people you can into senior positions in the government, judiciary, and civil service, that its pays its leaders high salaries including Cabinet ministers, Supreme Court Justices, judges, and senior civil servants handsomely down the line. From its early years, *good governance matters*" (Friedman, 2005).

In the United States, by contrast, our discipline seems to have faded. "Last year we cut the National Science Foundation budget, indulging in absurd creationist theories in our schools and passing pork-laden energy and transportation bills in the middle of an energy crisis" (Friedman, 2005). "Our economy seems to be fueled lately by either suing each other or selling each others' houses" (Friedman, 2005). When other nations saw the pictures of our own citizens left dead, uncollected on the streets, armed looters ransacking shops, survivors desperate to be rescued, and racial divisions—these images truly were out of sync with what we imagined our country was about. How can America be a world leader if we allow these things to happen? "But it is not only government that doesn't show up when government is starved of resources and leached of all of its meaning. Community doesn't show up either, sacrifice doesn't show up, pulling together doesn't show up. We're all in this together doesn't show up" (Friedman, 2005).

Most presidential elections in the United States, for instance, emphasize education as a major issue throughout the 20th century and continue to do so at the beginning of the 21st century. We will explore the many ways in which politics drive education.

New York City, the largest city in the United States, serves as an example of how money, class size, and mayoral politics interact (Robinson, 2005). Having once told voters to judge him on his management of education in the city, Mayor Michael Bloomberg reacted jubilantly to the news on May 18, 2005, that the reading scores of the city's fourth graders had risen dramatically that year. Of the students taking the test, almost 60 percent met state standards, an increase of about 10 percent more than the previous year. But amid this good news, the fact remained that city students did worse on this type of exam than anywhere in the state of New York—10 percent worse. To meet this disparity or achievement gap, two solutions were offered: *Give money and reduce class size*—two hot topics for the future mayoral race.

A quarter of the city's student population in the early elementary grades remains in classes of more than 25 students, whereas, statewide, the average is 20. Class sizes become progressively larger as children advance through public school, with high school classes in the city typically numbering 34 students. Advocates of smaller class size, including the Teachers Union of New York, stress that reducing class size works toward improving education. They say that smaller class will allow students to get the individual attention they need and deserve (Robinson, 2005).

The Bloomberg administration seems not to agree. Smaller class size is not a priority. The mayor proposed that the 2006 budget include increases in funding—particularly for the mayor's "cherished" program that creates more *small schools*—but the budget has no additional money to cut class size. The focus aims at leadership training, secondary school reform, early childhood education and special education, and instruction for non-English speakers.

THE CONSERVATIVE BACKLASH

Conservative reasoning has dominated many political efforts at school reform during the past several decades. This is especially true of urban school reform. This discourse has centered on such issues as the back-to-the-basics movement, instructional objectives, and minimum competency testing. Overtly, the "basic skills" push, centered on standardized testing, has been in response to the changing character of work in postindustrial America.

Before the 1960s, urban school districts had students from a heavily white, ethnic, working-class background. General and vocational education prepared these students for clerical and trade union jobs that were available. There was also a small college preparatory program for whose who aspired to more. The available jobs in industry to high school graduates were often routine and unrewarding, but the pay was relatively high and some offered job security. Manual skills took a priority over literacy requirements. The high school curriculum had socialized the working class by teaching students how to be cooperative workers, with more offerings for technical skills than college preparation.

By the 1960s, however, business and state leaders began to discuss the mismatch between the literacy skills of high school graduates and the literacy requirements of new jobs in urban areas. Enrollment in vocational education was relatively high, but fewer jobs were waiting for these students (Gray, 1991). Developing countries became recipients of manufacturing jobs, and the good trade union jobs became less available. Data processing, janitorial, clerical, and service industry jobs replaced them. New entry-level jobs increasingly required more literacy because workers frequently had to refer to sets of standards in operating equipment and in recording data on forms. Students needed reading and writing skills, and competencies of a certain minimal ability (generally defined at about ninth grade) that could be used and adapted to a number of diverse work settings (Livingstone, 1985).

To respond to the new jobs for Americans, conservatives believed the curriculum needed revision in terms of minimal language decoding, comprehension, and processing skills. These were needed for students to become effective workers in the new service industry, data processing, maintenance, and paraprofessional fields. The curriculum took the form of workbooks, drill sheets, and fragmentation of skills into tiny pieces. Students would encounter these year after year. After awhile, many students had to enroll in remedial basic skills classes to pass minimum competency tests. Many were also placed in low-ability groups or courses that emphasized basic skills over subject area knowledge.

After several decades of this basic skills reform, schools have failed to achieve even the most limited objective of certifying that students will be functionally literate by the time they graduate. In fact, many students from lower socioeconomic areas have not stayed in school long enough to graduate.

Like the Vietnam War and the War on Poverty, the War on Illiteracy and the War on the High School Dropouts in urban schools have become so problematic, little hope is held for solving these battles any time in the near future (Carlson, 1998). The goals of No Child Left Behind, the George W. Bush's initiative on education, will be discussed in great detail in Chapter 7. Although the goals are worthy, the likelihood of their accomplishment remains questionable.

ARE WE LOWERING STANDARDS?

"Liberalism must not only lower or eliminate standards in order to achieve equality of results, it must deny that is doing so" (Auster, 2002). The author continues to relate that the College Board and the Educational Testing Service (ETS) has added an asterisk to their official transcripts for students who had taken tests under "nonstandard conditions." These conditions may be such practices as allowing extra time or being given a room by oneself. A man with a disability with an asterisk on his test scores for the Graduate Management Admissions Test (GMAT) was rejected at two business schools. He sued the ETS for violating his rights with the Americans with Disabilities Act. In response, the ETS agreed to eliminate the "disabled" asterisk from the GMAT and some other tests. The College Board has now followed suit; it dropped the asterisk from the SATs. "As a consequence, college-bound students are flocking to doctors and psychologists to get themselves diagnosed as disabled, a designation that will not only let them get time-and-a-half or double time on the SATs, but will hide the fact from admitting colleges" (Auster, 2002).

This action of hiding data from personnel at college admissions can be "a double-edged sword." Comparing the scores of two individuals who took the test (SAT) under different circumstances is not particularly "useful." One also needs to consider those who practiced the test (SAT), took preliminary courses in preparing for the SAT, or hired coaches for the SAT (Freedman, 2003).

If equality always seeks to suppress facts, on what basis do we argue that the asterisk should remain in the transcript—*fairness, level playing field, equality* (Freedman, 2003)? The issue is not that standardized tests have no value. Rather, the value is likely overstated given the impossibility of knowing all the variables. "Saying that liberals categorically reject stereotyping is like saying that conservatives categorically embrace a simplistic two-dimensional world in light of evidence to the contrary. We can all find examples of both behaviors, but citing them as representative is clearly not useful" (Freedman, 2003).

DISPARITIES BETWEEN CURRICULUM AND STUDENT NEEDS

Why have schools not been more successful in ensuring that students from lower socioeconomic backgrounds learn the literacy skills that are necessary for gainful employment? Many reasons are postulated, but a standout is how the curriculum is packaged. The curriculum is so highly rationalized and regimented that it lacks interest about students. How can students in the 21st century who are used to being entertained find anything interesting in routine workbooks, drill sheets, or even computer programs with similar formats? Individual seat work and rounds and rounds of pre- and posttesting just "don't turn them on." The curriculum itself fails to hold much motivation for urban students after they leave school. The new working-class jobs pay low wages and leave little room for advancement. These jobs offer little job security or health benefits. Workers often have to work several jobs to supplement their income to maintain their family's level of poverty. Although some jobs may be out there, fewer "good" jobs exist, given the growing disparities of power and wealth in the United States. A "basic skills" curriculum has become increasingly more difficult to sell to the students who suffer through it.

WHO CONTROLS THE SCHOOLS?

Proponents of the conservative backlash give considerable voice to local control, but local control does not seem to be how the agenda works. Several conditions keep the control of schools basically out of local hands. State-mandated minimum competency testing, the growing financial dependency of urban schools on the state resulting from chronic fiscal crises in urban schools, and the growing threat of direct state takeover of failing urban school districts keep local school districts under control. To challenge these curricular and educational power relations, black and Hispanic groups will need to fight for involvement in substantive rather than merely technical educational decisions (Carlson, 1998). Many blacks and Hispanics were drawn to major urban areas in the 1970s and later because they were seeking space to assume control of their own institutions, away from the control of a repressive white power structure. Local control, however, still escapes both urban and rural areas in terms of school reform (Lefebvre, 1979).

The conservative basic skills school reform movement has also affected gender power relations in the school. The reforms have taken for granted the bureaucratic and hierarchical chain of command in urban schools that rigidly subordinated female teachers, particularly elementary teachers, to male administrators. In education, the teacherproofing of the curriculum, which has been advanced through basic skills reform, has also been based on the masculine presumptions that female teachers are not intelligent enough to be seriously involved in important curricular decisions (Freedman, 1988).

The Democratic–Progressive Discourse

Although liberal groups have exerted some influence on policy *thinking*, they have had little influence on policy *making*. Liberal discourse has advanced concerns about equity and excellence, and urged a curriculum organized around higher order literacy skills, a college preparatory curriculum for all students, the need to professionalize teachers rather than "deskill" them, the need to personalize instruction rather than regiment it, and the need to promote "site-based management" (McLaren, 1998; Sizer, 1984). Liberalism, however, has failed to deliver fully on its promises either, even when liberal politicians have gained control of the state. This failure has to do with a failure to take on certain difficult questions about whose interests are being served by the current system of structured inequalities and what it will take to change the way power is arranged and distributed in schools (Grubb & Lazerson, 1998).

Do We Have Other Choices?

We must have alternative ways of looking at education other than the traditional conservative-versus-liberal agendas. Carlson (1998) talks about a democratic–progressive discourse in education that might better address the current crises in education. First, although a democratic–progressive discourse would move beyond an economically functional analysis of the curriculum, it would not completely reject economic or workplace considerations in curriculum decision making. On the contrary, the relationship between schoolwork and work in other important institutional sites in society should be encouraged.

Second, although the conservative state discourse has promoted functional literacy and liberal discourse has emphasized higher order literacy, democratic–progressive discourse would reconceptualize the curriculum around "critical literacy." In urban, rural, and low-income-area schools, students need to learn how to critique the practices that keep them subordinated and reflect on their own role in the social construction of inequalities. For teachers, critical literacy education implies a reconceptualization of the role pedagogy plays. Teachers need to undertake social criticism, to engage themselves in the struggles of their students (Giroux, 1990).

Third, educators must insist on restructuring teachers' work and organizing the school so that it is consistent with democracy in the workplace. Drastic changes are needed in the way schools are organized and how educational decisions are made. A shift in substantive decision making—taking power from bureaucratic state officials and placing it within local communities, schools, and classrooms—must take place.

Finally, a democratic–progressive discourse focuses attention on linking educational theory and practice with social and cultural movements. Social movements involve a collective articulation and appropriation of cultural values in advancing particular agendas for changing the distribution of power in society. To feign off crises, dominant groups in education have become quite adept at crisis management. However, should the various groups who have been disempowered by basic skills reforms—in ways related to their class, gender, and race—articulate their concerns as part of a common movement to challenge bureaucratic state discourse and practice in education, it might yet become possible to build a new democratic–progressive voice for change that looks beyond crisis management toward crisis resolution (Carlson, 1998; McLaren, 1998).

FEDERAL, STATE, AND LOCAL CONTROL

Recent and Future Political Challenges

Education and politics are inextricably intertwined. One of the real dangers facing education is not the refusal of the general public to recognize how embedded power and privilege are at all levels of everyday life, but rather the public prefers to act as if there were no such political linkages. The danger is the ability of the public sphere to exist relatively uncontested (McLaren, 1998). Current issues in education and politics include attitudes, policy, and educational reform. These trends will likely extend well into the 21st century.

Attitudes about Schooling

Who is most supportive of the public school system and its current reform efforts? According to McLaren (1998), it is those groups most advantaged by *wealth* and *power*. Those individuals disempowered on the basis of race, socioeconomic status, or gender are understandably less enchanted with the public school system and its current reform efforts. Groups lobbying for minority positions on issues dealing with social, racial, and welfare concerns are being labeled within the conservative agenda by spokespersons such as Rush Limbaugh and Shawn Hannady as ethnocentric or separatist. This ideological position sounds an alarm for the demise of the white culture. It also shrouds domination in a white sheet of race, class, and gender purity by prohibiting questions of racism, sexism, homophobia, and class oppression (McLaren, 1998).

Another attitude that stirs the debate concerns values based on characteristics of *religion* and *education*. The legacy of U.S. Supreme Court Chief Justice Rehnquist, according to some (Farris, 2005; Stone, 2005) was to bring religion into the schools. The question avoided in this debate, according to Seljack

(1991), has to do with how religion and nationalism work together in ways that are debilitating to education and that promote racism. For instance, (religious and/or political) fundamentalists who make an issue of censorship have not been confronted by an educational system committed to curricular practices that examines the relationship among religion, nationalism, and racism in our schools (Seljack, 1991).

Although conservatives put forth their agenda and attitudes, critical theorists also have notions related to education and politics. Those who support a critical pedagogy perspective present an attitude of discontent and outrage that contests the hegemony of prevailing definitions of the every day as the "way things are." They believe teaching must be transformed into acts of dissonance, refusing to accept the existing relations of power. Students are encouraged to make critical judgments about what society might mean and what is possible or desirable outside existing configurations of power and privilege (Minh-ha, 1988).

POLICY ISSUES RELATED TO EDUCATION

Shapiro and Purpel (1998) described the Clinton years on the issue of education as policies without meaning. They acknowledge some accomplishments, although shallow in scope and effect. These include the shift in emphasis toward early childhood as welcomed and overdue, the Clinton initiative to make college loans more available, and the administration's proposals to encourage more flexibility and innovation in teaching and educational programs at lower levels.

However, the Clinton years brought an increased emphasis on the notion that public education exists to serve the needs of corporate America. Clinton defined education primarily in *vocationally related* terms. This discourse was not new, but it was disappointing that Clinton's administration tried to frame public discourse of education in economic terms. Public education is more than a place to teach workers how to use machines or master technology. Individuals need to learn about cooperative work, collective responsibility, the negotiation of priorities, and conflict resolution.

Little occurred during the Clinton years to change the decision-making process in schools. There was much rhetoric but little action. Schools must adopt a different approach to decision making in the 21st century. They will need to become what John Dewey called "laboratories of democracy." These are places where students of all ages begin to experience empowerment in their everyday lives. In this sense, vocational education becomes not simply job training, but a genuine form of critical, cultural education in which the broad human, economic, social, and environmental consequences of one's work can be and often are in question. Unfortunately, our public schools are rarely places where students learn what it means to live and work in a democratic environment (Shapiro & Purpel, 1998).

Goals 2000, the major education bill of the Clinton administration in 1994, was a push for national standards and methods of assessment throughout public education. This added emphasis on so-called performance standards, thereby reinforcing the uncritical and uncreative character of public education. Trends toward conforming were exacerbated. With Goals 2000 came more testing and more emphasis on accountability. Schools were already consumed and obsessed with testing. In fact, since the 1980s, the number of standardized tests administered to students has increased by almost 400 percent. The laudable notion of public accountability in education has been reduced to obsessive and harmful charting of test numbers. Teachers have been forced to teach to the test to keep their jobs. The result for teachers is content that is without creative or imaginative character (Shapiro & Purpel, 1998). The greatest disappointment in the Clinton administration was *not what had been proposed, but what was missing*. Clinton's approach was highly technocratic in its stress on making systems more effective and efficient, and in its view of education as an investment in human capital. Educationally, it was a perspective without "heart or soul." It was a time when the Right had been willing and able to invoke moral claims and purposes in its social and cultural agendas. The Left, in contrast, continued to defend church–state separation and academic freedom, but offered a view of education that was largely bereft of spiritual affirmation or moral conviction (Shapiro & Purpel, 1998).

Clinton and his advisors should have learned that education is more than higher test scores, advancing industrial productivity, and improving human capital. Real educational reform has to be linked to the struggle for a politics of meaning, asserting clearly that at the core of the educational enterprise are questions of human purpose and social vision: What does it mean to be human? How should we live together? Education should be understood as a cultural act, a process by which adults and children learn what it means to live with others in a community.

According to Shapiro and Purpel (1998), the Clinton legacy is a deep sense of social irresponsibility. This irresponsibility is mirrored in the callous and ubiquitous use of guns, fathers who refuse responsibility for their children, the rapacious corporate behavior that produces a toxic environment, and Wall Street speculators who make fortunes at the expense of the American workers. Communal values and concerns have declined (Shapiro & Purpel, 1998).

The George W. Bush Educational Initiatives

The current administration has identified three significant initiatives (Bush, 2001):

I. Leave no child behind.
   Current statistics indicate nearly 70 percent of American children entering the fourth grade are academically behind. This initiative is to be realized by the following.

- Increasing accountability for student performance
- Focusing on what works
- Reducing bureaucracy; increasing flexibility
- Empowering parents
- Limiting federal dollars to interventions that work

II. Rally the armies of compassion through faith-based community initiatives. This can be accomplished by
- Welcoming charities as partners
- Creating a White House panel
- Establishing five Cabinet departments committed to this initiative

III. Enact the New Freedom initiative. This can be accomplished by
- Removing barriers for Americans with Disabilities
- Continuing the spirit and process of the Americans with Disabilities Act (ADA) legislation signed by his father, George Bush
- Increasing federal funding
- Providing low-interest loans for educational use of technology

Misguided Educational Reform?

Although, to some extent, all times are unsettling because cultural development never stands still, in education the very existence of public education hangs precariously in the balance. Educational reform has taken many forms, but recent reforms have centered on either neoliberal thinking or neoconservative causes. Still, a crisis exists in the massive failure of urban school systems to reach inner-city youth and meet their needs. This failure is compounded by the collapse of job opportunities and fiscal crises of the postwelfare state. So where is the educational reform?

Giroux (1998) believes the United States is going through one of its most potentially dangerous historical junctures. Fear and racial hatred appear to be inspiring a major backlash against the gains of the Civil Rights Movement as affirmative action is openly attacked. Antiimmigration sentiment and legislation are sweeping the nation. At the state level, financial cutbacks and the restructuring of the labor force have weakened unions. Social services for the most vulnerable, including the poor, single women with small children, and older citizens are vastly undercut. Across the nation we are experiencing increasing discrimination and violence. Conservatives have well-organized campaigns to limit the rights and gains made by women. Acts of violence are increasing against women, homosexuals (both men and women), and racial minorities. A significant subtext of this conservative backlash is the increasingly growing attempt to decimate the public school system as part of a larger assault on the democratic foundations of political, social, and cultural life (Giroux, 1998).

As we have noted, schools are inextricably linked to the communities they serve through social, political, economic, and cultural interests. We have not realized the possibility for reforming public education and the fighting for social justice in education, particularly for those children of minority status. In the 1980s and 1990s, many school reform reports argued in favor of a wide range of additive reforms such as increased testing, more homework, a longer school year, and a longer school day. Others suggested a plethora of technical solutions ranging from the addition of specific course requirements to the public school curriculum to the addition or reduction of certain education requirements for teachers (Noll, 1997). For the most part, the reform efforts have been driven by what Giroux (1988) has called the ideology of the "quick fix."

Berliner and Biddle (1997) have tried to dispel some of the myths about educational reform created by federal politicians. They express the notion that some proposals for educational reform reflect only the personal experiences and prejudices of legislators, and that some are based on misunderstandings about problems of education (Waters, 1998). Many programs intended to improve our schools turn out to have little detectable effect, and result in creating serious problems for students and teachers.

Educators from diverse ideological and cultural backgrounds have drawn on the works of early scholars such as Dewey and Baldwin to show the political and ideological nature of schooling and ways in which schools often underserve the nonmajority students. The arguments have been ignored, dismissed, or have resulted in blaming the victims for educational inequalities. Schools ultimately bear the brunt of the broader economic and social problems that structure their existence.

Through recent school reform movements, the problems of American education have been systematically removed from public debate (Kretovics & Nussel, 1994). Giroux (1983) and Freire (1985) believe the schooling process is always structured on the values that embody specific cultural, social, political, and economic interests. Evaluators of educational reform must have a vision for change and the willingness to act on that vision. Evaluators must develop a framework that takes seriously issues of power and inequality as well as educational practice in the difficult process of reforming American public education (Shapiro & Purpel, 1998). Schools of education should adopt policies and practices that link their educational contributions closely with improved schooling for America's youth, or they should surrender their franchise (Maruyama & Deno, 1992).

Educational reform has not received much help from educational research and evaluation. For the most part, this discipline has remained both morally and politically innocent in theory, practice, and policy. Part of the innocence comes from the neglect of moral and political issues. The conception of social justice should not be considered a privilege for some, but rather a birthright for all (Sirotnik, 1990).

Another problem with educational reform is that issues of democracy, equality, race, gender, class, and poverty are rarely discussed in a comfortable forum of politics or education. The potential in education and the current crisis in public education are left basically in a silent space. Inquiry and discourse between public intellectuals remain fixed in a nonpolitical environment without values, beliefs, and passions. The ideology of neutrality has been internalized in the consciousness of most researchers in the modern university. However, no research, particularly on educational reform, can be politically neutral.

Social service institutions such as education are partly able to shape the systems to serve their own personal and professional goals at the expense of equitable delivery (Paul, 1991). Problems created by the limited voice of the politically weak are exacerbated in educational evaluation. When direct provision of services in virtual public monopolies of the "best teachers," the allocation of "best practices" in education, and the provision of high-quality curriculum and professional development training are centralized in higher socioeconomic communities, citizens within a lower socioeconomic community have limited capacity to improve public education.

Meanwhile, theoretical differences also abound. Neoconservatives are fighting efforts by progressives to make the curriculum more multicultural. Criticisms have been varied, but most substantive critical analyses have come from neo-Marxist and postmodern perspectives (Carlson & Apple, 1998). However, postmodernism brings with it some baggage that limits its critical potential. Postmodernism implies a dualism between the old and the new, which discourages us from seeing continuities and differences within modern and postmodern categories. In addition, some postmodern theorists have used language in a highly esoteric way that is quite hard to pin down to referents in the real world. Postmodern theory also risks abandoning the very idea of progress in a way that is dangerous culturally and politically. One of the characteristics of postmodernism is a growing cynicism about progress in education. Some limited progress has been made in public education that is worth keeping. Consequently, when the term *postmodernism* is used, it is with the recognition that it is a marker for a constellation of loosely related, contradictory discourses and practices (Carlson & Apple, 1998). So, once again, where is authentic educational reform?

CHALLENGES FOR EDUCATORS

Educators have *three major challenges* in the early part of the 21st century. First, we must be concerned with the *purposes* of our schools. Why have schools? Whether a teacher, school, or district elects to emphasize academic core subject matter, vocational training, or critical thinking, that choice is building toward the common purposes of helping students engage in lifelong learning, participate in a democratic society, and engage in productive life work. However, these choices limit or enhance certain opportunities for students. Careful consideration of what we teach, why we teach, and how the curriculum supports or marginalizes students is certainly a "top 10" issue facing us.

A second challenge is to rethink *how schooling in the 21st century will work.* How can schools make this transition? Many school districts are developing standards and working to redesign their schools. Still, much work remains regarding what these standards might be, how they can be framed, and how the curriculum, instruction, and organizational conditions can be reshaped to support the standards (Marsh, 1999).

A third challenge is *how schools and districts can embrace the new millennium as a source of celebration and reflection.* U.S. society and schools have found historical milestones to be important. For example, the World's Fair in Chicago set a sense of identity and momentum that shaped Chicago's progress for the next 50 years. The U.S. Bicentennial celebration and the 500th anniversary of Christopher Columbus's voyage were important events that shaped the American identity and the curriculum in U.S. schools (Marsh, 1999).

Change needs to occur in virtually all American school districts, including those serving the wealthiest suburbs. The success of the reform movement ultimately will be measured by its impact on our largest, most troubled public school settings. It is in our largest cities and our most rural districts that the job of schools is most difficult, given the often overwhelming social and economic circumstances of students who live in desperately impoverished neighborhoods (Oakes & Sirotnik, 1986).

The statement "All men are created equal" is found in the Declaration of Independence and Lincoln's Gettysburg Address. For educators, it has meant that American schools are charged with *offering every child equality of educational opportunity.* Throughout the period of public education in the 19th and 20th centuries, the concept of educational opportunity is one that has been implicit in most educational practices. No American white suburb, however, would tolerate the deplorable conditions taken for granted in the urban or rural public schools attended primarily by black, Hispanic, and poor children (Waters, 1998).

Big-city minority students by the tens of thousands are leaving school each year, some as dropouts, some as graduates, utterly unprepared to participate in and contribute to a democratic society (Oakes & Sirotnik, 1986). They lack the skills necessary for gainful employment and they lack the preparation to continue their education.

So what are we going to do about public education? This book looks closely at this and other related issues. In everything we do, politics plays a salient part, regardless of whether we choose to recognize it. As we look to the future, consider the following personal questions.

QUESTIONS

1. How have politics played a part in the educational system of my community?

2. What inequities exist in public education in my area?

3. What role do I play in educational reform?

4. Who decides what is taught and how it is taught in my state?

5. Is it possible for me to make a difference?

REFERENCES

Auster, L. (2002, October 7). The passing scene and what it's about viewed from the tradition-alist politically incorrect Right. *View from the Right*. [On-line]. Available: www.amnation.co/vrfr/archives/000838.html.

Berliner, D., & Biddle, B. (1997). *The manufactured crisis: Myths, fraud, and the attack on America's public schools.* New York: Longman.

Carlson, D. (1998). *The manufactured crisis: Myths, fraud, and the attack on America's public schools.* New York: Longman.

Carlson, D., & Apple, M. (1998). *Introduction to critical educational theory in unsettling times.* In D. Carlson & M. Apple (Eds.), *Power/knowledge/pedagogy* (pp. 1–38). Boulder, CO: Westview Press.

Dewey, J. (1952). *The school and society.* New York: Macmillan.

Farris, A. (2005, September 6). *Rehnquist leaves important legacy on church-state decisions.* Published by The Roundtable on Religion and Social Welfare Policy. [On-line]. Available: www.religionandsocialPolicy.org/news/article_print.cfm?id=3217.

Freedman, M. K. (2003). Disabling the SAT: Hoover Institution. [On-line]. Available: www.educationnext.org/20034/36.html.

Freedman, S. (1988). Teaching, gender, and curriculum. In L. Beyer & M. Apple (Eds.), *The curriculum: Problems, politics, and possibilities* (pp. 204–218). Albany, NY: SUNY Press.

Freire, P. (1985). *The politics of education.* South Hadley, MA: Bergin and Garvey.

Friedman, T. L. (2005, September 15). Storm shows meltdown in governance. *Birmingham News,* p. 13A.

George W. Bush Educational Initiatives. (2001, January 29). Updated. [On-line]. Available: http://pfie.ed.gov/inits.htm.

Giroux, H. (1983). *Theory and resistance in education: A pedagogy for the opposition.* South Hadley, MA: Bergin and Garvey.

Giroux, H. (1988). *Teachers as intellectuals: Toward a critical pedagogy of learning.* South Hadley, MA: Bergin and Garvey.

Giroux, H. (1993). *Border crossings.* London: Routledge.

Giroux, H. (1998). Education in unsettling times: Public intellectuals and the promise of cultural studies. In D. Carlson & M. W. Apple (Eds.), *Power/knowledge/pedagogy* (pp. 41–60). Boulder, CO: Westview Press.

Goals 2000: Educate America Act, Improving America's School Act of 1994, Washington, DC. [On-line]. Available: www.ed.gov/legislation/ESEA/toc.html.

GothamGazette.com [On-line]. Available: www.gothamgazette.com/article/education/20050520/6/1423.

Gray, K. (1991). Vocational education in high school: A modern phoenix? *Phi Delta Kappan, 72,* 437–445.

Grubb, W. N., & Lazerson, M. (1998). *The education gospel: The economic power of schooling*. Cambridge, MA: Harvard University Press.

Kretovics, J., & Nussel, E. (1994). *Transforming urban education*. Boston: Allyn & Bacon.

Lefebvre, H. (1979). Space: Social product and use value. In J. W. Freiberg (Ed.), *Critical sociology: European perspectives* (pp. 285–295). New York: Irvington Publishers.

Limbaugh, R. (1994). *See, I told you so*. New York: Simon and Schuster.

Livingstone, D. (1985). Class, educational ideologies, and mass opinion in capitalist crisis. *Sociology of Education, 58*, 8.

Marsh, D. (1999). Getting to the heart of the matter: Education in the 21st century. In D. Marsh (Ed.), *ASCD Yearbook: Preparing our schools for the 21st century* (pp. 1–12). Alexandria, VA: ASCD.

Maruyama, G., & Deno, S. (1992). Research in educational settings. Newbury Park, CA: Sage.

McLaren, P. (1998). *Life in schools: An introduction to critical pedagogy in the foundations of education* (3rd ed.). New York: Longman.

Minh-ha, T. (1988). Not you/like you: Post-colonial women and the interlocking questions of identity and difference, *Inscriptions, 3/4*, 71–77.

Noll, J. (1997). *Taking sides: Clashing views on controversial educational issues* (9th ed.). Guilford, CT: McGraw-Hill.

Oakes, J., & Sirotnik, K. (Eds.). (1986). *Critical perspectives on the organization and improvement of schooling*. Hingham, MA: Kluwer-Nijhoff.

Paul, S. (1991). *Accountability in public services: Exit, voice, and capture*. Washington, DC: The World Bank.

Robinson, G. (2005). *Money, class size, and mayoral politics.*

Seljack, D. (1991). Alan Davies on racism. *The Ecumenist, 29*, 13–14.

Shapiro, H., & Purpel, D. (1998). *Critical social issues in American education* (2nd ed.). Mahwah, NJ: Lawrence Erlbaum.

Sirotnik, K. A. (1990). Evaluation and social justice: Issues in public education. In K. A. Sirotnik (Ed.), *New directions for program evaluation* (Vol. 45). San Francisco: Jossey-Bass.

Sizer, T. (1984). *Horace's compromise: The dilemma of the American high school*. Boston: Houghton-Mifflin.

Sterling, B., & Sterling, F. (1996). *Will Rogers speaks*. New York: M. Evans.

United States Department of Education. (1998). *Twentieth Annual Report to Congress on the Implementation of the Individuals with Disabilities Education Act*. Washington, DC: Author.

United States Department of Education. (2005, November 17). *ED priorities and initiatives.* [On-line]. Available: www.ed.gov/about/inits/ed/index.html.

Waters, G. (1998, November 3). Critical Evaluation of Education Reform [On-line]. Available: http://olam.ed.asu.edu/epan/v6n20.html.

CHAPTER 2

CHANGING DEMOGRAPHICS AND DIVERSITY

People who understand demographics understand two-thirds of everything.
—David Foot

Canadian author David Foot (1996) titillates the reader by suggesting that most of us are not sure that we understand two-thirds of anything. We are swishing around the demographic tea leaves in an attempt toward enlightenment. Unfortunately, the future they predict may make us wish we had stuck with coffee.

POPULATION STATISTICS

According to The World Factbook (2005), the population in the United States is 295,734,134 and is growing by 0.92 percent yearly. Our people are living longer as well. The life expectancy at birth for females is 80.67 years; for males, 74.89 years. The following is the current breakdown of America by *race:*

White	77.1%
Black	12.9%
Asian	4.2%
Native American and Alaskan Native	1.5%
Native Hawaiian and Other Pacific Islander	0.3%
Other	4%

The following is the current breakdown of America according to *religion* (The World Factbook, 2005):

Protestants	52%
Roman Catholic	24%
Mormon	2%
Jewish	1%
Muslim	1%
Other	10%
None	10%

By further investigating the U.S. population, the reader will find the following demographics:

- One in four Americans is a baby boomer.
- By 2025, the nation's elderly population will have grown 80 percent.
- During the Revolutionary War, less that 10 percent of American households owned a gun.
- In the year 2000, Beverly Hills, California, which represents less than 1 percent of the population, donated more than $500,000 in presidential contributions. Watts, also in the Los Angeles area, donated a total of $250. (Frey, Abresch, & Yeasting, 2004)

Most Americans are immigrants or descendants of immigrants who arrived in the United States during the past 200 years. The majority of these migrants to the United States were European. The origins of immigrants change over time, as do their numbers and the effect they have on U.S. population growth. The volume of legal migration has fluctuated since the 1930s. Immigration has accounted for an increasing portion of population growth as American women are having fewer children. The U.S. Census Bureau projects that the U.S. population will reach more than 400 million (403,687,000 people) by 2050 (Population Reference Bureau, n.d.).

THE U.S. ECONOMY: AN OVERVIEW

The United States has the largest and most technologically powerful economy in the world with a per-capital gross domestic product (GDP) of $40,100 (The World Factbook, 2005). In this market-oriented economy, private individuals and businesses make most of the decisions, and the federal and state governments buy needed goods and services predominantly in the private marketplace.

The war in March/April 2003, between a U.S.-led coalition and Iraq, and the subsequent occupation of Iraq, required major shifts in national resources to the military. The rise of GDP in 2004 was undergirded by substantial gains in labor productivity. The economy suffered from a sharp increase in energy prices during the second half of 2004. Long-term problems include inadequate investment in economic infrastructure, rapidly rising medical and pension costs of an aging population, sizeable trade and budget deficits, and stagnation of family income in the lower economic groups.

TRENDS IN DEMOGRAPHY OF CHILDHOOD POVERTY

Fifty years after *Brown v Board of Education* and 40 years after President Johnson declared a war on poverty, many minority and lower income children still lack a fair chance to live, learn, thrive, and contribute in America. In a great nation such as the United States, where resources abound and democracy is the rule, individuals should be able to live in safety, security, and at a manageable comfort level. Unfortunately, this quality of life is not the case for many of our youngest residents. Although adults are vulnerable to injustices, children, by the nature of their dependency, are particularly vulnerable to victimization. One out of every five children is poor during the first three years of life—the time of greatest brain development. Marian Edelman, President of Children's Defense Fund (CDF), points out that an American child is born without health insurance every minute. "The United States is flunking the test that states that the morality of a society is how it treats its children" (CDF, 2003).

The underlying dynamics of poverty in the United States is changing. A troubling trend in recent decades is the growing disparity in the distribution of America's wealth. The number of Americans living below the poverty level in the United States has continued to increase during the past three decades. The rates for the number of children living in poverty have also increased (Fujiura, 1999). Poverty increasingly has become a phenomenon of children, the most vulnerable segment of the population. Nearly 4 in 100 black and Hispanic children live below the poverty threshold, and the majority of these live in female-headed single-parent households (Dalaker & Naifeh, 1998).

AMERICANS ON THE MOVE

The total population in the United States grew about 10 percent between 1990 and 1999, but the growth pattern varied across the country. The fast growth occurred in the West, especially among several "Rocky Mountain" states (Arizona, Colorado, Idaho, Nevada, and Utah). Slower population growth (a 5 percent change or less) was recorded among states in the Midwest and the Northeast.

Among the southern states, Georgia had the biggest gains, but substantial growth occurred in Florida and Texas (Hodgkinson, 1998). Most immigrants move for economic reasons. Some, however, move out of fear of political repercussions (Hodgkinson, 1998). Migration is the most difficult component to predict and is the most affected by government policies, such as control of borders. In 1998, 660,477 immigrants were admitted legally to the United States. Many foreigners, however, also enter this country illegally each year. The exact number of persons migrating illegally to the United States is unknown, but estimates range from 100,000 to 500,000 per year (Hodgkinson, 1998, p. 3).

An incredible number of people move every year—about 43 million. It may be possible, if not probable, for an elementary school teacher to report that she started the year with 24 students in September and still had 24 the following May, but that 22 of them were different children (Hodgkinson, 1998).

In the 21st century, the U.S. population continues to move south and west (Crowley, 2005). According to the U.S. Census Bureau (2000), by 2030, three states—California, Florida, and Texas—will encompass nearly half the nation's population growth. By 2011, Florida will surpass New York as the third most populous state. California and Texas will have the first and second largest populations respectively. Arizona and North Carolina are expected to displace Michigan and New Jersey on the top 10 list of the most populous states.

When examining population movement in the eastern half of the country, a picture emerges of suburban growth around declining urban cores in major cities. This pattern is very important when considering poverty among children. Although poverty is not increasing in cities as a whole, it is increasing in the *inner ring of suburbs*. If the criterion for poverty status is the increased number of children eligible for free and reduced-price lunches, then poverty exists in those inner rings of older suburbs.

Teacher Mobility

Each year teachers enter, leave, and move within the K–12 workforce in the United States. This move affects not only the composition of teachers at individual schools and the institutional stability of these schools, but also the demographics and qualifications of the teacher workforce as a whole. The U.S. Department of Education's National Center for Education Statistics (NCES, 2005), through surveys, tracks teachers' whereabouts to gather comprehensive information on many aspects of education that provide numbers and trends. Questions frequently asked include

- How many new teachers are hired each year?
- What are the characteristics of these new hires?
- How do the proportions of new hires differ by school control and poverty?
- How many teachers do schools lose at the end of the year?
- How do turnover rates differ by school control and poverty?

- How long have teachers been at the same school when they leave?
- Why do teachers leave? (National Center for Education Statistics, 2005)

The following data summarize the information collected from the 1999–2000 and 2000–2001 surveys that answers these questions.

New Hires

At the start of the 1999–2000 school year, 17 percent of the teacher workforce included new hires at their school. Only a relatively small percentage of the workforce (4 percent) included new teachers that school year.

- New teachers, delayed entrants, and recent graduates represent 27 percent of new hires. Experienced teachers, transfers, and returning teachers made up the majority (74 percent) of new hires in the 1999–2000 school year.
- In general, new hires were more likely to teach "out of field" than continue teaching. The average age of these new-hire teachers was 29, suggesting that many do not enter the teaching field right out of college.
- Private schools are more likely to have new hires than public schools. No measurable difference was found between low- and high-poverty public schools.

Transfers

- About half of teacher turnover can be attributed to the transfer of teachers between schools.
- Teachers transfer to public schools at higher rates than to private schools. Public school teachers in high-poverty schools are twice as likely as their counterparts in low-poverty public schools to transfer to another school.

Left Profession

- The percentage of teachers who retired at the end of the 1999–2000 school year was small relative to rates of total turnover—only 2 of 16 percent.
- The percentage of teachers who like teaching and took a job other than elementary or secondary teaching at the end of that school year was twice as large as that of teachers who retired (4 percent vs. 2 percent). Teachers who took a job other than elementary or secondary teaching were disproportionately male.
- The percentage of teachers who left teaching for family reasons, to return to school, or for other reasons was less than 2 percent. Virtually all teachers who left for family reasons were female. Teachers who left to return to school had an average of 4 years of teaching.
- Private school teachers are more likely to leave teaching than public school teachers.

- Teachers who left at the end of the school year most commonly identified retirement (20 percent) as a reason for leaving teaching, followed by family reasons (16 percent), pregnancy/childrearing (14 percent), wanting a better salary and benefits (14 percent), and wanting to pursue a different kind of career (13 percent).
- Both teachers who left teaching and teachers who transferred reported a lack of planning time, too heavy a workload, too low a salary, and problematic student behavior among their top five sources of dissatisfaction with the school they left. (National Center for Education Statistics, 2005, pp. 1–2)

The Average American Family

For the first time in U.S. history, fewer than 25 percent of all American households are made up of married couples with children. The "traditional" American family—two parents and one or more children younger than the age of 18—now represents only 23.5 percent of all American households. These statistics show the numbers are falling. In 1990, 25.6 percent represented traditional families; in 1960, 45 percent was the representation. Increasing by some 72 percent since 1990 is the number of unmarried persons living together as couples—in 1990, 3.19 million; in 2000, 5.47 million (Longley, 2002).

By the year 2056, "average" U.S. citizens will trace their descent to Africa, Asia, the Hispanic countries, the Pacific Islands—almost anywhere but white Europe. The statistical meaning of the word *minority* is quickly losing its significance, especially in U.S. classrooms (Valuing diversity, 2004).

CHANGING SCHOOL DEMOGRAPHICS

With the changing face of America and its public schools, valuing diversity is no longer merely a social goal. The future of our society depends upon our ability to talk effectively with one another, to reach mutual understanding, and to realize that in diversity there is strength (Kugler, 1999).

Consider the following challenges for education:

- Diverse groups are expected to comprise more than 40 percent of the population by 2020 and 50 percent by 2040.
- Poverty and single-parent families are the two variables that are most highly correlated with increased risk for childhood disability.
- Culturally and linguistically diverse students drop out of school at a much higher rate than white students.
- Culturally and linguistically diverse students are both underrepresented and overrepresented in special education (Heward, 2006).

THE OVER- AND UNDERREPRESENTATION
IN SPECIAL EDUCATION PROGRAMS

An educational trend that will not go away and continues to concern federal, state, and local educational policy makers is the overrepresentation and underrepresentation of certain "minority" populations in special education programs.

Since the Individuals with Disabilities Education Act passed in 1975, tremendous benefits have been experienced today. Approximately six million children with disabilities enjoy their right to a free, appropriate public education. These benefits, however, have not been equitably distributed. Minority children with disabilities all too often experience inadequate service—unnecessary isolation from their nondisabled peers, and low-quality curriculum and instruction. Moreover, inappropriate practices in both general and special education classrooms have resulted in the misclassification and hardship for minority students, particularly black and Native American students. For example, in most states, black children are identified at one and a half to four times the rate of white children in the disability categories of mental retardation and emotional disturbance. Nationally, Hispanic and Asian children are underidentified in cognitive disability categories compared with whites. These data raise questions about whether the special education needs of minority children are being met (Losen, 2002).

Consider the following data collected by the Civil Rights Program at Harvard University (Losen & Orfield, 2002):

- In wealthier districts, black children, especially males, are more likely to be labeled mentally retarded. Native American children also showed this finding, but to a lesser degree than black children.
- Minority children with disabilities are underserved. Black children with emotional disturbances received high-quality early intervention and far fewer hours of counseling and related services than white students with emotional disturbances.
- Disturbing racial disparities were found in outcomes and in rates of discipline. Among high schoolers with disabilities, about 75 percent of black students, compared with 47 percent of whites, are not employed two years out of school. Three to five years out of school, the arrest rate for blacks with disabilities was 40 percent compared with 27 percent for whites. New data also indicate substantially higher rates of school disciplinary action and placement facilities for black students with disabilities.

Keme'enui (2000) argues that at the beginning of the 21st century, the risk factors that plagued children with diverse learning and curricular needs a decade ago have not diminished. In fact the risks these students face are more intense now, at the beginning of the new millennium, than at any time before. The Information Age and global economy will be unforgiving to workers with poor reading and literacy skills (U.S. Department of Education, 1999). Jobs requiring the most education and training will grow the fastest and pay the highest. Occupations that require a bachelor's degree or higher will average a 23 percent growth—almost double the 12 percent growth for occupations that require less education and training (U.S. Department of Labor, 1995). Students who are unable to negotiate the "new basic skills" (Levy & Murnane, 1996) will be left behind in the new economy of the 21st century. This picture becomes increasingly chilly when the most recent reports of the National Assessment of Educational Progress (NAEP) are considered. At the close of the 20th century, two in five fourth grade children could not read at a basic level. This means they could not comprehend or make simple inferences about fourth grade material (NAEP Reading Scores, 1999).

Concurrent with the cultural, familial, and sociological changes that are now occurring in the new millennium, educational leaders are requiring more of all students (Keme'enui, 2000). Students and teachers are asked to go beyond the acquisition of basic knowledge and skills to integrate thinking and content area knowledge in authentic problem-solving activities. As Resnick (1987, p. 7) stated, "Although it is not new to include thinking, problem solving, and reasoning in *someone's* school curriculum, it is new to include it in *everyone's* curriculum." "Everyone" at the close of the last century means more than 46 million children who will attend nearly 88,000 pre-K–12 public schools (National Center for Education Statistics, 1997).

Educational leaders also are calling for *curriculum standards* or goals that indicate what students have learned upon their completion of public school education. These standards have been developed and promoted by a range of professional organizations, each calling for curriculum changes for *all* students.

By developing curriculum standards, educators can improve student learning outcomes. They need, however, effective strategies and programs to teach and manage students with diverse learning and curricular needs. Unlike middle- and upper middle-class students who may receive substantial support for academic pursuits outside of school, diverse learners, especially children from low-income families, are more dependent on schools for their academic development and educational achievement (Alexander & Entwisle, 1996). In the final analysis, these students are more dependent on effective programs and strategies that consider their learning characteristics, such as delayed language development or lack of background knowledge, in the design and delivery of the curriculum content.

The standards also require educators to scrutinize more closely innovations in curriculum and instruction. Although reasonable expectations must be set for diverse learners, failure to accommodate the unique learning and curricular needs of diverse learners can place these students at greater risk.

The motive for addressing diversity can no longer be liberalism or obligation, but a question of self-interest (Hodgkinson, 1985) since, as Yates (1987) predicted for the year 2050, half the U.S. population is projected to be Hispanic, black, of Asian/Pacific descent, or Native American (Council of Economic Advisors, 1998). Society must recognize the contributions of minority groups and implement procedures to permit them equal access to power within society (Bauer et al., 1997).

Schools have changed from predominantly white institutions to multicultural environments (McIntyre, 1997). The 25 largest school systems have a student population comprised mostly of students from diverse backgrounds. Nonurban areas are also seeing such developments.

Although minority children make up 40 percent of elementary and secondary enrollment nationwide, minority teachers account for only 13.5 percent of the teaching force (Johnston & Viadero, 2001). The contrast in cultural backgrounds between teachers and students applies to an even greater extent in special education, in which students from diverse backgrounds are overrepresented in various programs for the special needs youth. McIntyre (1997) cites researchers who attribute this overrepresentation to, in part, the difference between expectations from the students' parents and their schools.

Defining Culture

Culture is a complex concept that anthropologists and sociologists have defined in a variety of ways. Before the 1960s it was typically defined as a pattern of behavior and customs. Today it refers to the integrated patterns of human behavior that include communication styles, customs, beliefs, values, and institutions that give a group with a common heritage a sense of "peoplehood" (McIntyre, 1997).

"Most contemporary social scientists view culture as consisting primarily of the symbolic, ideational, and intangible aspects of human societies" (Banks & Banks, 1994, p. 83). Banks suggests six major elements of culture: (a) values and behavioral styles, (b) language and dialects, (c) nonverbal communication, (d) awareness (of one's cultural distinctiveness), (e) frames of reference (normative worldviews or perspectives), and (f) identification (feeling part of the cultural group).

The works of Edward T. Hall—*Beyond Culture, The Silent Language*, and *The Hidden Dimension*—are classics in the area of intercultural study and vividly describe how humans can be unknowingly influenced by their culture. People from different cultures may perceive the world differently, unaware that other perceptions are even possible. Hall (1976) argues that most of us hold unconscious assumptions about what is appropriate in terms of personal space, interpersonal relationships, time, and ways of seeking truth (for example, scientific inquiry, meditation).

Hall (1976) portrays a continuum of sociocultural tightness to distinguish among cultures. Specific cultures may be described according to where they lay on the continuum between *high-context* cultures at one end and *low-context* cultures at the other end. In low-context countries such as the United States, Germany, and Scandinavia, interpersonal communication can take the form of a verbal message, a memo, or a computer program. Meaning is gleaned from the message, and what is said is more important than who said it. High-context cultures, such as southern European, East Asian, Arab, Native American, and Mexican, and those found in portions of the rural United States, are generally the opposite. Meaning must be understood in the setting or context in which the communication occurs. For example, in the Chinese language, many words may be pronounced in several different ways, depending on the context within which they are used.

High- and low-context cultures differ along many dimensions. For example, reasoning among high-context cultures is knowledge gained through intuition, spiral logic, and contemplation. Feelings are important. In contrast, among low-context cultures, reasoning is linear and logical. Knowledge is gained through analytical reasoning (for example, the Socratic method). Words are important. Interpersonal relations also demonstrate a strong contrast. To high-context cultures, the group is paramount. Among low-context cultures, the individual is paramount (Bennett, 2003).

Cultural diversity means that significant differences exist in students' performance and interactions in broad areas such as verbal and nonverbal communication, and in orientation modes such as conceptions of time, social values, and cognitive tempo. Cultural differences in learning may be especially obvious in three areas: learning styles, communication styles, and language differences.

Minority groups are those groups that have unequal access to power. They are, for the most part, considered by the majority as inferior or less worthy of sharing power in some way (Mindel & Habenstein, 1984).

Too many widespread myths and misconceptions about multicultural education hinder the truth to be revealed, according to Banks and Banks (1994). One common misconception is that multicultural education is an entitlement program and a curriculum movement for blacks, Hispanics, poor, women, and other marginalized groups (D'Sousa, 1991; Glazer, 1997). Major researchers and theorists in multicultural education agree that is a reform movement designed to restructure educational institutions so that *all* students, including white, male, and middle-class students, will acquire the knowledge, skills, and attitudes needed to function effectively in a diverse nation and world (Banks & Banks, 1994; Gay, 1995; Grant & Sleeter, 1997).

Winzer and Mazurek (1998) show other common misconceptions about multicultural education. Another misconception is that multicultural education is the study of cultures that are *not* American. The reality is that no matter when they arrive, all Americans develop and share many common values and experiences. The curriculum in multicultural education should reflect the culture of various groups as well as the shared national culture. Goals of multicultural education are erroneously thought to be implemented quickly and easily. Research, however, indicates that these goals cannot be achieved in a short time; the process is ongoing. Lastly, it is an error to believe that multicultural education is too difficult for younger children and should only be part of secondary programs. The truth is that multicultural education should begin in preschool.

Multicultural education consists of four interactive dimensions: (a) equity pedagogy, (b) curriculum reform, (c) multicultural competence, and (d) teaching toward social justice. Equity pedagogy seeks to achieve fair and equal educational opportunities for all of the nation's children, particularly minorities and the economically disadvantaged. Curriculum reform expands the curriculum from traditional course contents that are primarily monoethnic (in the United States this means Anglo-European) to multiethnic and global perspectives. Multicultural competence is the process of becoming multicultural, whereby an individual develops competencies in multiple ways of perceiving, evaluating, believing, and doing. The focus is on understanding and learning to negotiate cultural diversity within a single nation and among nations. Teaching toward social justice involves clearing up myths and stereotypes associated with gender, different races, and ethnic groups, and stressing basic human similarities. It helps to put an end to prejudice and discrimination, and to solve basic problems of inequity (Burnette, 1998).

Today, more than 30 percent of this society's school-age children and youth are ethnic minorities. Every attempt must be made to reduce cultural conflict that may result from cultural bias. Research on the characteristics of effectively integrated schools shows that a policy consistent with integrated pluralism has the best potential for realizing good race relations, academic achievement, and personal development among students.

HIGH SCHOOL GRADUATION RATES

Students who fail to graduate from high school face a very bleak future because the basic skills conveyed in high school and higher education are essential for success in today's economy. Students who do not receive these skills are likely to suffer significantly reduced earnings and employment prospects. Among those persons older than 25 years who failed to complete high school or receive a General Education Degree (GED), 55 percent report no earnings in the 1999 Current Population Survey of the U.S. Census (2000) compared with 25 percent of those with at least a high school degree or GED. Students who failed to graduate high school are also significantly more likely to become single parents and have children at a younger age. These students who do not graduate high school are significantly more likely to rely on public assistance or be in prison. In essence, high school graduation is a very important predictor of young people's prospects in life (Kaufman, Kwon, & Klein, 2000). A recent revision of high school graduation rates in the United States (Greene, 2002) examined the rates for major racial and ethnic groups in each state as well as the nation. Main findings were the following:

- The national graduation rate for the class of 1998 was 71 percent. For white students the rate was 78 percent whereas it was 56 percent for black students and 54 percent for Hispanics.
- Among the 50 largest school districts in the country, Cleveland City had the lowest overall graduation rate with 28 percent, followed by Memphis, Milwaukee, and Columbus.
- The NCES finds a national completion rate of 86 percent for the class of 1998. The discrepancy between the NCES finding and this report's finding of a 71 percent rate is largely caused by the NCES, which counts GED graduates and others with alternative credentials as high school graduates, and it relies on a methodology that is likely to undercount dropouts.

President George Bush was asked at a March 2001 Education Conference in Washington, DC, two questions: (a) Why is so little attention paid to the high dropout rate among the nation's black children? (b) Why does the U.S. Department of Education (DOE) annually report incomplete and sometimes inaccurate dropout statistics to the general public? The president's aide responded: "The truth hurts, and few people want to share the truth about underperforming students these days" (Greene, 2001).

HIGH SCHOOL DROPOUT AND COLLEGE ENROLLMENT RATES

High school dropout and college enrollment rates for blacks have decreased substantially during the last 30 years (from 33.5 percent in 1974 to 17 percent in 2002). High school dropout rates, however, still remain *50 percent higher* than the white dropout rate in 2002 of 11 percent. College enrollments show a similar pattern of increase among blacks and whites during the 30-year span. Black college enrollment increased from 36 percent in 1960 to 57.7 percent in 2002. College enrollments for whites increased by 45 percent during the same 44-year time period (Greene, 2002).

EMPLOYMENT

Employment rates vary considerably over time as the U.S. economy cycles. The U.S. Department of Labor publishes labor statistics monthly. As of October 2005, both the number of unemployed persons, 7.4 million, and the unemployment rate, 5.0 percent, were little changed. The unemployment rate has ranged from 4.9 to 5.1 percent since May 2005. The unemployment rates of adult women (4.6 percent), teenagers (15.9 percent), whites (4.4 percent), and blacks (9.1 percent) showed little or no change during a month's period of time.

Generally black unemployment has been twice as high as white employment (Greene, 2002).

HEALTH

Although mortality rates have declined for both blacks and whites since 1954, a disparity persists. In 2002 the morality rate for black men was 27 percent higher than the mortality rate for white men. Mortality rates are 14 percent higher for black women than white women (Greene, 2002).

CRIME

Victimization rates for homicide have declined 27 percent for blacks but still are seven times the rate of white homicide victimization. The number of incarcerated blacks has increased 80 percent since the 1950s. In the late 1980s, the number of incarcerated blacks surpassed the number of incarcerated whites (Greene, 2002).

Gangs

A senior policy analyst for Latin America reported to a subcommittee on the Western hemisphere of the U.S. House of Representatives in Washington, DC, on April 20, 2005 (Johnson, 2005). He pointed out that, throughout history, youth gangs have flourished wherever there have been population shifts and unstable neighborhoods. However, recent growth in numbers and global affiliation of gangs poses a public security threat. Gangs that flourished in Los Angeles during the 1960s now have fraternal links to some 130,000 to 300,000 members in Mexico and Central America. They have expanded across the United States to both major cities and rural communities on the eastern seaboard. Activities range from defending neighborhood turf to extortion, armed robbery, alien smuggling, and drug and arms trafficking. Their transnational nature is facilitated by fluid migration across "porous" borders, incarceration with experienced criminals in U.S. prisons, and weak law enforcement in Mexico and Central America. Although no evidence links them with terrorist networks, these gangs could provide a source of willing young collaborators (Johnson, 2005).

Although gangs represent a tiny fraction of the general population, authorities have estimated that there are only 700,000 street gang members compared with some 280 million American residents. Yet the disproportionate growth and violence in gangs is now a major concern among law-abiding citizens. The number of cities reporting gangs went from 270 in 1970 to more than 2,500 in 1988 (about an 800 percent increase) (Johnson, 2005). In 2002, there were 21,500 gangs and 731,500 active gang members in the United States, 85 percent of whom reside in large cities. Gangs, however, are also present in rural areas as well. Twenty-seven percent of municipalities between 2,500 and 50,000 people now have had trouble with gangs (Johnson, 2005).

Most of the trouble starts with instability in neighborhoods. Broken homes, violent role models, and access to drugs feed the growth of gangs. In *migrant communities*, people forced to move as a result of difficult circumstances seldom have much choice but to settle in disorganized, transient neighborhoods. Foreigners, unprepared to compete in an adopted society, find their survival and integration especially difficult. In 2004, U.S. authorities caught some 10,000 unaccompanied juveniles trying to cross the southwestern borders hoping to join relatives already in the United States.

Estimates are that there are between 10 to 12 million Hispanic aliens in the United States who are attracted to seasonal work in agriculture and construction in both urban and rural communities. According to the *1999 National Youth Gang Survey* (Johnson, 2005), the racial and ethnic composition of U.S. gang members is 47 percent Hispanic, 31 percent black, 13 percent white, 7 percent Asian, and 3 percent "other."

ADDITIONAL TRENDS

- Persistent residential segregation, particularly in the Northeast and Midwest (Logan & Oakley, 2004)
- School district segregation (manifested at the regional level) (Losen & Orfield, 2002)

PEOPLE OF COLOR LIVING IN CONCENTRATED POVERTY

Poverty rates for both blacks and whites have declined since 1959 (60 percent and 50 percent respectively), but disparity persists. Black individual and family poverty rates are currently twice the rate of whites. The same pattern is true for *child poverty*—that is, black child poverty rates were approximately double the rates of white child poverty in the 1990s (Watson, 2003).

In 2000, more than two-thirds of people living in concentrated urban poverty were black or Hispanic. In 1999, half of poor rural blacks and Native Americans were found in concentrated poverty rural areas. One-third of all poor rural Hispanics are found in areas of high poverty. The Economic Research Services of the Brookings Institute summarizes the following results of its research: (a) Fifty years ago *Brown* offered a promise of desegregation. (b) Grutter challenged us to achieve it in another 25 years (Haskins, 2005).

IS DIVERSITY A MYTH? IS SINGLING OUT ONE GROUP FOR SPECIAL PRIVILEGES SIMULTANEOUSLY PATRONIZING AND BIGOTED?

When Burt Prelutsky was a story writer for the Dick Van Dyke TV series *Diagnosis Murder*, he worked with four other writers. He analyzed their geographical backgrounds: two were born in New York, one in New Orleans, one in Chicago, one in a small town in Utah. Regarding religion, three were Jews, one was an ex-Catholic, and one was a Mormon. Two believed in God, one was an atheist, one was an agnostic, and "one of us suspected that the higher power was none other than Dick Van Dyke" (Prelutsky, 2005). Two believed in capital punishment, two were opposed, and one wasn't certain. Looking at educational attainment, three were college graduates and two weren't. Regarding their leisure activities, two rooted for the Yankees, one for the Red Sox. Two thought the other three were nuts for liking baseball (Prelutsky, 2005). In Prelutsky's (2005) opinion, although they were all whites, all in their 50s, and all TV writers, they were as different as any random group of five adult Americans is likely to be. Hardly a day went by that "we were not arguing about something, and it was only rarely about a story point or a murder clue in one of our scripts. However, some would insist that because none of us was black or Hispanic, we couldn't possibly be a model of true diversity in the workplace" (Prelutsky, 2005).

The idea that the governing admissions body at the University of Michigan would award 20 points out of a possible 120 to a prospective student for merely being black, states Prelutsky, is simultaneously patronizing and bigoted. "After four decades of Head Start programs, court-mandated busing, and billions of dollars earmarked for minority education, why do black students require 20 points to compete?" (Prelutsky, 2005).

What Groups Are Considered Diverse Learners?

American education upholds the concept of the learner as an individual. When one provides a "list" of groups, other groups may feel omitted. Some groups also overlap, such as gifted learners and women. In this chapter we have omitted "learners with special needs," although they are recognized as a major category of diverse learners and those who have been victims of discrimination. Learners with special needs receive comprehensive discussion in the chapter on inclusion (see Chapter 9), as well as strategies for teaching (see Chapter 7) and exclusion from testing (see Chapter 6). In addition, any discussion of diversity needs to acknowledge that no one group is homogeneous in their characteristics. For purposes of discussion, however, some consensus needed to be reached. We therefore limited our "groups" of diverse learners in this chapter to the following: blacks, Hispanics (Latinos), Asians and Pacific Islanders, and Native Americans.

Blacks

Until recently, blacks were the largest distinct cultural group in the United States. As of April 1, 2000, 36.4 million persons fell into this group. This number represents 12.9 percent of the U.S. population (U.S. Census, 2000). However, recent statistics indicate that 13 percent of the population is now Hispanic (U.S. Census, 2002). This percentage indicates that the Hispanic population in the United States now exceeds the black population.

Acceptable nomenclatures for this cultural group include African Americans, black Americans, blacks, or people of color. *People of color* is preferred by many when addressing groups or discussion issues that affect several ethnic groups (Marofsky, 2005).

Although blacks are a diverse group, represented within every social, economic, and occupational status in U.S. society (Cartledge & Middleton, 1996), their lifestyle in the United States is characterized by some significant differences from the mainstream. The present-day black population, like many other ethnic groups, is several generations removed from their original land. Many practices and habits, therefore, have been lost, dropped, simulated, or modified. The greatest influence on many black families is the lifestyle of their parents or grandparents who lived in the southern United States (Cartledge & Middleton, 1996).

Historically, black rites revolve around food. The society is based on religious ceremonies, cooking, feasting, and growing food. The popular term for black cooking is *soul food.* Many of these foods are rich in nutrients—collard greens, yellow vegetables, legumes, beans, rice, and potatoes. Other parts of the diet, however, are low in calcium, potassium, and fiber, and high in fat. With the high incidence of diabetes, hypertension, obesity, and heart disease, some blacks have paid a high price for this lifestyle. Economically disadvantaged families may have little choice to eat what is available at low cost, because fresh fruits and vegetables, and lean meat and seafood are not as readily available at low cost. The educator may want to discuss ways of obtaining quality foods despite economic limitations, such as growing small gardens in community sites; shopping at large supermarkets rather than small, neighborhood markets; and developing budgeting clubs. Any opportunity to include information on exercise and teaching their children and teenagers good nutrition should be taken. Of course, not all blacks adhere to poor diets and have no concern about their health. Taboos about childrearing and nursing are usually common or adhered to if older grandparents are heads of households. Few teenage black mothers breast-feed, but it is common with older mothers.

Since the 1960s, various forces appear to have had a significant impact on the black family structure and other life circumstances. By 1992, the proportion of black households including married couples had dropped to 47 percent from the 68 percent recorded in 1970, with females heading 46 percent of the family households. At least 30 percent of black families lived below the poverty line. Approximately 62 percent of black children younger than 18 were reported to live in single-parent households, a circumstance that appears largely influenced by education and economics. Children living with two parents began to outnumber those in single-parent homes once the parents' education reached the college level.

Poor economic, educational, and racial conditions converge to create the most dismal of all statistics—those pertaining to mortality and crime. Beginning in infancy, blacks have a much higher mortality rate. Total life expectancy is lower than for whites.

The family is viewed as an extremely important and resilient cultural tradition in the black community (Franklin, 1988). The extended black family may assume various constellations, reaching as far as cousins or community members. Three times as many black children (compared with whites) younger than the age of 18 are likely to live with grandparents. Similarly, blacks have a greater tendency than whites to include extended family members in their households (Cartledge & Middleton, 1996). Although it may be debated whether this extended family phenomenon is more a function of economics or of culture, it is a well-established pattern within black families.

As with other groups, the black family plays a central role in the socialization of children, equipping them with "adaptive strategies" that will lead to a positive sense of self and attainment of desired social goals (Harrison, 1990). Although the "strong" black mother is often blamed for her children's failures, research shows the black mother to be a major force in the aspirations and achievement of her children (Hardy, 1993; Shade, 1994; Slaughter & Epps, 1987). However, the impact of unrelenting poverty, premature parenting, family isolation, and chronic joblessness has weakened the potential positive effects for families of low income.

The Kirwan Institute for the Study of Race and Ethnicity (2004) gives an academic overview of desegregation. The Institute compared social and economic measures over 50 years (1954–2004). Benchmarks of social/economic health included education, housing, poverty, employment, income, crime, health, and other contemporary concerns. When dealing with statistical data over a period of time, groupings may vary. For example, data taken from the 1960 time period included all nonwhite races (in other words, no individual black data was collected) (Freeman, 2004).

Rapid Hispanic* Migration to the United States

One of the pitfalls of using demographics for predictive purposes is that some have targeted geographical locations where the number of minorities is growing rapidly, whereas the actual number of minorities in those areas may be quite

*Note: U.S. Census Bureau (2005) identifies *Hispanic* as a person of Latin American descent (including persons of Cuban, Mexican, or Puerto Rican origin living in the United States who may be of any race or ethnic group (white, black, Asian, and so on). The U.S. Census Bureau recognizes that there are differences of opinion within the Hispanic or Latino community in terms of identification. For example, Hispanic may be considered a "colonialist" term, because Hispanic refers to Spain. However, we are using the identifiers used by the federal government or references by authors.

small. Los Angeles, in contrast, yields both large numbers of minorities and a rapidly growing population of Hispanics. Among the nation's 271 urban areas, Los Angeles is home to fully one-fifth of the Hispanic population. It also ranks first in total Hispanic population growth, netting 18 percent of all Hispanic population gains in the nation between 1990 and 1996. The city's Hispanic growth comes not only from Mexican and Latin American immigrants, but also from continued high birth rates among long-term Hispanic residents (Tumulty, 2001).

Growth Patterns during the Last Decade of the 20th Century

Since the 1990s, Hispanics have moved according to the "size-begets-growth phenomenon." The importance of the immigrant gateways in both attracting and maintaining large Hispanic populations was evident in the rankings of the top metropolises for numerical gains in Hispanics. The 10 metro centers with the largest Hispanic populations also had the largest population gain. Together they attracted more than half (52 percent) of new Hispanic immigrants between 1990 and 1996. The top 10 collectively house 58 percent of the nation's Hispanic residents (Frey, 1998). These metropolises include Miami, where Cubans have come; New York City, gaining Dominicans, Puerto Ricans, and other Caribbean-origin Hispanics; and Chicago, a continuing magnet for Mexicans. The other seven metro areas lay close to the Mexican border and continue to build on large, existing Latin American residents.

Politics: Hispanic Past Performance

By the end of the 20th century, the political ramifications of the increasing Hispanic population in the United States continued to intrigue observers. Where Hispanics were newly arrived, they only had just begun to "crack" the city school boards, councils, and county commissions. As one seemingly savvy politician remarked, "We're on the ground floor of political empowerment" (Tumulty, 2001, p. 74). Why had Hispanic political influence lagged behind the census? Several reasons were postulated. Hispanics in the United States are more dispersed than other minorities such as blacks. This means that legislators had to work harder to identify districts where potential voters live. In addition, the census figures could not yet accurately give the polls the true picture of voting power. More than one-third of Hispanics are younger than voting age, and those who are eligible to vote often do not. Although the Hispanic and black populations in the United States are roughly the same size, six million more blacks are registered to vote. Turnout rates for Hispanics are even more disappointing for the more educated and affluent.

On June 11, 2001, *Time* magazine published a special issue entitled "Welcome to Amexica." The article, "Courting a Sleeping Giant," reported:

> The biggest political news of the 2000 Census was that Hispanics—more than half of them tracing their roots to Mexico—have become the largest minority group in the U.S., surpassing African Americans at least six years sooner than expected. Where that's happening is turning out to be as surprising as how fast. Of the

congressional districts that saw the biggest increases in their Latino populations over the past decade, not a single one is in a state along the Mexican border. Rural areas saw huge growth in Hispanic populations. By the end of 2001, four of the eight largest U.S. cities may have Hispanic mayors. (Tumulty, 2001, p. 74)

Politics: Current Performance

The prediction has come true. The 2005 elections witnessed Hispanic mayors elected in Los Angeles, Tampa, Houston, San Antonio, and Austin, Texas, among other sites (Casey, 2004).

Irene Bustamante, diversity director for the MGM Mirage in Las Vegas, Nevada, and founder of the Latina Network, a nonprofit group affiliated with the Reynaldo Martinez Institute, said campaigns trying to win the Hispanic vote have not succeeded because they have not reached the right target audience— *women*. She contends that women are the decision makers in most Hispanic culture and "have the power to educate and influence future generations" (Casey, 2004, p. 3). Typically most Hispanic women have voted with the Democratic Party, but their message to Hispanics has been very generic and has alienated Latinas (Casey, 2004, p. 3). Bustamante said that the nation's two major parties have not delivered a message that focuses on education, crime, and social issues.

Undocumented Hispanics have become a major political issue. Recently, a U.S. senator proposed a fence be built from San Diego, California, to East Texas—a 2,000 mile fence. The justification to "keep out" undocumented immigrants is now being discussed as a national security issue as much as an immigration problem (Fine, 2006).

Asians and Pacific Islanders

Asian refers to those having origins in the Far East, Southeast Asia, or the Indian subcontinent, including (for example) Cambodia, China, Indian, Japan, Korea, Malaysia, Pakistan, the Philippine Islands, Thailand, and Vietnam. *Pacific Islander* refers to those having origins in Hawaii, Guam, Samoa, or other Pacific Islands. The Asian and Pacific Islander population is not a homogenous group. Rather, it comprises many groups who differ in language, culture, and length of residence in the United States. Some of the Asian groups, such as the Chinese and Japanese, have been in the United States for several generations. Others, such as the Hmong, Vietnamese, Laotians, and Cambodians, are comparatively recent immigrants. Relatively few of the Pacific Islanders are foreign born. While Asian Americans "only" make up about 5 percent of the United States's population as of May 2005, they are one of the fastest growing ethnic groups in terms of percentage increase in the United States. Although the Asian American community has received considerable scrutiny, some of its citizenry contend they still in many ways remain misunderstood (Asian Nation, 2005).

As with Hispanics, Asians have given the large gateway metros the greatest numerical growth. Together, Los Angeles, New York City, and San Francisco account for 39 percent of the nation's gains in Asian residents since 1990. Forty-three percent of all U.S. Asians live in these three urban areas. Chinese immigrants are heavily drawn to New York City, Filipinos to Los Angeles, and both show a large presence in San Francisco (Reeves & Bennett, 2003).

As stated, Asians do not fall into one homogenous group. Instead, their different cultures are based on their country of origin, region, social class, religion, and educational attainment. Although some basic beliefs and values are shared by all Asian groups, teachers need to recognize the diversity among Asian American students (Mathews, 2000). The value of honoring the family is very strongly embedded in South Asian and Southeast Asian children. Therefore, the sharing of personal problems with an outsider is regarded as a disgrace for the family. Furthermore, parents of these children tend to shy away from school involvement. The father is considered to be the head of the family and the decision maker. The mother is the nurturing parental figure who takes care of the household. Age is revered and, consequently, grandparents have a high status in the family. They are respected and cared for by other family members. Interpersonal relationships are more formal among this population than the informal and spontaneous nature found in the U.S. macro culture. Affection is not openly displayed. Rude and inappropriate behaviors are attributed to poor parental upbringing (House & Pinyuchon, 1998).

In terms of economic success, beyond a high school degree, a white person with a college degree can expect to earn beyond basic salary more than $2,000 per year. In contrast, returns on each additional year of education for a Japanese American is only $440, and for a Chinese American, $320. For blacks, it is even worse at only $284 (House & Pinyuchon, 1998).

Asian Americans also are underrepresented in the political arena. Just like blacks, Hispanics, and Native Americans, in the corporate world Asian Americans are also underrepresented as CEOs, board members, and high-level supervisors.

Asian Americans are still the targets of much prejudice, stereotyping, and discrimination. The persistent belief, for instance, that "all Asians are smart" puts a tremendous amount of pressure on many Asian Americans. Many, particularly Southeast Asians, are not able to conform to this unrealistic expectation, and in fact have the highest high school dropout rates in the country.

Research shows that Asian Americans are the fastest growing victims of hate crimes in the United States. Successful Asian Americans may have extraordinary levels of socioeconomic achievement, but it is very unlikely that many of them will say they no longer experience discrimination because of their Asian ethnicity (Asian Nation, 2005).

Native Americans

Native Americans include native American tribes, Alaskan natives, and Aleuts. They are referred to by a number of names. In common use they are native people, American Indians, and Native Americans. They comprise 1.5 percent of the total population (Smelser, Wilson, & Mitchell, 2001). According to the 2003

U.S. Census Bureau estimates, a little more than one-third of the 2,786,652 Native Americans in the United States live in three states: California, at more than 400,000; Arizona at about 300,000; and Oklahoma, at more than 275,000. As of 2000, the largest tribes in the United States by population were Cherokee, Navajo, Choctaw, Sioux, Chippewa, Blackfeet, Iroquois, and Pueblo. The U.S. Census data of 2000 also showed that Tlingit was the most populous Alaskan native tribe; 17,200 respondents reported being Tlingit alone or in combination with one or more other races or Native American or Alaskan native tribes. Other Alaskan native tribes with 5,000 or more responses were Alaskan Athbascan, Eskimo, and Yupi'ik.

More than half a million Native Americans lived on the reservation or other trust land. The most populous reservation was the Navajo Nation, which spans portions of Arizona, New Mexico, and Utah.

From the outset, European colonists had, at best, lived in an uneasy truce with the Native Americans (Native Americans, 2005). When Native Americans cooperated, they were inexorably displaced from the most favorable lands, and frequently the process involved violence. During the early 21st century, Native American communities are an enduring fixture in the United States, administering their own services like firefighting, maintenance of natural resources, and law enforcement. Most Native American communities have established their own court systems to adjudicate matters related to local ordinances and to deal with various forms of moral and social authority vested in traditional affiliations within the community. To meet the housing needs of Native Americans, Congress passed the Native American Housing and Self-Determination Act in 1996. This legislation replaced public housing with a block grant program directed toward Native American tribes.

Gambling has become a leading industry. Casinos operated by many Native American governments in the United States are creating a significant stream of gambling revenue that some communities are beginning to use as *leverage* to build diversified economies. Native American communities have waged and prevailed in legal battles to ensure rights to self-determination and use of natural resources. Tribal sovereignty has become a cornerstone of American jurisprudence. Although many Native American tribes have casinos, they are a source of conflict. Most tribes, especially small ones, feel that casinos and their proceeds destroy culture from the inside out. These tribes have refused to participate in the gaming industry.

Military defeat, cultural pressure, confinement on reservations, forced cultural assimilation, outlawing of native culture and languages, forced sterilizations, the termination policies of the 1950s and 1960s, and slavery have had deleterious effects on Native Americans' mental and ultimately physical health. Contemporary health problems include poverty, alcoholism, heart disease, and diabetes (Native Americans, 2005).

As a consequence of efforts first to eliminate them, and then to assimilate them, many Native Americans have experienced a sense of alienation from Euro-

Americans. Spindler and Spindler (1984), working with the Menominee tribe, describe the responses of Native Americans to this sense of alienation, which include reaffirmation, withdrawal, constructive marginality, biculturalism, and assimilation. One group working on reaffirmation tries to recreate and sustain a recognizable Native American way of life. Another group of Native Americans was so torn by cultural conflict that they identify with neither traditional Native American nor European American culture. This group either withdrew into self-destruction through substance abuse or simply did nothing about the conflict (Spindler & Spindler, 1984).

EDUCATORS' COPING WITH CHANGING DEMOGRAPHICS

Educators who are serving rapidly changing communities must study local and national distributions as well as economic and social patterns. Across the country, people are facing the challenge of living as multicultural citizens.

Studies on immigration, migration, and fertility patterns indicate that by the year 2010, about 38 percent of people younger than the age of 18 in the United States will be black, Asian American, or Hispanic. In the next decade, experts predict that most immigrants will arrive in this country from Asia and Latin America. Although 90 percent will settle in the largest American cities (New York, Los Angeles, and Chicago), each area in the United States will host its own unique cultural blend. For example, a large concentration of Asians will settle in the western coastal United States and a large concentration of blacks will settle in the East and Southeast (Native Americans, 2005).

Among these immigrants, a tremendous diversity in cultures, economic, family situations, and educational levels exist within each ethnic group. The number of low-income, single-parent, and homeless families is on the rise. Drug and alcohol abuse, teenage pregnancy, suicide, and school dropout rates continue to challenge educators.

As the nation's ethnic diversity increases, schools must develop ways to respond creatively to produce multicultural environments that accommodate diverse student backgrounds and native languages. Educators must commit to second-language learners. Issues of racism and ethnicity must be addressed. Teaching materials should be examined for racial, cultural, or gender biases (Klauke, 1989).

Some of the questions asked by members of a school team in San Diego are the following:

- Are all students actively involved in classroom instruction?
- Are reading materials provided in languages other than English for students who need them?
- Are there overt signs of racism in the school? (Klauke, 1989)

Is Diversity a Myth?

We continue to hear conflicting reports about diversity. Large numbers of international immigrants to the United States in the early 1990s fostered the perception that the United States is becoming truly diverse. Riding in cabs in downtown New York City may lead you to think that America is growing more racially and ethnically diverse by the day. According to William Frey (1998), however, the "melting pot" simply *is not real.* Frey, a demographer and doctoral research scientist, analyzed U.S. Census Bureau population estimates for 1996 and 1997. His research concluded that population shifts during the 1990s show a continued geographical concentration of minority groups into *specific regions* and a handful of metro areas. Frey proposes that this concentration is particularly true for new immigrant minorities, namely Hispanics and Asians. These minorities typically enter the United States through limited-gateway cities and remain in those regions.

Granted, the term *Hispanic* was invented in the 1980 census in an attempt to describe the large numbers of people from South and Central America who were moving to the United States. In Florida, they are not identified as Hispanics; rather, they are called Latinos and Latinas. In Texas and California, they are identified as Chicanos and Chicanas (Hodgkinson, 1998). For the purposes of this chapter, however, the term *Hispanic* is used in its comprehensive sense to include all these groups.

Although some of the Asian minorities are trickling out of the gateway metros, the pace is relatively slow. According to Frey, the largest blocks of these minorities are clustered in only a few geographical areas. Most places beyond these "melting pots" are largely white, or white and black.

The Impact of Diversity on U.S. Education

During the past 20 years, U.S. immigration has brought to the nation's shores countless newcomers representing countries, languages, traditions, and religions underrepresented here in the past. At the same time, the schools have continued to acknowledge a need for inclusionary programming, not only for immigrants, but for those students with special needs. Linda Darling–Hammond of Stanford University summed up the challenge in her 1997 book, *The Right to Learn:*

> If the challenge of the 20th century was creating a system of schools that could provide minimal education and basic socialization for the masses of previously uneducated citizens, the challenge of the 21st century is creating schools that ensure—for all students in all communities—a genuine right to learn. Meeting this new challenge is not an incremental undertaking. It requires a fundamentally different enterprise.

Arthur Schlesinger (1992) paints a different perspective on immigration. In his book *The Disuniting of America*, he warns against the cult of multiculturalism.

Today's immigrants do not feel what our grandfathers did: the "pressure to assimilate." Because most immigrants come from nearby countries in this hemisphere, they do not experience what is called the *psychological guillotine* of being severed from their old country by distance and the difficulty of transoceanic travel.

Student Ethnic Demographics

The new language diversity in U.S. schools contrasts significantly with that of previous influxes of immigrants. It is extensive. For example, in Long Beach, California, once known as a haven for people moving from the American Midwest, more than one-third of the total enrollment of students in the public schools, K–12, today is from Southeast Asia. Furthermore, ties with the "old country" are easier to keep. Modern transportation and communication allow immigrant families to keep up contacts, and thus their languages and cultures. In one middle school in Long Beach, Cambodian families established daily lessons in Khmer for their children.

At one time schools fostered the concept of the melting pot—a policy that minimized one's cultural background in favor of assimilation. Although in today's schools, literacy in English is stressed, they also focus on understanding different cultures. Textbooks and other classroom resources attempt to provide a wide exposure to diverse cultures. Many teacher recruitment efforts are aimed at building much greater diversity among the teaching force.

Federal and some state programs provide funding for bilingual education—the strategy of learning some academic subjects in the native language while studying English. This strategy was used during the early part of the last century to keep German-speaking students in midwestern U.S. cities in public schools. Fear of foreigners after World War I led to a backlash against bilingual programs. A U.S. Supreme Court decision in the 1970s guaranteed language-minority students an appropriate education, and thus a return of bilingual or similar programs. Concern about the surge in immigration in California, however, contributed to voter approval of a referendum that severely limited bilingual classes in the state. U.S. Secretary of Education Richard Riley, however, endorsed dual-language immersion programs to help language-minority students maintain fluency in the home language while learning English, and to give English-speaking students a full opportunity to learn another language.

The impact of language diversity varies among states. Five states—California, Texas, Florida, New York, and Illinois—are experiencing the largest growth in language-minority enrollments. Diverse enrollments also tend to concentrate in central city schools. Almost all large urban districts now have more minority students than white students. Yet, even rural schools in states such as Kansas and Alabama are finding a growing number of language-minority families in their schools, attracted to the communities by low-skill industries.

What is different about the racial ethnic diversity in schools today is how these institutions are responding. In the past, school officials usually expected student achievement among minorities to be lower than that of white students. This expectation resulted in large percentages of ethnic and racial minority students being placed in remedial and/or vocational programs. They often dropped out of school before obtaining a high school diploma at much higher rates than white students. Education reforms, however, focus on higher standards for *all* students. The reforms present a special challenge to low-performing schools, which enroll mostly minority and/or low-income children. "Closing the gap" in achievement has become a priority for these schools, and there is some evidence of progress. Hispanic students, unfortunately, still lag far behind. Some states such as Texas require schools to show improved achievement among "subgroups" of students, meaning that overall scores cannot hide problems with minority students. Schools that are focusing on special help for low-performing minority students (for example, smaller classes, research-based early reading strategies, and motivation to prepare for college) show that minority student achievement often exceeds national averages (Lewis, 2000).

Religious Diversity

The United States, unlike many other countries, conducts a strict separation of church and state in its schools. Public funds are to be used for public school only, although a few states and cities now are experimenting with voucher programs that allow public funds to be spent at schools outside the public system, including religious (parochial) schools. Because of this separation, there is a private and parochial school sector in the United States. About five million students, or 10 percent of the K–12 enrollment, attend private primary and secondary schools. Although Catholic schools comprise half of private school education, the most rapid expansion is within the Muslim community.

CBS News (Brewer, 2005) reported a demographic trend toward "spirituality" among the United States yuppie population as this segment of the population approaches their 60s. According to the research undertaken by CBS, yuppies are seeking out "spirituality," whether in the form of established, organized religion or new formats for religion/spirituality.

Gender Bias—Girls as a Disadvantaged Population

Contrary to popularly held beliefs, girls continue to be a disadvantaged group relative to their male peers in the development of their gifted level abilities (American Association of University Women Educational Foundation, 1998). In a comprehensive review of studies across many cultures, the conclusions reached were that boys tended to be significantly more self-assured and better adjusted than girls. The boys demonstrated better self-control, less vulnerability, more pride, and higher subjective well-being. At early adolescence, girls showed evidence of lower self-esteem across all domains. A major longitudinal research program that followed high school valedictorians into adulthood catalogued a steady lowering of women's aspirations and goals, accompanied by a drop in their self-esteem—a decline that was not experienced by their male counterparts (Hulbert, 2006; Arnold & Sibley, 1995; Petersen, Silbereisen, & Sorensen, 1996).

Diversity in Achievement

Although schools are moving toward higher standards for all children, American K–12 education is providing for the exceptionally gifted and talented as well. Home schooling has become increasing popular as another route beyond public education to provide the standards that families want maintained. Church-affiliated schools also have served to reflect the standards of families. A more comprehensive discussion of this alternative can be found in Chapter 8. Affluent families maintain their separate education through exclusive private, college preparatory schools—a route that was taken by many of their forebears. Still, public education promises to provide a range of programs for all levels of ability. This promise led to the development of programs for the gifted and talented. Because of the differences in state laws and local practices, the number of students enrolled in these programs varies greatly—from 5 percent in some states to more than 10 percent in others. Although advocates always say more efforts and better funding are needed, schools use a number of methods to challenge the gifted. There are, for example, "pull-out" programs, in which students leave their regular classrooms several times a week to participate in enrichment activities. This is the most common program at the primary school level. Magnet high schools that focus on the arts, math, or sciences offer students more intensive work in these areas. High schools also offer a number of means for high-ability students to be challenged. They can, for example, take part in such programs as Future Problem Solving, Odyssey of the Mind, or the Great Books reading series. More than 60 percent of public high schools and 46 percent of nonpublic schools participate in the advanced placement (AP) program of the College Board. Very able teachers volunteer to teach AP courses that offer advanced work in academic subjects. AP exams are offered, and a good score on the exam qualifies the student for credit and/or enrollment in advanced courses at almost all four-year colleges and universities. About 30 percent of the students in AP courses in 1999 were minorities. Efforts continue to encourage high schools without AP courses, most of them in high-poverty, high-minority areas, to prepare teachers and students for AP courses (Lewis, 2000).

INADEQUATE ASSUMPTIONS ABOUT HUMAN DEVELOPMENT

Hundreds of theories of human development and intelligence have been offered since the recorded philosophical assumptions of Plato (Ceci, 1996). Modern psychological theories have been motivated by either genetic (Jensen, 1973) or contextual (Coles, 2000) assumptions. The nature/nurture controversy debated elsewhere (Ceci, 1996; Kamin, 1974) has revolved around assumptions and interpretations of IQ tests. Kamin (1974) argues that the IQ tests used in the United States have been fostered by men committed to a particular social view. The view, basically, is that those at the bottom of the scale are genetically inferior; consequently, the tests serve as instruments of oppression against the poor, the foreign born, and racial minorities.

Research and theories of scholars from diverse disciplines (Ceci, 1996; Coles, 2000; Dewey, 1938; Wozmak & Fischer, 1993) currently have converged to support a framework of human development that builds on developmental, cognitive, and social psychology, as well as anthropology, sociology, and genetics. Ceci (1996) suggests, "One's cultural context is an integral part of cognition because the culture arranges the occurrence or nonoccurrence of events that are known to affect cognitive developments, e.g., literacy" (pp. 95–96). Coles (2000) shares an illuminating quote from the anthropologist Theodor Adorno: "Culture might be precisely that condition that excludes a mentality capable of measuring it" (p. 7).

What is culture? How and by whom is it defined? Culture is closely intertwined with concepts of ethnicity, social class, and race. Williams (1999) offers the following definition: "Culture is the lens, crafted by history, tradition, and environmental conditions, through which groups view themselves, their environment, and their future, and shape their decision making, problem solving, and behavioral responses" (p. 93).

ETHNICITY IN AMERICA: BRIDGING THE GAP BETWEEN A HISTORY OF RACISM AND A FUTURE TOWARD EQUALITY IN DIVERSITY

America's strength has come from its origins—with a remarkable native population and many people from many places. Our strength has often come from our diversity. It would be a mistake, however, to believe that the United States has been free of racism. We have had a comparatively positive view of our immigrants and the lack of racial genocide compared with the levels seen in Germany and other places. However, our Jim Crow laws, our Japanese internment camps, and the fate of the Cheyenne in the San Creek massacre are but a few of the examples of the racism that has existed in the United States (Stoler, 1997).

Racism refers to the beliefs and practices that assume inherent and significant differences exist between the genetics of various groups of human beings. Racism assumes that these differences can be measured on a scale of "superior" to "inferior." These differences result in the social, political, and economic advantage of one group in relation to others (Stoler, 1997). Racism is a belief that race is the primary determinant of human capacities. There is a growing, but somewhat controversial opinion, that racism is a *system* of oppression, a nexus of racist beliefs (whether explicit, tacit, or unconscious), practices, organizations, and institutions that combine to discriminate against and marginalize a class of people who share a common racial designation (Stoler, 1997).

In the 20th century, thoughts of racial superiority and inferiority as inherently problematic and wrong began to grow. In the United States, much of the discourse relating to racial theory of this sort emerged in the years after the American Civil War, and European thinkers began to think of people in terms of linguistic "nations" more than they did "races." A turning point in racial thinking came with the rise of Adolf Hitler's nazism, which built much of its political agenda upon the rhetoric of anti-Semitism and overt statements of racial superiority and inferiority. Ironically Judaism is a not a race, but a religion. Full opposition to Germany's ideas did not begin until the outbreak of WWII. A large part of Allied propaganda efforts was to label Nazi Germany as a racist state, thus distinguishing their own states from them. By the end of the war, the association of racism with the Nazis and the genocidal policies they undertook thoroughly established the theme that racism was something to be opposed in the United States. The experiences of the Civil Rights Movement further emphasized the evil inherent in racism.

One view of the origins of racism emphasizes "stereotyping." People generally respond to others differently based on what they know, which may include superficial characteristics associated with ethnicity—for example, the perceived danger associated with a white person walking in a black neighborhood or a black person walking in a white neighborhood.

Concepts of race and racism often have played central roles in major conflicts. Debaters over the concepts often use the term *racism* to refer to more general phenomena such as xenophobia and ethnocentrism. In most cases, national conflicts arise over ownership of land and strategic resources.

In the Western world, racism evolved, twinned with a doctrine of white supremacy, and helped fuel European exploration, conquest, and colonization of the rest of the world, especially after Christopher Columbus reached the Americas. The justification of slavery in the Americas as an "equal-opportunity employer" was denounced with the introduction of Christian theory in the West. Maintaining that Africans were "subhuman" was the only loophole in the then-accepted law that "men are created equal" (Wolf, 1982) Some people even argued that Native Americans were natural slaves. In Asia, the Chinese and Japanese empires were both strong colonial powers. The Chinese made colonies and vassal states of much of the mainland of Asia. The Japanese did the same in the West Pacific. In both empires, the Asian imperial powers believed they were ethnically and racially superior to their vassals, and entitled to be their masters.

Racism may be divided into three major subcategories. The first two are (a) *individual racism*, wherein a person, for example, is not hired by a particular employer because of his race; and (b) *structural racism*, wherein discrimination is based on a widespread established belief system. An example of this widespread discrimination in the workplace was underscored by researchers at the University of Chicago (Bertrand) and Harvard University (Mullainathan) in 2003. The study found that job applicants whose names were merely perceived as "sounding black" were 50 percent less likely than candidates perceived as having "white-sounding names" to receive callbacks for interviews, no matter their level of previous experience. Examples of *ideological racism*, the third subcategory, are when government policy discriminates and legislates against groups such as apartheid in South Africa or, in the 1970s, when Uganda expelled tens of thousands of ethnic Indians. Until 2003, Malaysia enforced discriminatory policies limiting access to university education for ethnic Chinese and Indian students, although they were citizens by birth of Malaysia. Russia launched anti-Semitic pogroms against Jews in 1905 and after. During the 1930s and '40s, attempts were made to prevent Jews from immigrating to the Middle East. Following the creation of Israel, land ownership in many Israeli towns was limited to Jews. Many Muslim countries expelled Jewish Arabs and continue to refuse entry to Jews.

In the United States, racial profiling of minorities by law enforcement officials continues to be controversial. Some believe that profiling young Arab male fliers at airports will only lead to increased recruitment of older non-Arab and female terrorists. Some critics of racial profiling claim that is an unconstitutional practice, because it bases questioning individuals on what crimes they might commit, not on those they have actually committed.

Although racism is usually directed toward minority populations, it may also be directed against a majority population. In the United States, federal legislation has been interpreted by some as mandated preferential treatment for nonwhites. These politics have become known as *reverse racism*. Although this is a controversial concept, it is usually applied to instances of perceived discrimination against members of a dominant rather than a minority group. In the United States, some people, mostly conservatives, criticize policies such as *affirmative action*—the practice of favoring or benefiting members of a particular race in areas such as college admissions and workplace advancement. The purpose is an attempt to create an atmosphere of racial diversity and racial equality. Although lauded by many as a boon to society, giving the less privileged a chance at success, the practice is condemned as racially discriminatory by others (Stoler, 1997).

Critics of affirmative action emphasize that insofar as these policies provide preference to certain racial groups and not others, they are race-based discrimination, regardless that their goal is to correct a previous act of discrimination. Supporters of affirmative action argue that these policies counteract systemic and cultural racism by providing a balancing force. Affirmative action does not qualify as racist because these actions are enacted by politicians, most of whom are part of the majority and directed toward their own race.

Increasingly significant numbers of white people (with European ethnicity) believe that political correctness has led to a denigration of the white race through "special attention" paid to minority races. For example, they consider the existence of Black History Month in February, but not a White History Month, Native American History Month, or Asian History Month to be *de facto* racism directed at a majority—nonblack minorities. Others would argue that the absence of a White History Month is because much of the school year is devoted to teaching history from a Eurocentric perspective.

The number of white Americans, however, who believe affirmative action programs are "reverse racism" is increasing. According to Bennett (2003), feelings of alienation appear to be especially strong among white men.

"Race appreciation is a lifelong developmental process that begins with a healthy sense of one's own racial/ethnic identity" (Ponteratto & Pederson, 1993, p. 39). Before people can feel good about themselves, they must feel good about others.

Many whites actively support affirmative action programs because they believe these programs are needed to counteract centuries of racial inequities in education, job opportunities, health care, political opportunities, and so on. Unfortunately, past inequities as in gender seem to continue:

- Full-time white working women earn 74 percent of what men earn.
- Full-time black working women earn 63 percent of what men earn.
- Women comprise 46 percent of the workforce, but only 5 percent of top management in Fortune 200 companies.

TEACHERS' RESPONSES TO DIVERSITY

Research has identified a positive correlation between the higher achievement of culturally diverse poor students and teachers who demonstrate culturally responsible instructional strategies (Ladson–Billings, 1994). There is an assumption that teachers will do what is best to improve academic outcomes for students. Lipman (1999) reports research describing teacher decision making that negates this assumption. Issues at the core of many black students' experiences in school—misinterpretation of discourse (language, style, social interactions), academic tracking, negation of student strengths, the exclusion of diverse students' experiences and histories in the curriculum, and the problematic implications of an emphasis on individual competition—were not touched.

A large-scale, systematic study uncovering the instructional practices of approximately 140 classrooms in 15 elementary schools serving diverse students reports a range of teacher responses to diversity (Knapp, Shields, & Turnbull, 1995). Teachers approached the tasks of dealing with cultural and social diversity in a variety of ways. Responses to diversity ranged from approaches that actively excluded children from learning opportunities because of their backgrounds to attempts to use students' backgrounds as a positive basis for learning in the classroom.

Corbett, Wilson, and Williams (1997) researched another dimension of teachers' responses to diversity. They found that teachers overwhelmingly agreed (79 percent of 50 teachers interviewed) that "all students could succeed in school and that the teachers themselves could make a difference" (p. 102). One segment of the teachers maintained that it is the *teachers' responsibility* to ensure that diverse students succeed. Another segment claimed that all children can succeed if the students put forth the necessary effort.

Teachers vary in their perceptions of recognizing and valuing the diverse experiences of students. Many believe that the responsibility for learning in school resides in the student—a perception that may affect a teacher's approach to classroom instruction. The assumption or perception that all students should come to school ready to learn and that it is the teacher's job to teach them and to treat them equally raises issues and questions about the understanding of equity.

CONCLUSION

No single way to ensure success for all student learners appears best. An increased awareness among staff of the need to *know the learner* and to strengthen their relationships with culturally diverse students seems to be a key element. Williams (1999) states that the challenge is to systematize such awareness by providing caring environments and strategies that connect learners to instruction. She further acknowledges that much remains to be resolved. Brain research continues; new information will influence perceptions of diversity and learning. Technology continues to explode and changes rapidly occur. Populations continue to move and grow. Will adjusting learning experiences to ensure success for diverse populations continue to be ignored and resisted?

Educators must continue to learn about human development and learning. We must continue to *learn about ourselves*—the strengths and concerns (for example, skill deficiencies and/or biases) we may bring to the learning relationship. We must continually evaluate the implications of technology for skill development. New professional development studies (for example, study groups, action research) face a constant challenge to reach all students. We need to define "success" in terms of the 21st century. We need to stress cooperation, not competition. We have a wonderful opportunity . . . let's go for it!

REFERENCES

Alexander, K. L., & Entwisle, D. R. (1996). Schools and children at risk. In A. Booth & J. F. Dunn (Eds.), *Family school links: How do they affect educational outcomes?* [On-line]. Available: www.summerlearning.org/summer/learningday/factsheet.pdf.

American Association of University Women Educational Foundation. (1998). *Gender gaps: Where our schools fail our children.* Washington, DC: Author.

Arnold, E., & Sibley, D. (1995). Gender, place, and culture. [On-line]. Available: www
.emporia.edu/socshi/fembib/shtm.

Asian Nation. (2005). *Asian American history, demographics, and issues.* [On-line]. Available: www
.asianamerican.net.

Banks, J. A., & Banks, C. A. (1994). *Handbook for research on multicultural education.* New York:
Macmillan.

Bauer, A. M., Boyle, J., Danforth, S., & Shea, T. M. (1997). *Cases in special education.* New York:
Muse Inc.

Bennett, C. I. (2003). *Comprehensive multicultural educational theory and practice.* Boston: Allyn &
Bacon.

Bertrand, M., & Mullainathan, S. (2003, May 27). *Are Emily and Greg more employable than La-
kisha and Jamal? A field experiment on labor market discrimination.* [On-line]. Available:
http://ssrn.com/abstract=422902.

Brewer, J. (2005, November 28). *Religion and spirituality.* CBS News. [On-line]. Available:
listserv.maiami.edu/scripts/Waexe?A1=ind0511&L=5tradarch.

Burnette, J. (1998). *Reducing the disproportionate representation of minority students in special education ED417501.* ERIC Clearinghouse on Disabilities & Gifted Education. ERIC/OSEP
Digest #E566. Reston: VA.

Cartledge, G., & Middleton, M. (1996). African Americans. In G. Cartledge (Ed.), *Cultural diversity and social skills instruction: Understanding ethnic and gender differences* (pp. 133–201).
Champaign, IL: Research Press.

Casey, J. V. (2004, February 16). Political power: Hispanic influence growing. [On-line]. Available: www.reviewjournal.com/lvrj_home/2004/Feb-16-Mon-2004/news/23201579.html.

Ceci, S. (1996). *On intelligence: A bioecological treatise on intellectual development.* Cambridge, MA:
Harvard University Press.

Coles, R. (2000). *Lives of moral leadership.* New York: Random House.

Corbett, D., Wilson, B., & Williams, B. (1997). *Assumptions, actions, and performance: First-year
report to OERI and the participating school districts.* Philadelphia: Unpublished report.

Council of Economic Advisors. (1988). *U.S. Economic Data.* [On-line]. Available: docs.lib.duke
.edu/federal/guides/us_econdata.html.

Crowley, A. (2005, April 23). U.S. population continues moving south, west. [On-line]. Available: www.eyebeam.org/reblog/archives/2005/04/us_population_continues_moving_s_1
.html.

D'Sousa, D. (1991). Illiberal education: The politics of race and sex on campus. [On-line].
Available: upload.mcgill.ca/sociology/EthnicRelations-redinglist.rtf.

Dalaker, J., & Naifeh, M. (1998). *Poverty in the United States: 1997.* Washington, DC: U.S.
Government Printing Office.

Darling–Hammond, L. (1997). *The right to learn: A blueprint for creating schools that work.* San
Francisco: Jossey-Bass.

Dewey, J. (1938). *Experience and education.* New York: Macmillan.

Edelman, M. W. (2003). *30 Years of action, poverty.* Boston: Beacon Press.

Fine, R. (2006). Russ and Dee (Fine) in the Morning. 101.1 F.M. Radio, Birmingham, AL.

Foot, D. (1996). *Boom, bust, and echo: How to profit from the coming demographic shift.* Toronto:
Macfarlane, Walter & Ross.

Franklin, D. L. (1998). Race, class, and adolescent pregnancy: An ecological analysis. *American
Journal of Orthopsychiatry, 58,* 399–403.

Freeman, C. (2004). *Trends in educational equity of girls and women.* National Center for Education Statistics. Washington, DC: U.S. Department of Education.

Frey, W. (1998). *The diversity myth.* [On-line]. Available: www.demographics.com/publications/
ad98_ad/9806_ad/ad/980626.htm.

Frey, W. H., Abresch, B., & Yeasting, J. (2004). America by the numbers: A field guide to the
U.S. population. [On-line]. Available: www.ssdan.net/abn.shtml.

Fujiura, G. T. (1999). *Commentary on the meaning of race and income inequity to disabilitites.* [On-
line]. Available: www.dimenet.com/dpolicy/archive.php?mode=P&id=10.

Gay, G. (1995). *A synthesis of scholarship in multicultural education.* [On-line]. Available: www .edchange.org/multicultural/sites/essays.html.

Glazer, N. (1997). Memoir and autobiography: Pathways to examining the multicultural self. [On-line]. Available: www.findarticles.com/p/articles/mi_qa3935/is_20031/ai_n9322310-34.

Grant, C. A., & Sleeter, C. E. (1997). Race, class, gender, and disability in the classroom. In J. A. Banks & C. A. Banks (Eds.), *Multicultural education: Issues and perspectives* (3rd ed., pp. 61–84). Boston: Allyn & Bacon.

Greene, J. P. (2001, March). *Report/high school graduation rates in the United States.* [On-line]. Available: www.manhattan-institute.org/html/cr_baeo.htm.

Greene, J. P. (2002, April). High school graduation rates in the United States. [On-line]. Available: www.manhattan-institute.org/html/cr_baeo.htm.

Hall, E. T. (1959). *The silent language.* New York: Doubleday.

Hall, E. T. (1966). *The hidden dimension.* New York: Doubleday.

Hall, E. T. (1976). *Beyond culture.* New York: Doubleday.

Hardy, F. (1993). The power of hands: African American women as shapers of creative expression in adolescent black females. [On-line]. Available: www.uscs.edu/academics/se/other_pdfs/hardy.pdf.

Harrison, B. (1990). Making the connections. In H. Shapiro & D. Purpel (Eds.), *Critical social issues in American education: Transforming in a post modern world.* Boston: Beacon.

Haskins, R. (2005). Poverty and income in 2004. The Brookings Institute. [On-line]. Available: http://www.brookings.edu/comm/.events/20050830.htm.

Heward, W. L. (2006). *Exceptional children: An introduction to special education* (8th ed.). Upper Saddle River, NJ: Pearson, Merrill Prentice Hall.

Hodgkinson, H. (1985). *All one system: Demographics of education, kindergarten through graduate school.* Washington, DC: Institute for Educational Leadership.

Hodgkinson, H. (1998). Demographics of diversity. *Education Digest, 64* (2), 1–4.

House, R. M., & Pinyuchon, M. (1998). Counseling Thai Americans: An emerging need. *Journal of Multicultural Counseling and Development, 26* (3), 194–195.

Hulbert, A. (2006, February 1). *Will boys be boys? Why the gender lens may not shed light on the latest educational crisis.* [On-line]. Available: www.slate.com/id/213543?nav=wp.

Jensen, A. R. (1973). *Educability and group differences.* New York: Harper & Row.

Johnson, S. (2005, April 20). *North American youth gangs: Patterns and remedies.* [On-line]. Available: www.heritage.org/Research/LatinAmerica/tst042105a.cfm.

Johnston, R. C., & Viadero, D. (2001, May/June). *Unmet promise: Raising minority achievement.* Washington DC: Brookings Institute. [On-line]. Available: www.edletter.org/past/issues/2001-mj/gap.shtml.

Kamin, L. J. (1974). *The science and politics of IQ.* Hillsdale, NJ: Lawrence Erlbaum Associates.

Kaufman, P., Kwon, J., & Klein, S. (2000, November). *Dropout rates in the United States: 1999.* Statistical analysis report. Washington, DC: National Center for Education Statistics, p. 1.

Keme'enui, E. J. (2000). *Reading first.* [On-line]. Available: www.educationation.org/reading-resources.html.

Kirwan Institute for the Study of Race and Ethnicity. (2004, April). *An academic overview of desegregation.* [On-line]. Available: http://kirwaninstitute.org/mulitmedia/presentations/4-7%20CLE%20Final.ppt#2256,1,An Academic Overview of Desegregation.

Klauke, A. (1989). *Restructuring the schools.* ERIC Digest Series (Eugene, Oregon) ERIC Clearinghouse on Educational Management, Number EA 37.

Knapp, M. S., Shields, P. M., & Turnbull, B. J. (1995). *Academic challenge for the children of poverty: Summary report.* Washington, DC: U.S. Department of Education, Office of Policy and Planning.

Kugler, E. (1999, December). Diverse schools: A first-class educational environment. In *Updating school board policies,* National School Boards Association. [On-line]. Available: www.embracediverseschools.com/resources.htm.

Ladson–Billings, G. (1994). *The dream keepers: Successful teachers of African American children.* San Francisco: Jossey-Bass.

Levy, F., & Murnane, R .J. (1996). *Teaching the new basic skills.* New York: Free Press, Simon & Schuster.

Lewis, A. (2000, June). Diversity in U.S. education. *U.S. Society & Values.* [On-line]. Available: http://usinfo.state.gov/journals/itsv/0600/ijse/diversity.htm.

Link, R. (2003, Autumn). *The children's defense fund: 30 years of action.* [On-line]. Available: www.cpag.org.uk/info/Povertyarticles/Poverty116defensefund.html#12.

Lipman, P. (1999). *Race, class, and power in school structuring.* Albany: State University of New York Press.

Logan, J. R., & Oakley, D. (2004). *The continuing legacy of the Brown Decision: Court action and school segregation, 1960–2000.* [On-line]. Available: http://mumford.albany.edu/census/norsegregation/Brown01.htm.

Longley, R. (2002). *The lone American grows in number.* U.S. government information/resources. [On-line]. Available: http://usgovinfo.about.com/library/weekly/aa051601a.htm.

Losen, D. J. (2002). Minority overrepresentation and under-servicing in special education. *Principal 81* (3): 45–46.

Losen, D. J., & Orfield, G. (Eds.). (2002). *Racial inequity in special education.* Boston: The Civil Rights Project, Harvard University.

Marofsky, M. 2005. Job outlook showing signs of life for minorities. [On-line]. Available: http://juantornoe.blogs.com/hispanictrending/2004/06/job_outlook_sho.html.

Mathews, R. (2000, November). Cultural patterns of South Asian and Southeast Asian Americans. *Intervention in School and Clinic, 36,* 101–104.

McIntryre, A. (1997). *Making meaning of whiteness: Exploring racial identity with white teachers.* Albany: State University of New York Press.

Mindel, C. H., & Habenstein, R. W. (Eds.). (1984). *Ethnic families in America: Patterns and variations.* New York: Elsevier.

NAEP Reading Scores. (1999). [On-line]. Available: www.house.gov/ed_workforce/issues/107th/education/nclb/hr1chart4.pdf.

National Center for Education Statistics. (1997). *The condition of education, 1997.* Washington, DC: Department of Education, Office of Educational Research and Improvement.

National Center for Education Statistics. Institute of Education Sciences. (2005). *Special analysis 2005: Mobility of the teacher workforce.* [On-line]. Available: http://nces.ed.gov/programs/coe/2005/analysis/sa10.asp.

Native Americans. (2005). *Native Americans in the United States.* [On-line]. Available: www.crystalinks.com/nativeamericans.html.

Peterson, A. C., Silbereisen, R. K., & Sorensen, S. (1996). Adolescent development: A global perspective. In K. Hurrelmann and S. F. Hamilton (Eds.), *Social problems and social contexts in adolescence: Perspectives across boundaries* (pp. 3–37). New York: Aldine De Gruyter.

Ponterratto, J. G., & Pederson, P. B. (1993). *Preventing prejudice: A guide of counselors and educators.* Newbury Park, CA: Sage.

Population Reference Bureau. (n.d.). *Human population: Fundamentals of growth effect of migration on population growth.* [On-line]. Available: www.prb.org/Content/NavigationMenu/PRB/Educators/Human_Population/Migration2/Migration1.htm.

Prelutsky, B. (2005, February 23). *Diversity, schmiversity.* The Squeaky Wheel. [On-line]. Available: www.worldnetdaily.com/news/article.asp?ARTICLE_ID=42975.

Reeves, T., & Bennett, C. (2003). *The Asian and Pacific Islander population in the United States, March 2002.* Current Population Reports, P20-540, U. S. Census Bureau, Washington, DC.

Resnick, L. (1987). *Education and learning to think.* Washington, DC: National Academy Press.

Resnick, L. (1995). From aptitude to effort: A new foundation for our schools. *Daedalus, 124,* 55–62.

Schlesinger, A. Jr. (1992). *The disuniting of America.* New York: W.W. Norton.

Shade, B. J. (1994). Understanding the African American learner. In E. R. Hollins, J. E. King, & W. C. Hayman (Eds.), *Teaching diverse populations: Formulating a knowledge base* (pp. 175–189). New York: State University of New York Press.

Slaughter, D., & Epps, E. G. (1987). The home environment and the academic achievement of Black American children and youth: An overview. *The Journal of Negro Education, 56*, 3–20.

Smelser, N. J., Wilson, W. J., & Mitchell, F. (Eds.). (2001). *America becoming: Racial trends and their consequences.* [On-line]. Available: www.rand.org/pubs/research-_briefs/RB5050/index1 .html.

Spindler, G., & Spindler, L. (1984). *Dreamers without power: The Menonini Indians.* Prospect Heights, IL: Waveland Press.

Stoler, A. L. (1997). Racial histories and their regimes of truth. *Political Power and Social Theory, 11*, 183–206.

The World Factbook. (2005, June 14). [On-line]. Available: www.cia.gov/cia/publications/ factbook/geos/us.html.

Tumulty, K. (2001, June 11). Courting a sleeping giant. *Time*, Special Edition: Amexica.

U.S. Bureau of the Census. (2000). *Statistical abstract of the United States: 2000.* (120th ed.) Washington, DC: Author.

U.S. Bureau of the Census. (2005, April 21). *Florida, California and Texas to dominate future population growth, Census Bureau reports.* [On-line]. Acknowledgments. [On-line]. Available: www.census.gov/PressRelease/www/releases/archives/population/004704.html.

U.S. Department of Education. (1999). *Reading is fundamental.* National Center for Education Statistics. [On-line]. Available: www.riforg/who/newsroo/leteracy_ata_glancemspx.

U.S. Department of Labor. (1995). Private pension plan bulletin. [On-line]. Available: www.dol.gov/asp/programs/history/herman/reports/futurework/report/chapter2/main.htm.

Valuing diversity in the schools: The counselor's role. (2004). ERIC Digest, The Public School Parent's Network. [On-line]. Available: www.psparents.net/culturalSensitivity.htm.

Watson, G. (2003). Can natural assets help address urban poverty? [On-line]. Available: www.umass.edu/peri/pdfs/CDP1.pdf.

Williams, B. (1999). Diversity and education for the 21st century. In D. Marsh (Ed.), *Preparing our schools for the 21st century* (pp. 89–114). Alexandria, VA: ASCD.

Winzer, M., & Mazurek, K. (1998). *Special education in multicultural contexts.* Columbus, OH: Merrill.

Wolf, E. R. (1982). *Europe and the people without history.* Los Angeles: University of California Press.

Wozmak, R., & Fischer, K. (Eds.). (1993). *Development in context: Acting and thinking in specific environments.* Hillsdale, NJ: Lawrence Erlbaum.

Yearbook 2001: The state of America's children. (2001). Washington, DC: Children's Defense Fund.

CHAPTER 3

RIGHTS OF STAKEHOLDERS IN EDUCATION

Although the rights of children still are paramount, parents, teachers, and the community have rights too. This team of stakeholders—students, parents, educators, administrators, other school personnel, and community citizenry at large—must complement one another. Their positive synergy will ensure that children will thrive in the school atmosphere in which children live. This complementary group also has *responsibilities* that imply taking an *active role* whether as a learner (student), a teacher in the home (parent) or in the school, or a citizen in the community.

Topics presented in this chapter include children and youth at risk for failure, for poverty, homelessness, violence, abuse, and neglect. Additional material discusses the state of child health and the moral dilemmas facing our children. The debate continues regarding who should be responsible for our children's character.

THE RIGHTS OF CHILDREN

A child is a person who is going to carry on what you have started. He is going to sit where you are sitting, and when you are gone, attend to those things which you think are important. You may adopt all the policies you please, but how they are carried out depends on him. He will assume control of your cities, states, and nations. He is going to move in and take over your churches, schools, universities, and corporations. All your books are going to be judged, praised, or condemned by him. The fate of humanity is in his hands.

—Abraham Lincoln

Within the four-year span since the publication of the first edition of this book, many changes have occurred in education. Unfortunately, the rights of children continue to be problematic. When comparing the *welfare status* of U.S. children during the past four years, statistics show a similar truth: The numbers of children on welfare continue to be *high* and continue to *increase* (Edelman, 2004). According to Marian Wright Edelman (2004), founder and president of the Children's Defense Fund, "America is jeopardizing its future and its soul" (p. 9). Consider the following data in moments in America for children:

- Every 9 seconds a high school student drops out
- Every 12 seconds a public school student is corporally punished
- Every 20 seconds a child is arrested
- Every 36 seconds a baby is born into poverty
  (Children's Defense Fund, 2004)

Although the largest group of children in low-income families is white, black and Hispanic children are significantly more likely to live in families with low incomes than white children, and they account for the increase in low-income children (Schuck, 2005). U.S. Census Bureau information cites the *growing poverty* among children of immigrants in the United States (Bernstein, 2002; Van Hook, 2003).

The Disparity Continues

Fifty years after *Brown v Board of Education* and 40 years after President Johnson declared a War on Poverty, many minority and lower income children still lack a fair chance to live, learn, thrive, and contribute in America. In a great nation such as the United States, where resources abound and democracy is the rule, individuals should be able to live in safety, security, and at a manageable comfort level. Unfortunately, this quality of life is not the case for many of our youngest residents. Although adults are vulnerable to injustices, children by the nature of their dependency are particularly vulnerable to victimization. One out of every five children is poor during the first three years of life—the time of greatest brain development. The US is flunking the test that states that the morality of a society is how it treats its children. (Children's Defense Fund, 2003)

CHILDREN AND YOUTH AT RISK: AN OVERVIEW

Maria comes from a large family, originally from Mexico. She is a first grader who does not speak English and has been identified by readiness tests and by her teacher as a child at risk. Is Maria at risk for failure because others believe she is not ready to learn in school? If so, what does this mean? Children from Mexico come to school with a wealth of knowledge (Moll, Amanti, Neff, & Gonzales, 1992). It is a mistake to believe that children who do not speak "standard English" must first be filled in by the school before they can learn (Erickson, 1968, p. 19). A massive school readiness problem exists, but who owns that problem? The children are ready for school. Are the teachers ready for the children?

Beth Swadener and Sally Lubeck (1995) prefer to look at children and families "at promise." They believe that the whole notion of "children at risk" places a negative perspective on how we define children, youth, families, and communities who are different—who are poor, of color, or speak a primary language other than English.

The term *at risk* is a generic one that can be used to describe a range of problems of school-age children and youth. Low achievement, absenteeism, grade retention, and behavior problems all indicate that a student may be at risk of school failure (Henley, Ramsey, & Algonzzine, 1999). Risk factors most often relate to home, school, and community (Barr & Parrett, 1995). Risk factors interact synergistically. As the number of risk factors increases, chances rise for teenage pregnancy, incarceration, unemployment, welfare, suicide, and other negative long-term outcomes (Barr & Parrett, 1995).

During recent years, research has successfully identified and documented factors that place children at risk (Barr & Parrett, 1995). Using only a relatively few identified factors, schools can now predict with better than 80 percent accuracy students *in the third grade* who will later drop out of school. These factors are so powerful that researchers agree if a poor child (1) attends a school composed largely of other poor children, (2) is reading a year behind by third grade, and (3) has been retained a grade, the chances of this child ever graduating from high school are near zero (McPartland & Slavin, 1990). Two of the three characteristics are school related: learning (or not learning) to read and grade retention related to school issues. Why are these children at risk? Is it because of their own personal and familial characteristics or are they at risk because the schools are failing to meet their needs?

Approximately 15 percent of all high school students leave school before their graduation date. After infants, the most vulnerable at-risk population is adolescents, according to Henley, Ramsey, and Algozzine (1999).

Overwhelmingly, the majority of at-risk students are students whose appearance, culture, language, values, communities, and family structures do not match those of the dominant white culture that schools were designed to serve and support (Hixson & Tinzmann, 1990). School efforts to help at-risk children and youth primarily have focused almost exclusively on students from low socioeconomic backgrounds. Compensatory education is used to describe federal programs that are targeted for disadvantaged children who are at risk for academic failure (Henley, Ramsey, & Algonzzine, 1999; Peterson, 1987).

Too often these at-risk students are identified and placed in special education classes. This overrepresentation occurs also among culturally diverse students. When students are identified as at risk for low achievement or school failure, schools often respond by *labeling* them as disabled and placing them in restrictive educational programs. These practices appear to be especially problematic in urban settings (Atler, Gottlieb, & Wishner, 1994). Since the passage of the Individuals with Disabilities Education Act, the number of students with learning disabilities has increased beyond all reasonable expectations. Slavin (1989) points out that "special education has assumed a substantial burden in trying to meet the needs of students at risk of school failure. Yet research comparing students with mild handicaps in special education to similar students left in regular classrooms finds few if any benefits for this expensive service" (p. 15). A comprehensive discussion of the pros and cons of inclusion can be found in Chapter 9.

The annual dropout rate for students with disabilities is 5.1 percent. Students with behavior disorders have a higher rate than any other type of disability, and older secondary students are more likely to drop out than younger ones.

The tendency to blame school failure on characteristics *within* the students, their families, and communities has supposedly diminished somewhat or at least has become less overt. The terminology used is less pejorative, although some educators still use the term *educationally disadvantaged* (Natriello, McDill, & Pallas, 1990).

Defining *at risk* continues to remain controversial because it reflects ideological and philosophical divisions among educators, policymakers, and the general public about the role and responsibility of schools, families, and students themselves.

A PROMISING APPROACH FOR ADDRESSING AT-RISK STUDENTS

An ecological approach (Bronfenbrenner, 1989; Hixson & Tinzmann, 1990) can be used to recognize education as a process that takes place both inside and outside school and is affected—not determined—by (a) the social and academic organization of the school; (b) the personal and background characteristics and circumstances of students and their families; (c) the community contexts within which students, families, and schools exist; and (d) the relationship of these factors to one another (Natriello et al., 1990).

Maria would be better served by this approach because the teachers would consider how the school was organized to meet her needs with regard to her personal characteristics, family background, language, and neighborhood, which is predominantly Mexican. All these factors and the relationship among them will influence whether Maria succeeds in first grade.

When Maria gets to high school, promising practices will help her complete her schooling. These practices address the ecological or contextual systems in which Maria lives and attends school. Some factors that may help are (a) individual attention such as tutoring, (b) smaller class sizes, (c) help from an instructional aide or peer tutor, (d) job-specific vocational education, and (e) socialization with other students outside of school and involvement in extracurricular activities (Werner & Smith, 1992).

CHILDREN LIVING IN POVERTY

In 2000, 11.3 percent or 31.1 million people in the United States lived in poverty (U.S. Department of Education, 2002). Although the number of poor people has decreased slightly in recent years, *the number of people living in extreme poverty has increased.* In 2000, 39 percent of all people living in poverty had *incomes of less than half the poverty level.* This statistic remains unchanged from the 1999 level. The 2000 poverty rate of 16.2 percent for children is significantly higher than the poverty rate for any other age group.

If we look at the *working poor,* we know they tend to be just one accident away from losing their job (Phillips, 2004, p. 3). Scientific evidence indicates that life in *near* poverty is almost as detrimental to children's development and health as living *just below* the poverty line (Zill, Moore, Smith, Stief, & Coiro, 1991). Moreover, extreme poverty early in life is especially deleterious to children's chances for a future life (Duncan, Brooks–Gunn, & Klebanov, 1994; Children's Defense Fund, 2003).

Susan Phillips, the executive editor of Connect for Kids, an organization that summarizes economic impact and public policy toward children and advocates for children, calls for political leadership in helping our young (Phillips, 2004). The United States seems to address poverty and income distribution through tax codes. Although many countries use tax codes, the difference for the United States is that it "tends to be pretty much the only instrument we use" (Phillips, 2004, p. 3). We do not have a good system to deliver benefits to children on a regular basis through a family allowance, for example, the way other countries are able to do it. She says, "Somewhere somebody has to understand we're not talking about helping welfare mothers—there are very few of them left, in any case" (Phillips, 2004, p. 3).

In George W. Bush's first inaugural address, he stated: "America, at its best, is compassionate. In the quiet of America's conscience, we know that deep, persistent poverty is unworthy of our nation's promise. And whatever our views of its cause, we can agree that children at risk are not at fault" (Children's Defense Fund, 2001).

An overview of low-income children in the United States indicates that one-third of children in the United States live in low-income families. This means their parents earn up to double what is considered poverty in the country. The federal poverty level of a family of four as of 2004 is $18,850 (Phillips, 2004).

Raymond is five years old and has just begun attending a public kindergarten. Raymond and his family live below the poverty line. He comes to school hungry most mornings. He has just survived a summer of oppressive heat because there is no air-conditioning in his building. In the winter he will suffer from limited heating in his home. Question: *How will all of this affect Raymond's experiences in school?*

Two common misconceptions about children in low-income families are the following:

1. They live with single mothers who are unemployed. In truth, most children in low-income families have parents who are employed full-time and year round.
2. Two out of three children in low-income families live either in the South or the West. In truth, in the Northeast and Midwest, children in *urban areas* are more likely to live in low-income families whereas in the South and West, children in *rural areas* are more likely to live in low-income families (Phillips, 2004).

Let us consider the following data:

- Poor children come in all colors and live in every family type and region.
- Seventy-eight percent of poor children live in families where somebody worked all or part of the time in 1999.
- More than any other age group, young children are more likely to be extremely poor, poor, or nearly poor. The poverty rate for young children is well over double the rates for adults or the elderly. The poverty rate for young children is also significantly higher than the poverty rates for children age 6 through 17. (Children's Defense Fund, 2001)

The Face of Poverty among Young Children Is Changing

After a decade of decline, the rate of children living in low-income families is rising again (Schuck, 2005). Although the largest group of children in low-income families is white, black and Hispanic children are significantly more likely to live in families with low incomes, which accounts for the increase in low-income children (Schuck, 2005).

The problems of poverty among young children extend beyond the stereotypical image of the poor minority child in an urban setting. Young-child poverty is a *mainstream problem*, affecting children from all racial and ethnic backgrounds, from all types of residential areas, and from all regions of the United States. Less than a third of the families of poor young children depend exclusively on public assistance.

The age of the household head appears to be a telling factor. Among families with children in which the household head is younger than 25, the poverty rate rose from one-fourth in 1974 to nearly half in 1994 (Schuck, 2005).

Families headed by a single parent run an exceptionally high risk of being poor. In 1994, the poverty rate for female-headed families with children was 44 percent compared with 8.3 percent for married-couple families with children. The poverty rate for single mothers has hovered around 45 percent for the last 20 years. Several reasons are proposed: (a) single-parent families have fewer potential breadwinners than a two-income family, (b) most single-parent families are headed by women who traditionally earn less than men, and (c) single mothers with dependent children, on average, have lower levels of educational attainment than married mothers, thus limiting their employment opportunities further. Educational attainment has been one of the most powerful personal characteristics that protect people from poverty. The economic penalty for failing to attain at least a high school diploma has risen steadily since the 1970s. In 1994, the poverty rate was 31 percent for high school dropouts ages 22 to 64 (Schuck, 2005).

Concentration of Poverty.   The rate of poverty among children is significantly higher in the United States than in any other Western industrialized nation. This rate is at least a third higher and usually two to three times as high as the poverty rate of young children in any of the 12 other Western industrialized nations (Schuck, 2005; Shinn & Weitzman, 1996).

Poor Kids in a Rich Country.   The Russell Sage Foundation compared data from 25 "rich" countries throughout the world and over several decades. How did U.S. children compare with other children in rich nations? The U.S. poverty rate for children is *highest* in a group of 15 rich countries (Phillips, 2004). A child in the United States is more than five times as likely to be poor as a child in Denmark, Finland, Norway, or Sweden.

The poor most often live in neighborhoods in which their neighbors are also poor. This geographical concentration of poverty exacerbates the negative social and economic consequences of being poor, especially for children (Duncan et al., 1994). Few neighbors have the financial resources to help a poor family through a poverty spell, or the social connections to pass along information about job possibilities. The trend toward geographical concentration of the poor is most evident in the cities.

Katrina, a fourth grader, lives with her father under a bridge in a large urban area. They sometimes stay in a homeless shelter on cold nights, but most evenings they huddle with other homeless families just beneath the bridge. Katrina's attendance at school is sporadic, but in some ways she's lucky even to attend school. Just a few years ago she would have been denied schooling because she did not have a permanent address.

The Costs of Poverty among Young Children.   The experience of poverty on young children takes a serious toll. Young children in poverty are more likely to

- Be born at a low birthweight
- Be hospitalized during childhood
- Die in infancy or early childhood
- Receive lower quality medical care
- Experience hunger and malnutrition
- Experience high levels of interpersonal conflict in their homes

- Be exposed to violence and environmental toxins in their neighborhoods
- Experience delays in their physical, cognitive, language, and emotional development that will affect their readiness for school
- Experience difficulty in adolescence and adulthood (They are more likely to drop out of school, have children out of wedlock, and be unemployed [Klearman, 1991].)

In addition to the costs to the children themselves, large economic costs to the nation result from the poverty of children. Several economists working with Nobel Laureate economist Robert Solow placed the cost of child poverty to the United States at between $36 billion to $177 billion annually (Sherman, 1994). If one in four children continues to grow up in poverty, enormous constraints will be placed on our nation's labor force in terms of productivity and competitiveness.

HOMELESSNESS

Poverty and homelessness are inextricably linked (National Coalition for the Homeless [NCH], 2001). The experience of homelessness can devastate a family. It disrupts virtually every aspect of family life, harming the physical and emotional health of family members, interfering with children's education and development, and frequently leading to the separation of family members.

Families with children are the fastest growing segment of the homeless population. Declining wages have put housing out of reach for many workers. In every state, more than the minimum wage is required to afford a one- or two-bedroom apartment at "fair market rent." In Miami, for example, a family needs to work 126 hours a week at minimum wage to afford a moderately priced two-bedroom apartment (NCH, 2001). Approximately 40 percent of people who become homeless include families with children (Shinn & Weitzman, 1996). A 1997 survey of 29 U.S. cities found that children accounted for 25 percent of the homeless population (NCH, 2001). In rural areas these proportions are likely to be higher. Research (Vissing, 1996) indicates that single mothers, families, and children constitute the largest group of people who are homeless in rural areas. Moreover, the 1997 survey revealed that about one-third of the requests for shelter by homeless families was denied access because of lack of resources. More than 90 percent of the cities surveyed expected an increase in the number of requests by families with children for emergency shelters in 1998.

Causes of Homelessness

Poverty and *lack of affordable housing* are the principal causes of family homelessness (NCH, 2001). *Domestic violence* also contributes to homelessness among families. When a woman leaves an abusive relationship, she often has nowhere to go—particularly with women with few resources.

Stagnating wages and changes in welfare programs—principally, the erosion of benefits and restrictive eligibility requirements—account for increasing poverty among families. The welfare benefit levels have not kept up with increases in the cost of rent and therefore do not provide families with adequate allowances for housing.

Consequences of Homelessness

Homelessness severely affects the health and well-being of all the members of a family. When compared with *housed* poor children, homeless children experience more severe consequences: worse health; more developmental delay; more anxiety, depression, and behavioral problems; and lower educational achievement (Shinn & Weitzman, 1996). Homeless children face barriers to enrolling and attending school, including problems with transportation, inability to obtain previous school records, lack of a permanent address, lack of immunization records, and lack of clothing and school supplies. A study of mothers of homeless and poor housed families (Bassuk, 1996) found that both groups experienced higher rates of depressive disorders than the overall female population. One-third of homeless mothers had made at least one suicide attempt compared with one-fourth of housed mothers. In both groups, more than a third of the sample had at least one chronic health condition.

Families often break up under the stress of homelessness. Shelter policies that deny access to older boys or fathers may separate families. Separations may also be caused by placement of children into foster care. Moreover, parents may leave their children with friends or relatives to permit them to continue attending their regular school or to save them from the ordeal of homelessness. Shinn and Weitzman (1996) have documented the phenomenon of the breakup of families because of homelessness. In New York City, 60 percent of the residents in shelters for single adults did not have children with them. In Chicago, although 54 percent of the homeless samples were parents, 91 percent did not have children with them.

Domestic violence is the second leading cause of homelessness among women. Battered women who live in poverty often are forced to choose between homelessness and abusive relationships. Nationally, approximately half of all women and children experiencing homelessness are fleeing domestic violence (NCH, 2001).

Homelessness frequently deprives children of their right to a free, public education. It demeans their sense of worth. The following profiles reflect the experiences and feelings of homeless children:

> *I've been in four schools this year. It's rough, always having to move and change and get used to people and make new friends. It takes a little while. And right when I get it, then right when I get friends and get used to stuff, then we have to move again.*
>
> —Ryan (Public Justice Center, 1997)

Kendrick Williams, a homeless boy excluded from Washington, DC, schools for one month while officials searched for his records spoke the following words while giving his testimony before the Congressional Subcommittee on Employment and Productivity of the Senate Commission on Labor and Human Resources (May 22, 1990): *"It's hard being homeless and going to school. People make fun of you and tease you. . . . I love to read and learn, so that month was hard on me. I really missed school. . . . They shouldn't try to ruin the one chance we've got."*

Policy Issues on Homelessness

To end homelessness we must include jobs that pay livable wages. To work, families with children need access to *quality child care* that is affordable to them. However, jobs and child care are not sufficient. *Decent housing* is necessary so that people can keep their jobs and remain healthy. *Welfare reform* must include serious efforts to link cash benefits and job assistance to affordable housing. Preventing homelessness and poverty also requires access to *affordable health care.* According to NCH (2005), no known community or school has solved all the problems homelessness presents. Federal, state, and local housing, education, and health agencies must work collaboratively to enhance homeless children's access to needed services. Only concerted efforts to meet these needs will end the tragedy of homelessness for America's families and children (NCH, 1997).

CHILD ABUSE AND NEGLECT

Child abuse thrives in the shadows of privacy and secrecy.
It lives by inattention.

—David Bakan, *Slaughter of the Innocents*

Child abuse and neglect rob children of their right to safety and security. Their victims *know most perpetrators.* If a child is victimized, it is likely the perpetrator is an adult who should be ensuring the well-being of children. Instead, the adult has betrayed the child. The child has lost his/her innocence.

The topic of child abuse is so abhorrent that it shocks the collective conscience of all people of good will. So alarming is its existence, that often there has been a reluctance by many people to bring it to a conscious level let alone to *discuss, understand, remedy, or prevent it.* Today, the public is growing increasingly aware of child abuse (Goldman, 2005).

PREVALENCE DATA ON CHILD ABUSE: A CONTINUED ISSUE OF UNCERTAINTY

The National Child Abuse and Neglect (NCCAN) Data System, developed by the Children's Bureau of the U.S. Department of Health and Human Services in partnership with states, collect statistics yearly on child maltreatment from state child protective services (CPS). CPS agencies respond to referrals regarding harm to children caused by parents or primary caregivers. Incidents of harm to children caused by other people such as acquaintances and strangers are *not* included in these data (NCCAN, 2005).

An estimated 906,000 children were determined to be victims of child abuse or neglect in 2003. Although the rate of victimization per 1,000 children in the national population has dropped from 13.4 children in 1990 to 12.4 in 2003, we need not be proud of these figures. Experts agree that whatever the figures might be, they are still considerably underestimated (Goldman, 1994b, 2005; Sobsey, 1992). Reasons for the underestimation of abuse and neglect are several:

- Inconsistencies among reporters still exist regarding what constitutes child abuse.
- Cases of child abuse cover several "types" of abuse and may be recorded differently.
- Children who have truly been abused may recant their testimony.
- Children are reluctant to report abuse because they fear repercussions from perpetrators and have been "sworn to secrecy."
- Adults are reluctant to become involved and/or fear repercussions from perpetrators.

Although teachers and other professionals are mandated by law in the United States to report suspicions of abuse, many fail to do so (Goldman, 1994b, 2005). Some reasons given for failure to report include (a) insufficient information and/or signs of abuse, (b) fear of reprisal, (c) discouragement by supervisors, (d) concern for the destruction of the family unit, and (e) avoidance of the emotional and legal "hassle" that is likely to ensue once disclosure has occurred.

Systematic inquiry into the impact of child maltreatment on subsequent development has been a clear need since the modern recognition of the scourge of child abuse (Kempe, Silverman, Steele, Droegemuller, & Silver, 1984). The data collected by CPS and the Longitudinal Studies of Child Abuse and Neglect (LONGSCAN) have shown different descriptions of maltreatment based on different definitions (Runyan et al., 2005). LONGSCAN is a consortium of five longitudinal studies of child abuse, begun in 1991, that uses common measures, definitions, interviewing approaches, and data entry systems. A study comparing the recording systems of child maltreatment used by CPS and those used by LONGSCAN over an extended period of time revealed significant differences. Nearly 10 percent of physical and sexual abuse reports were classified as neglect by CPS agencies. The researchers recommend additional work to improve classifications of types of maltreatment and to examine patterns of classification over time. More children than ever are victims of maltreatment, regardless of increased sensitivity (Goldman, 1994b). Numbers of serious injuries *have quadrupled* since the previous NIS-2 study was undertaken in 1984 (Sedlak & Broadhurst, 1996).

What Do Abuse and Neglect Mean?

The answer is generally unclear because both *abuse* and *neglect* are generic terms. Similar to many phrases or expressions, a universally accepted understanding of the construct continues to elude us (Goldman, 2005). Many reasons cause this elusion; many cases overlap specific categories or types (for example, with sexual abuse, also certainly emotional abuse and often physical abuse occur). Which category should take precedence? The construct of abuse continues to be culturally determined:

- Meier and Sloan (1984) asserted that abuse varies over time, across cultures, and between dissimilar cultural and social groups.
- Maher (1985) noted that "different societies accept and condone different levels of violence towards its members, including their children" (p. 54).

Despite the problems of offering a definition that is acceptable to various professionals and that satisfies differing community standards, it is necessary to attempt to facilitate and establish a language of understanding. For the purposes of discussion, therefore, the following descriptions are used.

Physical abuse according to the National Clearinghouse on Child Abuse and Neglect (2005) is inflicting a nonaccidental physical injury upon a child. This may include burning, hitting, punching, shaking, kicking, beating, or otherwise harming a child. Physical abuse continues to affect large numbers of children, with 166,920 reported victims in the United States in 2002, including 1,390 fatalities (U.S. DHHS, 2005). Young children and infants are at particular risk for severe physical injury and death given their small size and immaturity. The highest rates of child maltreatment are noted in children younger than 3 years of age (Christoffel et al., 2003).

State CPS agencies have identified recurrence risks ranging from 1 to 2 percent for "low-risk" families to more than 50 percent for "high-risk" families over five years (DePantilis & Zuravin, 1998). Higher rates of reoccurrence were noted in children younger than 3 years of age (Ellaway et al., 2004). Additional risk has been suggested in families with domestic violence, criminal convictions, mental health needs, and substance abuse problems (Ellaway et al., 2004).

Neglect is the failure to provide for a child's basic needs. Neglect can be physical or emotional (for example, inadequate physical supervision; refusal to seek, allow, or provide medical treatment; poor nutrition; disregard of health hazards in the home; inadequate or inappropriate clothing; and chronic school truancy) (NCCAN, 2005). Since the National Center for Child and Abuse began collecting data in 1976, neglect continues to be the most commonly reported form of abuse. Incidence data range between 60 and 67 percent of reported cases. Although the public in general, and educators in particular, perceive this category as the most benign, researchers for years have concluded that this form can have the most insidious effect on its victims. Somehow it is easier for children to believe that the caretaker beats or molests them, because at least they care. To be ignored by someone a child trusts and loves can be the worst type of abuse (Goldman, 2003).

Sexual abuse refers to any sexual act with a child by an adult or older child. It includes fondling or rubbing the child's genitals, penetration, incest, rape, sodomy, indecent exposure, and using the child for prostitution, the product of pornographic materials, or adult sexual behavior with a child (NCCAN, 2005).

Other types of child abuse include *emotional abuse* and *verbal abuse*. *Emotional abuse*, according to Brenner (1984), occurs when adults attempt to shape children's behavior through the use of severe disparagement, humiliation, rejection, guilt, and fear. Emotional child abuse is maltreatment that results in impaired psychological growth and development. This "type" of abuse seems to be inherent in all kinds of earlier identified "types" of abuse, because in the vast majority of instances, emotional or psychological injury is a consequence of physical abuse, neglect, and sexual abuse. The child is often sworn to secrecy by threats of harm including death, abandonment by nonabusing parents, and/or nonbelief by the child's immediate community.

Although there is a federal law against child abuse, each state has its own laws. To understand the law and its ramifications, teachers may need lawyers to interpret the law for them when needed. Each school district needs to set its own *policy* as determined by its legal representatives and each teacher needs to know *beforehand* the necessary steps to take when he or she suspects, has a child disclose to him or her, or reports to the police or the CPS. The questions most frequently asked by teachers is why they do not hear from the persons to whom they reported (personal communications, 1986–2005).

How Do We Recognize It?

Signs and symptoms of abuse often overlap and some signs may not be abuse. However, the following signs and symptoms are highly suspicious:

- The child has broken bones or *unexplained* bruises, burns, or welts in various signs of healing.
- The child is unusually frightened of a parent or caretaker, or is afraid to go home.
- The child shows signs of malnutrition or begs, steals, or hoards food.
- The child has poor hygiene, dirty skin, or severe body odor.
- The child displays age-inappropriate play with toys, self, or others.
- The child has inappropriate knowledge about sex. (NCCAN, 2005)

Child Fatalities

"Children are not supposed to die," says Dr. D. E. Williamson (2002), the State Health Officer of Alabama. Children dying are often the most tragic consequence of maltreatment. In 2003, 1,500 children died as a result of *known abuse or neglect.* Seventy-nine percent of children who were killed were younger than four years old. Infant boys had the highest rate of fatalities with 19 deaths per 100,000 boys of the same age in the national population. Infant girls had a rate of 14 deaths per 100,000. These children died primarily because of physical abuse and neglect.

For the victims, the subsequent events following revelation also can be worse than the abuse. Victims face the trauma of not being believed, particularly if their credibility is in question. *Children with special needs* often make poor reporters or witnesses. If a child is cognitively delayed, the perpetrator's defense may argue that "slow"-thinking children often get things wrong. Children in general and special children in particular have difficulty remembering the exact dates and times these events may have occurred. Sadly, special children are more vulnerable to abuse because they are typically more dependent on caregivers for longer periods of time (Goldman, 2005). Younger children are more vulnerable to abuse because they cannot get away, are more dependent on caregivers, and have normal developmental difficulties remembering time and place. Children ages birth to three years continue to have the highest rate of child maltreatment (16.4 per 1,000 children). Girls were slightly more likely to be victims than boys (NCCAN, 2005).

Child Care

The public still remains concerned about the quality of care that others give our children. During the last decade, child maltreatment involving daycare centers and foster care homes attracted considerable attention. Such publicity created the perception that abuse is more commonplace in these out-of-home settings than in-home settings (Finkelhor, Mitchell, & Wolak, 2000). Reports from 18 states on abuse in daycare, foster care, or other institutional care settings represented only about 3 percent of all confirmed cases in 1997 (Wang & Daro, 1998). This percentage has remained consistent over the past 11 years (National Commission to Prevent Child Abuse, 1998). A recent research study examined differences in two areas that may be associated with evidence of deficits among maltreated children in foster care (Fisher, Burraston, & Pears, 2005). Results indicated that maltreated children in foster care placements (a) show poorer skills at recognition of facial expressions of emotions when cognitive ability is controlled and (b) did not appear to be more sensitive to the emotion of anger than maltreated children living at home. Today, nannies and babysitters are being screened and monitored more carefully among those parents who can afford to do so. Still, children from various economic, racial, and religious groups continue to die from maltreatment. Adult victims increasingly have come forward to attack clergy as perpetrators of child maltreatment. Although the Catholic Church has undergone mass media coverage as of late, pedophiles can be found anywhere. It just makes sense that pedophiles would place themselves in positions that give them easy access to children (Goldman, 2004b).

Substance Abuse

The link between *substance abuse* and child abuse has increased over the years. In 1997, 88 percent of respondents named the influence of substance abuse as one of the top two problems presented by families reported for maltreatment. This percentage is higher than that reported in previous years, suggesting that after several years of some improvement, substance abuse again is surfacing as a primary contributor to child maltreatment (Wang & Daro, 1998).

CHARACTERISTICS OF VICTIMS

Age

Federal statute names the maximum age of a child—victim or perpetrator—as 18, but *state law* determines the specific age. What about a victim (or perpetrator) who is cognitively delayed and therefore has the mind of a child? Recent statistics indicate that some children are physically abused before the age of three years. *Recurrence rates* for child abuse or neglect are grossly misunderstood. The rates reported in the literature range from 9 to 67 percent, depending on the age of the child, length of follow-up services provided, and type of initial or subsequent abuse, and whether the study looked at repeat reports, hospitalizations, or actual maltreatment (Palusci, Smith, & Paneth, 2004). In the United States the DHHS (2005) indicates that children in the age group of *birth to three years* have the highest overall rates of victimization, followed by the *four-to-seven years* age group (Scannapieco & Connell–Carrick, 2005). Teenagers (13–18 years old) constituted about 21 percent of all reported abuse victims.

Gender

Girls are sexually abused about three times more often than boys—a disturbing statistic that has been stable over time (Dube et al., 2005; Sedlak & Broadhurst, 1996). However, prevalence estimates range from 20 to 30 percent for girls and show a great range for boys (4 to 76 percent). For both genders, risk of child sexual abuse is correlated with family-related factors such as divorce and domestic violence, and having family members who abuse substances or who are emotionally unavailable (Dube et al., 2005). Boys had higher incidence rates than girls in some arenas. Boys were at somewhat greater risk of serious injury (24 percent higher than girls' risk) and boys were significantly more likely to be emotionally neglected (18 percent higher than girls' risk).

Ethnicity

Whites represented almost 56 percent of all victims of maltreatment according to data provided by 47 states. Black victims constituted the second largest group at about 26 percent, Hispanic victims made up about 9 percent, Native American victims made up about 2 percent, and Asian/Pacific Islander victims accounted for less than 1 percent. The remaining 6 percent of all victims were of unknown or other racial/ethnic backgrounds (DHHS, 2005). To explain the black–white disparity in maltreatment is to look at risk factors such as poverty, female-headed families, and urbanization (Schuck, 2005). In addition to these risk factors, investigators question the differences in parenting practices, cultural aspects of childrearing, and discrimination by child welfare workers, which could also contribute to the overrepresentation (p. 551; Sedlack & Broadhurst, 1996).

People with Special Needs

The relationship between disabling conditions and abuse has received increasing attention (Akuffo & Sylvester, 1983; Sobsey, 1992; Sullivan & Knutson, 2000). Experts (Finklehor, 1979; Straus & Kaufman–Kantor, 1986; Zirpoli, 1986) have noted that research shows some common characteristics among victims that increase their vulnerability—particularly persons with a wide variety of physical, mental, and sensory disabilities. These characteristics include greater dependency on adults, more difficulty with communication, impulse control, social interaction, and people-pleasing behaviors.

A disproportionate number of children and youth with intellectual and learning disabilities appear as victims of sexual abuse (Goldman, 1993; Martorella, 1998; Malmgren and Meisel, 2004; Sobsey & Doe, 1991). American psychologist Skeels (1966) chronicled the detrimental effects that abuse and neglect play on cognitive development and language acquisition in a longitudinal study that spanned 30 years. He also showed the positive effects adult intervention played in the lives of institutionalized and adopted children. Conversely, children who are subjected to abuse show more intellectual and physical disabilities than even previously suspected (Akuffo & Sylvester, 1983). Low socioeconomic status also seems to place children at higher risk for abuse and neglect. Two National Incidence studies (1996) conducted with similar research protocols over a seven-year period (1986–1993) support this finding. Children from families with annual incomes less than $15,000 were *22 times* more likely to experience maltreatment compared with children from families with annual incomes more than $30,000. Other strongly implicated family characteristics that contribute to abuse and neglect risk were single-parent status, substance-abusing parents, and large family size, especially when considering neglect.

CHARACTERISTICS OF PERPETRATORS

People Known to the Child

Nearly 80 percent of perpetrators of child maltreatment were parents, according to NIS-3 data from 41 states. An additional 10 percent were other relatives of the victim. People who were in other care-taking relationships to the child victims represented only 2 percent of the perpetrators (e.g., foster parents, facility staff, and child care providers). The remaining 5 percent of all perpetrators were non-caretakers (Child Maltreatment, 1997).

Stranger Danger

A youngster survived in the wilderness for five days but hid from others calling his name on day four, because they did not call his family password. As of June 23, 2005, officials changed their stand on stranger danger training of youngsters. Officials warn that parents should train their youngster to respond to help from people in uniform who call their name. Within smaller confines such as stores, they should be trained to inform cashiers (CNN interview with senior law enforcement agent, A. Scofield).

Gender

Female perpetrators were somewhat more likely than males to maltreat children. Sixty-five percent of the maltreated children had been maltreated by a female, whereas 54 percent had been maltreated by a male. Of the children who were maltreated by their birth parents, the majority (75%) was maltreated by their mothers, and a sizable minority (46%) was maltreated by their fathers. Both parents maltreated some children. In contrast, children who were maltreated by parent substitutes or by other persons were more likely to have been maltreated by a male than by a female (80–85% were maltreated by males; 15% by females) (Sedlak & Broadhurst, 1996). Abused children presented a different pattern in connection with the gender of their perpetrators than did the neglected children. Children were more often *neglected* by female perpetrators, congruent with the fact that mothers and mother substitutes tend to assume the role of primary caretakers and persons held responsible for omission of care (Sedlak & Broadhurst, 1996).

THE HISTORY OF CHILD ABUSE

Child abuse and neglect are not recent phenomena. Unfortunately, the maltreatment of children has endured a long and tragic history (Goldman & Wheeler, 1986). Segal (1978), citing child historian, De Mause, noted that "the history of childhood is a panorama of incredible cruelty and exploitation" (p. 171):

> A child, only seven, but appearing ancient, has become a grotesque satire of youth—the product of chronic abuse and mutilation by his elders. His feet are crushed, his shoulders bent out of shape, his head held at a tilt, the result of repeated insult to the brain. As he walks alone in the busy market, he excites the curious gaze and revulsion of passersby.

This description is chronicled in the archives of ancient Rome. One of the earliest recorded descriptions of child abuse occurred more than 5,000 years ago in ancient Sumer, where a clay tablet tells of a young girl who was sexually abused (Goldman & Wheeler, 1986). Religious beliefs and practices frequently contributed to maltreatment. Boys were flogged by their parents before altars erected to the goddess Diana (Goldman & Wheeler, 1986). Isaac, accompanied by his father, Abraham, went to the mountain top where he was to be slaughtered as a test of his father's obedience to his lord. In the days of the Roman Empire, the doctrine of *Patria Potestas* gave a father absolute authority over his children and allowed him, should he desire, to sell, kill, or otherwise dispose of his offspring in any manner he desired (Goldman & Wheeler, 1986).

Throughout history, adults assumed that they had the right to treat children in any way they desired, regardless of whether they were rich or poor, famous or unknown. Henry VI was regularly beaten by his tutor, as was Charles I, although Charles I was "fortunate" to have a whipping boy accept punishment meant for him (Radbill, 1974). In the typical English and American schoolhouse, the hickory stick was a common instructional tool. Beethoven was known to have abused his pupils with a knitting needle and, on occasion, by biting them (Segal, 1978). The advent of the Industrial Revolution introduced a systematic means to use children as sources of cheap labor. Stories are rampant about the maiming and deaths of children in industrial settings (Goldman & Wheeler, 1986).

During the Victorian era, human sexuality was not understood. Women were viewed as basically sexless. Men, however, were encouraged to be ambitious in pursuit of wealth and sex (Goldman & Wheeler, 1986). Men of letters were preoccupied with the "cult of the little girl." Edgar Allan Poe, Charles Dickens, John Rustin, and Lewis Carroll all extolled the virtues of little girls.

Child pornography has been in existence since at least 1780. The industrial and technological advances of the 19th and 20th centuries made possible the widescale production and distribution of child pornography. Prostitution in Europe by the mid 19th century was widespread. In London alone it was estimated that 1 out of 16 women was a prostitute. Great numbers of homeless children lived by any means available. Often the boys became involved in thievery, whereas the girls became prostitutes. In the late 1900s, more than 20,000 street children lived and died of disease or starvation in London. In America, children were also victimized. Indentured girls often were sexually exploited. Prostitution in America flourished. Children brought premium rewards—as much as $60 to $70 a night in a bordello (Goldman, 1990).

Child Victims and the Law

The law has traditionally treated children differently than adult victims. State criminal codes define many crimes against children separately from the same offenses committed against adult victims. These crimes include

- Abduction by stranger or by family
- Neglect or abandonment
- Physical, emotional, or sexual abuse
- Pornography or exploitation of children
- Statutory rape

All states recognize their duty to protect children. Specified classes of professionals in every state must report child abuse. These professionals usually include educators, child care workers, and medical professionals. States are also establishing child victim and offender registries to assist in the investigation and prevention of child maltreatment. Since the expanded awareness of the potential for child abuse in institutions such as school or daycare facilities, states are requiring criminal history background checks for employees and license applicants for child care facilities and other institutions.

To protect children, state laws allow police and other officials to take a child into protective custody in emergency cases. State laws also permit courts to issue protective orders and require hearings at which the accused has an opportunity to contest reports and present evidence in his/her favor. The law of most states provides privacy protection for child victims by deleting identifying information or prohibiting the release of information regarding an offense committed against a child. States have also adopted laws relating to missing children. States often require a child's birth certificate or school records to be marked in some way when a child is reported missing (Office for Victims of Crime, 1998).

Recently, pedophile tracking has increased. Many states have pictures of child pedophiles and their dwellings. There are increasingly stricter laws regarding where these perpetrators can live and how close they can live to a public school.

THE EFFECTS OF CHILD ABUSE

On Children

Children who are abused suffer a range of maladaptive, antisocial, and self-destructive behaviors and thoughts by trying to cope with the abuse, by trying to understand the situation and why the abuse is happening (Newton, 2001b). The psychological effect on an adult who is robbed or attacked is often daunting. Adult victims may blame themselves because they think they did something to encourage the attack. Children experience similar thoughts when they suffer abuse, except they are much more immature. Their thoughts often make much less sense because the violence is occurring in their own family, and nothing makes sense in that situation. By developing bizarre ideas about how to avoid the abuse next week, or whenever, children develop a range of maladaptive behaviors that can become pathological problems.

In addition to distorting children's thoughts, abuse also forces children into a position of having to "hide the family secret" (Newton, 2001b, p. 2). This secrecy prevents children from having real relationships and has lifelong effects. A history of abuse prevents forming healthy social relationships with others because they have been deprived of many skills necessary to navigate the social world. Their entire concept of a relationship is distorted. This leads to problematic relationships in life and even on the job.

The secrecy also places restraints on child initiative. If children fear doing anything new because of the chance that it will lead to another attack or because an abusive parent maintains a tight control, they will lose their sense of curiosity and wonder at the world. They will stop trying new things and exercising their mind. These children will never achieve their intellectual potential.

"Another disturbing aspect of abuse is the experiential restraint it puts on children" (Newton, 2001b, p. 1). Multiple exposures to violence or stress can cause what is known as *autonomic and endocrine hyperarousal*. Basically, it means the victim gets "stressed out." If this is a repetitive experience, there are physiological changes. These changes can be seen as overreactions to stimuli, as in being easily startled; generally being emotionally numb; craving high-risk, stimulating, or dangerous experiences of self-injury; difficulties in attention and concentration; cardiovascular problems; and immune suppression, which leads to a higher risk for colds and more severe illnesses (Newton, 2001a, p. 2). Children have different levels of resiliency or hardiness and different personality attributes. Different children, therefore, respond differently to similarly abusive situations. That is why the list of warning signs seems so general. Also, a child may endure abuse without developing any symptoms.

On Adults Who Were Abused as Children

Compared with people without a history of childhood abuse, adults with such a history are more likely to have a partner with a substance abuse problem; anxiety disorders; chronic head, face, or pelvic pain; eating disorders; musculoskeletal complaints; depression; gastrointestinal distress or symptoms; asthma or other respiratory ailments; obesity; insomnia; panic; sexual dysfunction; substance abuse; suicidal ideation or behavior; pseudoneurological symptoms (dizziness, and so forth); unintended pregnancy; and self-injury; and they are more likely to abuse their own children (Newton, 2001a; Goldman, 2005).

THE COSTS OF ABUSE

Abuse of children costs everyone. Even a simple economic analysis shows the *enormous direct costs:* medical care for injuries; medical care for the long-term effects of survivors; mental health care for survivors; substance abuse treatment for survivors; mental health treatment for abuses; the criminal justice system costs of police intervention, arrests, prosecution, and incarceration; legal system costs for lawyers, judges, and courtrooms; costs to our educational system for special education services; counseling services; and social service costs for shelters, foster care, emergency housing, and case workers.

Adolescents who have been sexually abused are more likely to have a greater number of sexual partners and not to use contraception—behaviors that increase their risk of unintended pregnancy. One in five unintended first pregnancies was associated with the woman's history of abuse and household dysfunction during childhood (Newton, 2001a).

Experts underscore two categories of cost: *direct* (those costs associated with the immediate needs of abused or neglected children) and *indirect* (those costs associated with the long-term and/or secondary effects of child abuse). Data were drawn from a variety of sources, including the DHHS, the Department of Justice, the U.S. Census, and others. In all instances, the summary has "opted to use *conservative estimates*" (Fromm, 2001, p. 1). For instance, only children who were identified as abused or neglected according to the Harm Standard—the most stringent classification category established by the U.S. DHHS—were included in the analysis. "For this reason, we believe the estimate of *$94 billion per year* is conservative" (Fromm, 2001, p. 1).

A breakdown of direct costs follows:

DIRECT COSTS	ESTIMATED ANNUAL COST, $
Hospitalization	6.2 billion
Chronic health problems	3 billion
Mental health care system	425 million
Child welfare system	14.4 billion
Law enforcement	25 million
Judicial system	340 million
Total direct costs	**24.5 billion**

A closer examination reveals "hidden" costs that may dwarf the direct costs discussed here. How much damage is done to our gross domestic project yearly as a result of the loss of productivity in the workforce alone? What is the cost of the lost potential of millions of children? "How much does it cost a society to look away from the suffering of its children?" (Fromm, 2001, p. 1).

THE NEED FOR PREVENTION

For the past 14 years, the National Committee to Prevent Child Abuse (NCPCA) has commissioned national public opinion polls to determine the public's attitudes and actions regarding child abuse prevention. Since the first survey in December 1986, and each year thereafter, the survey has sought to identify shifts in public attitudes and behaviors in several areas: (a) the public's attitudes toward specific parenting behaviors, (b) the frequency of various discipline practices, and (c) the public's optimism toward and involvement in child abuse prevention of children. Each survey involved a representative telephone survey of 1,250 randomly selected adults across the country, of which approximately 36 to 38 percent were parents with children younger than 18 living at home. Key findings were the following:

■ Physical punishment and repeated yelling and swearing continue to be viewed by the majority of respondents as potentially detrimental to a child's well-being. For the past 11 years, the public consistently expressed greater ambivalence over the potential harm of physical punishment (in other words, hitting or spanking).

■ Parents in the samples continue to report less use of physical punishment today than was true in the initial 1988 survey. One-quarter fewer parents reported the use of corporal punishment and repeated swearing and yelling today than did so in 1988. Furthermore, the use of *alternatives* to these behaviors, such as denying privileges or "time out" strategies, has been consistent or has increased.

■ The decrease in potentially harmful discipline practices has been virtually universal across income levels, race, educational status, residential location, and political and religious preferences.

■ In contrast to the general decline, an increase has been seen in the reported use of spanking among the youngest survey respondents, those ages 18 to 24. During the 11-year reporting period, the percentage of young parents who reported the use of spanking and hitting rose from 45 percent in 1988 to 59 percent in 1998.

■ Public commitment to and involvement in the prevention of child abuse virtually has been unchanged during the past 12 years. Each year, roughly one out of four of the general public and one in three parents have taken personal action to prevent child abuse and neglect (NCPCA, 1998).

STUDENT DISPOSITION—PERSONALITY: DETERMINANTS OF RIGHT OR WRONGDOING

Are there personality "traits" or dispositions that predispose some youth toward inappropriate behavior? If so, can we determine what these traits are to help prevent, identify, and/or alter them before serious and irreversible consequences occur?

Alchohol, Drug Abuse, and Violence

Research indicates a strong relationship between drinking and violent crime. Aggression and heavy drinking may be associated in the same people (McMurran, 1999). A longitudinal study was undertaken to examine the childhood and adolescent personality determinants of young-adult drug use. The conclusions of this study were that the personality characteristics remained stable from childhood to adolescence. Despite this personality stability, other results suggested ways to modify drug use (Brook, Whiteman, Cohen, Shapiro, & Balka, 1995).

Proclivity toward Violence

In order for students to fulfill their potential, The National Center for Education Statistics (NCES) (2004) summarizes data based on indicators of school crime and safety. As of 2004, for example, the following statistics were collected on such topics as victimization, fights, bullying, classroom disorder, teacher injury, weapons, and student perceptions of school safety. The following are the key findings of the report.

■ *Violent deaths*—Although considerable press has been devoted to school shootings, youth, ages 5 to 19, are much *safer at school* than away from school. From July 1, 1999, through June 2000, there were 32 school-associated violent deaths reported in the United States. Twenty-four of these violent deaths were homicides; eight were suicides. Only 1 percent of the homicides of children ages 5 to 19 occurred at school. Away from school, there were a total of almost 2,000 suicides of children ages 5 to 19 during the 2000 calendar year.

Nonfatal student victimization: student reports—Although the victimization rate for students ages 12 to 18 generally declined both at school and away from school between 1992 and 2003, no difference was detected between 2001 and 2002 in total crime rate, the rate of theft, or the rate of violent victimization either at or away from school. Conclusion: The trend stays fairly consistent both at and away from school for nonfatal student victimization.

Student perception of safety—Nationally, five percent of youth said they missed at least one day of school the past month because they had felt unsafe at school or when traveling to or from school (NCES, 2004). Although most crimes at the elementary school level (compared with secondary school levels) were relatively less serious incidents, such as fistfights, vandalism, or theft, about 4 percent of elementary principals and 19 percent of middle school principals reported at least one serious crime during the year such as rape or other types of sexual battery, physical fights or attacks with weapons, or robbery. In 1997, more than 100,000 students brought weapons to school daily (Kaufman, Walker, & Sprague, 1997). With zero tolerance for weapon possession in many schools among all ages of youth, the current data of weapon possession is drastically reduced. The Center for Safe Schools has compiled a resource guide on school-based strategies to assist in prevention and response to threats of violence.

Bullying

CNN reported a study by Price (2001) in which about 550 Midwestern middle school students were interviewed regarding bullying behavior. The results were disconcerting.

■ Eighty percent said they acted like bullies at least once a month. Their behavior included physical aggression, social ridicule, teasing, name calling, and issuing threats. Earlier reports indicated about 15 percent.

■ "A lot more goes on in junior high than the teachers or supervisors really know about," said one girl (Espelage, 1999).

■ "Different" kids are likely targets. When one boy was asked why he thought he was picked on, he replied, "because I'm fat" (Espelage, 1999).

■ "Kids don't have the skills to stop it. They also fear that if they try, attention will turn to them," according to a psychologist (Espelage, 1999).

Why do students bully? "It's fun," said one unrepentant bully. "These kids, they're like helpless—I mean they've got the big glasses and the fat stomachs" (Espelage, 1999). School shootings have spotlighted bullying behavior. The shooters in these tragedies complained that they were treated like social outcasts. There is a concern that by ignoring bully behavior, parents, teachers, and school administrators are in essence condoning it. Bullying is *not* just a normal part of growing up. Several resources exist that give parents and educators the simple language to explain to their child/student what a bully is and what to do about it.

Cheating

According to the literature, cheating has become a serious problem among Americans attending school in today's society (Puett, 2004). It is most prevalent at the college level. There, however, have been numerous reports of cheating incidents occurring at the high school level. Because it is such a serious problem, Puett's study attempted to determine at what age children begin to recognize what cheating is and the age at which they begin cheating themselves. In this study, first through sixth grade students attending two schools of different socioeconomic status participated. The student participants listened to a survey consisting of six scenarios dealing with different aspects of cheating and dishonesty. From the data collected, distinct differences between child's responses at each elementary school and grade level occurred. The results indicated that children who attended the lower socioeconomic school were more likely to view cheating behaviors as being okay. Fewer children attending the higher socioeconomic status school viewed cheating behaviors as acceptable. As children grew older, they were less likely to view cheating behaviors as acceptable. Although more studies are needed, the value of identifying possible determinants could lead to a way of prevention.

VIOLENCE AND CHILD DEVELOPMENT

Consider the following statistics from *Yearbook 2001* (p. 100):

- More children died in 1998 from gunfire than from cancer, pneumonia, influenza, asthma, and HIV/AIDS combined.
- Ten children and teens die each day from gunfire in America—one child every two and a half hours.
- Juvenile arrests for violent crime have declined 23 percent since 1995.
- The United States accounts for one-third of the world total of persons sentenced to death for crimes committed while younger than age 18.
- Between 50 to 75 percent of incarcerated youths have a diagnosable mental health disorder.
- The average American child watches 28 hours of television a week and, by age 18, will have seen 16,000 simulated murders and 200,000 acts of violence.
- The unemployment rate for teens is more than four times the adult rate.

Violence continues to run rampant in the United States, claiming thousands of lives and costing hundreds of millions of dollars annually in medical care and lost wages (Wallace, 1994). Violence refers to child abuse or other domestic conflict, gang aggression, and community crime, including assault. The developmental consequences of violence for children who are victims of or witnesses to family and community violence can be enormous.

Violence during the Preschool Years

Children growing up surrounded by violence are at considerable risk for pathological development. According to Erik Erikson's (1968) theory on developmental milestones, an infant's primary task during the first year of life should be learning to trust. Trust provides the foundation for later development of self-confidence and self-esteem. The infant's ability to trust is dependent upon the family's ability to provide consistent care and to respond to the baby's needs for love and nurturance. Caregiving is greatly compromised when the baby's family lives in a world wracked by violence and when the family fears for its safety (Halpern, 1990). In such a world, otherwise simple tasks like going to work or shopping take careful planning and extra effort.

During toddlerhood, children are learning to walk, jump, and climb—skills best learned in playgrounds and parks, not crowded apartments. Because of fear of the outside, parents restrict their children's activities to indoors. Toddlers do not understand these restrictions and often resent them, leading to disruptive relationships with the rest of the family (Wallace, 1994).

During the preschool years, children seek new relationships to learn about other people. Because of fear for safety, adults limit children's activities. Childcare programs may be located in areas where violence occurs frequently.

Violence during the School Years

During the school years, children develop academic and social skills that are necessary to function as adults and citizens. Violence in the community or at home takes its toll. Consider the following:

- When children's energies are drained because they are defending themselves against outside dangers or internal fears, difficulty in school may ensue (Craig, 1992).

- When children have been victims or witnesses to violence, they may have difficulty getting along with others.

- Children learn social skills by identifying with adults in their lives. Children may have difficulty learning nonaggressive ways of interacting with others when their only models, including those of the media, use physical force to solve problems (Garbarino, Dubrow, Kostelny, & Pardo, 1992).

- Children who live with violence may repress feelings to control their fears. This defensive maneuver may lead to pathological development. It can interfere with their ability to feel empathy for others. They are more likely to become insensitive to brutality in general (Gilligan, 1991).

- Children need to feel they have some control over their current existence and future.

- Children, however, who live with violence learn that they have little say in what happens to them. Beginning with the restrictions on autonomy when they are toddlers, this sense of helplessness continues as they go through their school years.

■ Research indicates that children who experience some form of violence in their homes are more likely to behave violently throughout their adolescence and into adulthood (Children's Defense Fund, 2003, p. 100).

Violence during College

In the mid 1980s we were alerted to crime on college and university campuses by the media. Civil suits filed by victims and surviving family members of homicide victims against universities and administrators served as a prelude to a successful advocacy for federal legislation that requires colleges to compile and publish annual campus security reports. These laws, programs, policies, and procedures have served to enhance safety, security, and crime victim assistance on many campuses. Although violence on college campuses continues to be acknowledged, two points should be remembered: (a) *college campuses have federal requirements to report crimes* and (b) *victims have rights* (Campus Sexual Assault Bill of Rights passed in 1991). However, the *barriers* to reporting campus crime are as follows:

■ How to *define* campus crime (in other words, campus crime should include, for legal purposes, the campus proper and embody the community in which the college is located). Victims can include students, faculty, staff, outside contractors, and visitors (Bureau of Justice Statistics, 2005).
■ How campus crime is *reported*—in other words, fear of retaliation. Unique to college campuses is the fear of victims to tell their parents out of fear of parents limiting their financial support.

When compared with persons of similar ages (18–24) in the general population, student victimization is less than for those not in college. More specifically, for women, nonstudents were more than 1.5 times more likely than college students to be victims of a violent crime.

TEACHER STRESS AND BURNOUT

Many sources create stress. Obvious losses include death of a loved one, breakup of an affair, separation, and divorce. Other sources of stress, however, that are not so obvious include loss of money, moving, illness, change of teachers or schools, loss of a pet, leaving school, and leaving home (Colgrove, Bloomfield, & McWilliams, 1981).

Many school districts have trouble attracting and retaining teachers. The impending retirement of a substantial fraction of public school teachers raises the specter of severe shortages among some public schools. Schools in urban areas that serve poor and minority students appear particularly vulnerable. The following factors—pay, student characteristics, and school policies—according to this study, affect the probabilities that teachers switch schools or exit the public schools entirely.

Pay

Higher teacher pay reduces the probability that teachers will leave the profession, particularly after differences in alternative earnings opportunities are taken into consideration (Hanushek, Kain, & Rivkin, 2003).

Student Characteristics

Student characteristics were more important, particularly among female teachers, than money in teacher retention according to a study that included research data from three institutions of higher learning: Stanford University, the University of Texas at Dallas, and Amherst College (Hanushek, Kain, & Rivkin, 2003). Teachers in schools serving large numbers of academically disadvantaged black or Hispanic students lost a substantial fraction of teachers each year both to other districts and to out-of-state public schools entirely. Studies show that student racial composition is an important determinant of both the probability of teachers switching districts or leaving the public school system entirely. For white teachers, the influence on switching districts holds across the experience distribution. For black teachers, the reactions of varying concentrations of black students are almost exactly the opposite than for whites in both sign and magnitude. More important, the interpretation of this differential racial effect throughout has been heavily conditioned by the possibility of explicit school district personnel policies to place minority teachers in schools with higher concentrations of minority students. But the fact that exiting teaching is more closely related to the individual teacher than to the district—in other words, follows the same pattern—suggests that the minority composition effects are more deeply rooted in *individual* teacher decisions. In summary, studies have indicated the following (U.S. Department of Education, 2002):

- Schools serving academically disadvantaged students have more difficulty retaining teachers, particularly those early in their careers.
- Teaching lower achieving students is a strong factor in decisions to leave public schools, and the magnitude of the effect holds across the full range of teacher experience.
- There is strong evidence that a higher rate of minority enrollment increases the probability that white teachers exit a school.
- Increases in percent black and percent Hispanic students tend to reduce rather than increase the probability of transition for black and Hispanic teachers respectively.

- Salary issues need to offset the labor market disadvantages of certain schools.
- Schools with 10 percent more black students would require about 10 percent higher salaries to neutralize the increased probability of leaving.
- Similarly, a one-standard deviation decrease in school average achievement equates to 10 to 15 percent higher salaries to hold exit rates constant.
- Women are clearly much less responsive to salary differences than men in determining whether to transition out of a school.
- The availability of black or Hispanic teachers may also substantially reduce the costs of hiring for these schools but remain underrepresented (20 percent) relative to the student population.

School Policies

According to critics of school hiring practices (Hanushek, Kain, & Rivkin, 2003) new teachers on the average are *lower performing* than more experienced ones. If exit rates increase when schools have larger concentrations of low-achieving and disadvantaged populations, these same schools are more likely to have higher proportions of new teachers, thus exacerbating their difficulties. Salary adjustments designed to reduce teacher turnover will affect both high-quality and low-quality teachers, tending to increase the retention of both. Good policy, therefore, is to increase salaries for teacher quality measured in terms of effectiveness in the classroom. Unfortunately, the supply function for teacher quality measured in those terms is currently basically unknown (Hanushek et al., 2003).

Several books and articles address teacher burnout. Some of the following "related resources" address what *causes* teacher burnout and how to *remedy* it:

- Stress and stress management
- School climate
- Classroom climate
- Teacher–principal relationship
- Teacher–student relationship
- Parent–teacher relationship

Striving for Solutions

Researchers (Sprague, Sugai, & Walker, 1998) suggest schools must go beyond a "discipline handbook." Schools need information about *expectations* for acceptable behavior. "All students, but especially students with antisocial behaviors, must be exposed to clearly specified and consistently implemented discipline system that both encourage pro social behaviors and discourage rule violations."

The following steps were recommended so that educators and school leaders can take a positive role to foster values and expectations associated with a safer school setting: building and reinforcement of life skills and social competencies; health promotion, problem prevention skills; coping skills, and social support for periods of transitions and crises, and for making positive social contributions. Teach students to

- Integrate social and emotional learning with traditional academics to enhance learning in both areas
- Build a caring, supportive, and challenging classroom and school climate to ensure effective social and emotional teaching and learning
- Integrate and coordinate social and emotional learning programs and activities with the regular curriculum and life of the classroom and school
- Foster enduring and pervasive effects in this type of social and emotional learning through collaboration between home and school (NCCAN, 2005, p. 5)

What Parents Can Do

A parent educator and advocate on school violence prevention wrote *Ten Talks Parents Must Have with Their Children about Violence* (Capello, 2000). The author refers to the dictionary's definition of character education with three important words: *personality* and *moral strength*. Parents are to ask themselves: What kinds of personality traits does your child exhibit? Is he/she curious, empathetic, tolerant, detached, angry, or fearful? When your child is asked to make ethical and moral decisions, what behaviors did he/she exhibit? Is your child's moral strength as strong as you would like? Preparation for talking to a child is not always easy. Certainly parents want to have talks with their children that empowers them, talks that give their children an opportunity to discuss important issues and reinforce them as they think critically and solve problems. The last but a most significant chapter in Cappello's book (pp. 291–323) for discussion is entitled, "Rules to Live By." Parents must communicate with their children and let them know

- They can depend on you to talk about *your* values
- You have expectations about their behavior
- Family rules exist and consequences follow if they break them (p. 293)

How closely this resembles teacher communication! As a teacher you must talk about your values, expectations, classroom rules, and the consequences that follow. Your expectations must conform to at least two beliefs:

1. Know different families have different beliefs.
2. Each family has its own standard for right and wrong.

INFLUENCE OF THE MEDIA

We did not have Play Stations, Nintendo's, X-boxes, no video games at all, no 99 channels on cable, no videotape movies, no surround sound, no cell phones, no personal computers, no Internet or Internet chat rooms. . . . WE HAD FRIENDS and we went outside and found them.

—Author Unknown

- When did you as a parent or teacher last see a television program, watch a movie, or a video that agreed with your standards for right and wrong?
- What is your child (student's) favorite television personality? How would he/she describe his/her morals or ethics?

Just 60 years ago, we watched television as an unknown curiosity. TV was a mix of black-and-white ghostly figures on a screen so small hardly anyone in the room could see them. Today that curiosity is a constant companion to many, including our children. The TV has all but replaced the printed page. TV programs report the news and weather, persuade us to buy certain products, and provide programs that influence our opinions and shape our actions. TV programs also provide programs that glorify violence. TV affects our "family value system" in both positive and negative ways (Family Support America, 2005). TV violence has been related to aggressive behavior in children, although how much of an impact TV violence actually has is still not clear (American Academy of Child & Adolescent Psychiatry, 1999; Garbarino et al., 1992; Gilligan, 1991). According to the American Academy of Child & Adolescent Psychiatry (1999), hundreds of studies of the effects of TV violence on children and teenagers have found that children may

- Become "immune" to the horror of violence
- Gradually accept violence as a way to solve problems
- Imitate the violence they observe on TV
- Identify with certain characters, victims, and/or victimizers

Also, children may become more fearful of the world around them. The Academy (1999) suggests the following ways in which parents can protect children from excessive TV violence:

- Pay attention to the programs your children are watching and watch some with them.
- Set limits on the amount of time they spend with TV; consider removing the TV set from the child's bedroom.
- Point out that although the actor has not actually been hurt or killed, such violence in real life does result in pain or death.
- Refuse to let your children see shows known to be violent, and change the channel or turn off the TV set when offensive material comes on, with an explanation of what is wrong with the program.

- Disapprove of the violent episodes shown in front of the children and stress the belief that such behavior is not the best way to resolve a problem.
- Offset peer pressure among friends and classmates; contact other parents and agree to enforce similar rules about the length of time and type of program the children may watch.

A national survey undertaken in 2001 indicated that about one in five youth are solicited for sex over the Internet annually (Dombrowksi, LeMasney, Ahia, & Dickson, 2004; Finkelhor & Wolak, 2001). The Internet has changed the way in which many people interact. It is now a seemingly much more acceptable forum for seeking out friendships and romantic relationships, particularly among the younger generations (Wolak, Mitchell, & Finkehor, 2003).

VIOLENCE PREVENTION IN THE COMMUNITY

Violence can be prevented through family strengthening strategies. Paramount to this hope are the following principles (Family Support America, 2005):

- Families are *resources* to other families and to communities.
- Programs should be embedded in communities and contribute to the community building process.
- Programs should advocate with families for services and systems that are fair, responsive, and accountable to the families served.
- A list of programs both nationally and statewide is provided.

SAFETY ISSUES

Cell Phones

Today, the use of cell phones is very common. Concerns have been expressed regarding the health safety (radiation) of having a cell phone constantly in one's ear (Iannelli, 2005). The main reason for a cell phone for children, according to a pediatrician (Iannelli, 2005) in the *Guide to Pediatrics*, is a way for everyone to stay in touch—in the case of a real tragedy, like a school shooting or terrorist attack.

In a remembrance of things past the question was asked:

(How come): No one was able to reach us all day . . . and we were OK?

> ("To All the Kids Who Survived the [19] 30s, '40s, '50s and
> '60s," Author Unknown, 2005)

Certainly, the world has changed. For our gains there are always some losses. Today, kidnappings of our children—by enraged noncustodial parents or persons wanting ransom or holding a grudge or a passing pedophile or a serial killer—are happening. Pictures of *nondesirables* line the walls of school secretaries in a similar manner to the walls of wanted persons at our post offices.

- Consider this question: *How young does a child need to be before he is given his own cell phone?*
- *How many times does the classroom teacher have to put up with cell phones ringing in the classroom?*

DISCIPLINE

Of all the issues that concern teachers, discipline generally tops the list (Bluestein, 2004). Without the cooperation and attention of our students, all our preparation, enthusiasm, and instructional expertise won't get us much. As an insight into what makes for successful discipline, one needs to look at some of the topics discussed at workshops for both parents and teachers provided by the author. These include

- Attacking problems, not people
- Grownups, kids, parents, teens, and boundaries—how to draw the line
- Positively positive—keeping the focus you want (at home and school)
- Using boundaries to build responsibility, cooperation, and mutual respect
- Boundary setting 101—the basics of accountability and self-care
- Dealing with difficult students—practical strategies for success with defiant, defeated, and other at-risk kids

For children in abusive families, a physician writes that discipline is neither educational nor constructive. It does not teach proper behavior attitudes. It simply produces injury—either physical or emotional—that frequently requires some sort of medical intervention (Tokarski, 2001).

Corporal Punishment

Child Physical Abuse and Corporal Punishment. The physical maltreatment of children has its roots in western Judeo-Christian culture wherein youngsters are perceived as easily spoiled, stubborn, or in some instances "born with original sin." John Calvin reportedly preached that it was the parent's duty to God to "break the will" of the child at the earliest possible age (Segal, 1978).

In some instances, children were flogged for displaying inappropriate behaviors. In 1646, however, Massachusetts adopted a law whereby unruly children encountered the death penalty. Connecticut soon followed the lead of its neighboring state. Fortunately, public whippings were frequently substituted for the death penalty for many young persons (Radbill, 1974).

Corporal punishment historically and currently remains a major issue among advocates against child abuse. The U.S. Supreme Court has upheld the right of schools to utilize corporal punishment. In a 1977 decision (*Ingram v. Wright*) the court ruled, by a five-to-four margin, that corporal punishment administered by public school teachers and administrators was not a violation of the cruel and unusual punishment clause of the Eighth Amendment. Although some states have abolished corporal punishment in schools, many states have continued to maintain this practice, if not endorsing it. Advocates against corporal punishment would emphasize that this commonly used practice is so harmful to children that it can lead to physical injuries that, if inflicted by a parent, would be considered child abuse (Parents and Teachers, 1987). American organizations opposed to corporal punishment in schools have included The American Academy of Pediatrics, the American Psychiatric Association, the American Psychological Association, the National Education Association, and the National Mental Health Association (Parents and Teachers, 1987).

Many states have exceptions for corporal punishment written into their laws on child abuse. These same states have exceptions written into their laws for children denied medical treatment for religious reasons. Proponents of corporal punishment frequently justify their actions by religious doctrine (Newton, 2001c). Although the phrase "Spare the rod and spoil the child" is not a biblical text, it no doubt reflects the meaning of two or three of the strongest biblical proverbs on childrearing. These passages from the book of Proverbs read, "He who spares the rod hates his son, but he who loves him is diligent to discipline him" (Proverbs 13:24, King James Version [KJV]) and "Folly is bound up in the heart of a child but the rod of discipline drives it far from him" (Proverbs 22:15, KJV). All other biblical texts that speak of childrearing, with the possible exception of Hebrews 12:6, which speaks of "chastising" ("scourging" in the authorized KJV), use more general, positive terms such as *discipline, nurture,* and *train up.* Some texts from the Bible would even seem to contradict the Proverbs texts (Newton, 2001c). A primary example is from Ephesians 6:4: "Fathers, do not provoke your children to anger, but bring them up in the nurture and instruction of the Lord."

Professionals who deal daily with child physical abuse uniformly speak of the fact that most physical abuse results from attempts to punish or control the child, which escalated to produce physical harm. One pediatrician who works with physically abused children in a hospital emergency room situation has said, "I do not understand that quote from Proverbs which says, 'If you beat him with a rod he will not die.' The fact is many do die" (Newton, 2001c, p. 2).

Biblical scholars and other theologians must deal with the questions of the justification of corporal punishment. The manner in which this is resolved theologically must be left to each minister, priest, rabbi, or imam.

Parents and educators also seem to have taken the theme exposed by pro and con proponents of corporal punishment. In the southern regions of the

United States, corporal punishment is practiced more in homes and schools than in other geographical locations. The relationship between the South and "The Bible Belt" cannot be ignored (Personal communication with Goldman).

Researchers investigated the antisocial behavior of adolescents who as children had received physically abusive discipline (Herrenkohl, Tajima, Whitney, & Huang, 2005). Antisocial behaviors were identified as violence, delinquency, and status offenses. Results revealed that certain factors *protect* youth: (a) the importance of school commitment, (b) the disapproval by parents/peers of antisocial behavior, and (c) being involved in a religious community. When the researchers controlled for age, gender, and demographics, these protective factors may independently lower risk for antisocial behavior during adolescence. Another study (Widom, 1999) in the *American Journal of Psychiatry*, reported that victims of sexual and physical child abuse and neglect are at increased risk for developing posttraumatic stress disorder (PTSD), but childhood victimization is not a sufficient condition. Individual, family, and lifestyle variables also place individuals at risk and contribute to the symptoms of PTSD.

NEED FOR TEACHERS TO DEAL WITH ABUSE

Protecting Our Children and Our Teachers (against Litigation)

False Allegations. Concerns about allegations of child sexual abuse against teachers. Of 3,000 questionnaires sent out to a random sample of New York state teachers, about one-sixth (n = 515) were returned. Those who responded were similar to those on the original mailing list in terms of gender, age, and racial/ethnic distribution. The results indicated that 56 percent were aware of false allegations made against a teacher in their own school district. About one-third expressed concern that a child abuse allegation could be made against them. The conclusion of the study indicated that *fears among teachers for their own vulnerability* against false allegations may limit their contact with students, resulting in potentially adverse consequences for students and the teaching environment (Anderson & Levine, 1999).

Still, teachers remain hesitant to report abuse. They are often not informed of the necessary steps needed to report abuse. Some do not know they do not need hard evidence, merely suspicion. Because children fall often, educators are still not sure which bruises are normal and which are highly suspicious of abuse. If they tell a superior, they may be told, "Stay out of it. Family business is not school business." The repercussions often can be worse than the revelations. Educators are often afraid of reprisals from the family. In some states the law varies regarding whether they can report anonymously and/or whether they will be told of the subsequent happenings. They fear they will be called to testify.

We (our children) fell out of trees, got cut, broke bones and teeth, and there were no law-suits from these accidents.

—Author Unknown, 2005.

The number of lawsuits against schools/educators is growing phenome-nally. In the past few years, special education has been an active participant in lit-igation. With the reality of *inclusion* hitting the general education classroom, more and more general educators will likely be involved with their special edu-cation colleagues in the classroom. Because special educators are more chal-lenged in training requirements than general education teachers to be "highly qualified" at the elementary level, the two groups are more likely to share class-rooms, share students, and share lawsuits.

Today's schools have lawyers that address what teachers should say, read, and write. In the past, schools had lawyers, but they were called only when an ed-ucator made a grievous error, such as falling in love with a younger student (Le-tourneau, 2005) or allowing "so-called" obscenities to invade the classroom. Lawsuits occur regarding what teachers should read to their students or allow their students to read. Queries constantly arise about topics such as homosexual-ity, biblical references, and the degree of sexual innuendo (Lax, 2005).

The criterion for avoiding liability may vary among school systems in the same geographical area (Rogan, 2005) as well as liability coverage of administra-tors versus teachers. Pity the teacher that moves from one system to the next and has not asked about teacher liability. Never say a student is "lazy" in the teacher's lounge or off campus, even if he does not turn in assignments regularly, fails tests, and/or sleeps in class. The student may be "driving the teacher nuts," a possibly justified emotion, although not a pathological one. Jerome Sattler (2001) advises observers of human behavior to speak and write in clear, descriptive language (pp. 698–699). As Sattler (2001) says, "Communicate clearly" (p. 706). All be-havior has a cause. Humans owe one another respect. Teachers, however, have feelings too. They should not be expected to like all their students all the time, nor equally. Some behavior is not likeable. If a teacher has to vent anger, it is best to take up anger management, aerobics, or kick boxing.

Teachers may be innocent of intentional wrongdoing, but the idea of being sued is often frightening to them. After all, they are teachers. Confrontation is not a skill teachers are taught or admire. Rather, teachers are taught conflict res-olution. Experience, unfortunately, often has taught otherwise. Although we want to model for our student independent communication, we teachers are taught and highly encouraged to cooperate and, in the end, to submit to author-ity figures such as the administration or the parent—if we want to consider these possible outcomes: not gain tenure, not be known as a professional "trouble-maker," and avoid general harassment. In the "old" days, when something was amiss at school, all authority figures were right and children were basically wrong. Certainly teachers were highly regarded, deservedly or not. Is this the case today?

We have affirmed the long history of child abuse. But is this scourge on humanity getting any better? Professionals highly invested in the prevention of child abuse still disagree in which category to place cases of known abuse. Consider these questions:

- Do all kinds of abuse overlap each other?
- Is one category of abuse worse than any other?
- Why is child abuse on the rise if the public no longer questions its existence (Goldman, 1980, 2005)?
- Why is our record keeping on child abuse still so *underreported?*
- Why do educators, who are the number one group of people to whom children reveal their abuse, still fail to report abuse?
- Do teachers know how many teenagers who are addicted to drugs or who run away from home become so vulnerable as victims themselves to prostitution, pornography, and even early death by suicide or violence?
- Do teachers know the relative numbers of perpetrators of child abuse with regard to their age, gender, racial, and economic dispositions?
- Do teachers know the relative numbers of victims according to their age, gender, racial, and economic dispositions?
- Can students be trusted to tell the truth? If so, why do they often recant their story?
- *Should a course in the prevention of child abuse be mandatory for every preservice and practicing teacher?*
- Under which category should one or the other types of abuse be recorded? Which is worse?
- Because chronological age is a significant determining factor in abuse, what happens to children and youth who are developmentally delayed (in other words, those whose cognitive abilities are immature)?

Consider for example a 20-year-old woman, living in an institutional setting, whose mental age has been measured as that of a child. She is unable to understand adult relationships and to make adult choices and decisions regarding her well-being. A caretaker has lured her into sexual intercourse. Is she a consenting adult or does she fall under the category of a *child* victim of sexual abuse?

Although we cannot eradicate abuse, each step we take as an individual helps. We, as teachers, are in a unique role to help. Let us do so.

REFERENCES

Akuffo, E., & Sylvester, P. (1983). Head injury and mental handicap. *Journal of Royal Society of Medicine, 76,* 545–549.

American Academy of Child & Adolescent Psychiatry. (1999, April). *Children and TV violence.* [On-line]. Available: www.aacap.org/publications/factsfam/violence.htm.

Anderson, E., & Levine, M. (1999, August). Concerns about allegations of child sexual abuse against teachers and the teaching environment. *Child Abuse and Neglect, 23.* (8), 833–843.

Atler, M., Gottlieb, B., & Wishner, J. (1994). *Special education in urban America: It is not justifiable for many.* [On-line]. Available: www.msu.edu/jonesna6/Courses/CEP900/Matrix.doc.

Bakan, D. (1971). *Slaughter of the innocents.* San Francisco, CA: Jossey-Bass.

Barr, R., & Parrett, W. (1995). *Hope at last for at-risk youth.* Boston: Allyn & Bacon.

Basler, R. P. (Ed.). (2006). *Collected works of Abraham Lincoln.* NJ: Rutgers University Press.

Bassuk, E. L., Weinreb, L. F., Buckner, J. C., Browne, A., Salomon, A., & Bassuk, S. S. (1996). The characteristics and needs of sheltered homeless and low-income housed mothers. *Journal of the American Medical Association, 276* (8), 640–646.

Bernstein, R. (2002, September 24). *Poverty rate rises, household income declines, Census Bureau reports.* Washington, DC: United States Department of Commerce News.

Bluestein, J. (2004). *Building responsibility, cooperation, and self management—21st century discipline.* [On-line]. Available: www.janebluestein.com/workshops/21cd.html.

Brenner, A. (1984). *Helping children cope with stress.* Lexington, MA: Lexington Books.

Bronfenbrenner, U. (1989). Ecological systems theory. In R. Vasta (Ed.), *Annals of child development* (Vol. 6, pp. 187–251). Greenwich, CT: JAI Press.

Brook, J., Whiteman, M., Cohen, P., Shapiro, J., & Balka, E. (1995). Longitudinally predicting late adolescent and young adult drug use: Childhood and adolescent precursors. *Journal of the American Academy of Child & Adolescent Psychiatry, 34* (9), 1230–1238.

Bureau of Justice Statistics. (2005). *Violent victimization of college students, 1995–2002.* [On-line]. Available: www.ojp.usdoj.gov/bjs/abstract/vves02.htm.

Bush, President George W. (2001, January 20). Inaugural Address. [On-line]. Available: www.whitehouse.gov/news/inaugural-address.html.Cappello, D. (2000).

Cause of homelessness. [On-line]. Available: www.camillushouse.org/camillus_resources/homelessness.php.

Cappello, D. (2000). *Ten talks parents must have with their children about violence.* New York: Hyperion.

Child Maltreatment. (1997). *Child maltreatment 1995: Reports from the states to the national child abuse and neglect data system.* [On-line]. Available: www.acf.dhhs.gov/programs/cb/stats/ncands/index.html.

Children's Defense Fund. (2004, August). *Moments in America for children.* [On-line]. Available: www.childrensdefense.org/data/moments.aspx.

Children's Defense Fund. (2003). *The state of America's children: Yearbook 2003.* [On-line]. Available: www.childrensdefense.org.

Children's Defense Fund. (2001a). *The state of America's children: Yearbook 2000* (2nd ed.). Washington, DC: Author.

Children's Defense Fund. (2001b). *The state of America's children: Yearbook 2001.* Washington, DC: Children's Defense Fund.

Clearinghouse on educational policy. (2001). *Trends and issues: School safety.* [On-line]. Available: cepm.uoregon.edu/trends_issues/safety/.

Colgrove, M., Bloomfield, H., & McWilliams, R. (1981). *How to survive the loss of a love.* Toronto: Bantam Books.

Craig, S. E. (1992). The educational needs of children living with violence. *Phi Delta Kappan, 74,* 67–71.

Creighton, L. (1997). *The public justice center: Individual homeless families.* [On-line]. Available: www.browngold.com/pd/Creighton.pdf.

Cristoffel, K. K., Scheidt, P. C., Agran, P. F., Kraus, J. F., & McLoughlin, M. (2003). *Child maltreatment.* [On-line]. Available: www.menstuff.org/issues/byissu/childmaltreatment.html.

DePanfilis, D., & Zuravin, S. J. (1998). Rates, patterns, and frequency of child maltreatment recurrences among public CPS families. *Child Maltreatment, 3,* 27–42.

Dombrowski, S. C., Ahia, C. E., & McQuillan, K. (2003). Protecting children through mandated child abuse reporting. *The Educational Forum, 67* (2), 76–85.

Dombrowski, S. C., LeMasney, J. W., Ahia, C. E., & Dickson, S. A. (2004). Protecting children from online sexual predators: Technological, psychoeducational, and legal considerations. *Professional Psychology: Research and Practice, 35* (1), 65–73.

Dube, S. R., Anda, R. F., Whitfield, C. I., Brown, D. W., Felitti, V. J., Dong, M., & Giles, W. H. (2005). Long-term consequences of childhood sexual abuse by gender of victim. *American Journal of Preventive Medicine 28* (5), 430–438.

Duncan, G. J., Brooks–Gunn, J., & Klebanov, P. K. (1994). Economic deprivation and early childhood development. In A. C. Huston, C. Coll, & V. C. McLoyd (Eds.), Special issue: Children in poverty. *Child Development, 65* (2), 296–318.

Edelman, M. W. (2000). *Lanterns: A memoir of mentors.* Boston: Beacon Press.

Edelman, M. W. (2004, July 13). "The State of America's Children."

Ellaway, B. A. Payne, E. H., Rolfe, K., Dunston, F. D., Kemp, A. M., Butler, J., & Sibert, J. R. (2004). Are abused babies protected from further abuse? *Archives of Disease in Childhood, 89,* 845–846.

Erikson, E. (1968). *Childhood and society* (2nd ed.). New York: W. W. Norton.

Espelage, D. (1999, August 20). Study: Bullying rampant in U.S. middle schools. [On-line]. Available: www.cnn.co/US/9908/20/bullies/.

Family Support America (February 5, 2005). Brief No 5. *Community Violence Prevention as a Family Strengthening Strategy.* [On-line]. Available: www.nassembly.org/fspc/practice/brief5-practicesfromfield.htm.

Family Works. (2005). *Effects of violence on television can impact family values.* University of Illinois Extension. [On-line]. Available: www.urbanext.uiuc.edu/familyworks/values-04.html.

Finkelhor, D. (1979). *Sexually victimized children.* New York: Free Press.

Finkelhor, D., Mitchell, K. J., & Wolak, J. (2000). *Online victimization: A report on the nation's youth.* Alexandria, VA: National Center for Missing and Exploited Children.

Finkelhor, D., & Wolak, J. (2001). *The crimes against children.* [On-line]. Available: www .unh.edu/ccrc?child_Vic_Papers_pubs.html.

Fisher, P. A., Burraston, B., & Pears, K. (2005). The early intervention foster care program: Permanent placement outcomes from a randomized trial. *Child Maltreatment, 10,* 61–71.

Foscarinis, M., & Ernst, G. (1995, December). Education of children and youth in homeless. *Clearinghouse Review 29.* [On-line]. Available: www.nclchp.org/Pubs/index.Cfm?startRow= 6&FA=2&TAB=1.

Fromm, S. (2001). *Total estimated cost of child abuse and neglect in the U.S.: Statistical evidence. Prevention of Child Abuse in America.* The Edna McConnell Clark Foundation. [On-line]. Available: www.emcf.org.

Garbarino, J., Dubrow, N., Kostelny, N., & Pardo, C. (1992). *Children in danger: Coping with the consequence of community violence.* San Francisco, CA: Jossey-Bass.

Gilligan, J. (1991). Shame and humiliation: The emotions of individual and collective violence. Paper presented at the Erikson Lectures, Harvard University, Cambridge, MA, May 23, 1991.

Goldman, R. (1990). An educational perspective on abuse. In R. Goldman & R. Gargiulo (Eds.), *Children at risk: An interdisciplinary approach to child abuse,* pp. 37–72. Austin, TX: Pro-Ed.

Goldman, R. (1993). Sexual abuse of young children with special needs. Are they safe in day care? *Day Care & Early Education, 20,* 4.

Goldman, R. (1994a). Abuse among the elderly and adolescents with behavior disorders: A comparative study. *Programming for Adolescents with Behavioral Disorders, 5,* 21–34.

Goldman, R. (1994b). Child abuse in child care settings. *Day Care and Early Education 22,* 6.

Goldman, R. (1994c). Children and youth with intellectual disabilities: Targets for sexual abuse. *International Journal of Disability, Development, and Education, 41* (2), 89–102.

Goldman, R. (2005). Educating teachers about abuse. *Focus: Teacher Education, 5* (3), 1–4.

Goldman, R., & Wheeler, V. (1986). *Silent shame: The sexual abuse of children.* Danforth, IL: Interstate Publishers & Austin TX: Pro-Ed.

Goodlad, J., & Keating, P. (Eds.). (1990). *Access to knowledge: An agenda for our nation's schools.* New York: The College Entrance Board.

Halpern, R. (1990). Poverty and early childhood parenting: Toward a framework for intervention. *American Journal of Orthopsychiatry, 60* (1), 6–18.

Hanushek, E. A., Kain, J. F., & Rivkin, S. G. (2003). Why public schools lose teachers. *Journal of Human Resources.* [On-line]. Available: www.all4ed.arg/publications/tappingthePotential .html.

Henley, M., Ramsey, R., & Algozzine, R. (1999). *Characteristics and strategies for teaching students with mild disabilities* (3rd ed.). Boston: Allyn & Bacon.

Herrenkohl, T. I., Tajima, E. A., Whitney, S. D., & Huang, B. (2005). Protection against antisocial behavior in children exposed to physical abuse. *Journal of Adolescent Health.* [On-line]. Available: ww.ncbi.nlm.nih.gov.

Hixson, J., & Tinzmann, M. B. (1990). *Who are the at-risk students of the 1990's?* [On-line]. Available: www.ncre/.org/sdrs/areas/rpl_esys/equity.htm.

Homeless Families with Children, National Coalition for the Homeless. (June 2001). [On line]. Available: www.nationalhomeless.org/families.html.

Iannelli, V. (2005a). *Guide to pediatrics.* [On-line]. Available: www.pediatrics.about.com/ mbiopage.htm.

Iannelli, V. (2005b). Kids and cell phones. *About Pediatrics.* [On-line]. Available: www.fda .gov/cellphones/.

Kaufman, M., Walker, H., & Sprague, J. (August 1997). *Translating research on safe and violence free schools into effective practices.* Eugene, OR: Institute on Violence and Destructive Behavior.

Kempe, C. H., Silverman, F. N., Steele, B. F., Droegemuller, W., Silver, H. E. (1962). Battered child syndrome. *JAMA, 252* (24), 3288–3294.

KidsHealth. [On-line]. Available: http://helpguide.org/mental/childabusephysicalemotional sexualneglect.htm.

Klearman, L. V. (1991). The association between adolescent parenting and childhood poverty. In A. C. Huston (Ed.), *Children in poverty: Child development and public policy.* New York: National Center for Children in Poverty, Columbia University School of Public Health.

Lax, S. (2005). *The function of profanity in modern English.* [On-line]. Available: www.essay sample.comessay/002655.

Lazere, E. (1995). *In short supply: The growing affordable housing gap.* Washington, DC: Center on Budget and Policy Priorities.

Leonhardt, D. (2004). A 30% chance that statistics never lie. The happy guy humor column, p. 1. [On-line]. Available: www.hotlib.com/articles/show.pdpit=A.

Letourneau, M. K. (2005). *Teen centre forums.* [On-line]. Available: www.theteencentre .net/forum/archive/index.php/t-11563.html.

Link, R. (2003, Autumn). *The Children's Defense Fund: 30 years of action.* [On-line]. Available: www.cpag.org.uk/info/Povertyarticles/Poverty116/defensefund.htm.

Lucier, J. P. (1992). Unconventional rights: Children and the United Nations. *Family, 5,* 1–16.

Maher, P. (1985). Child abuse: The secret epidemic. *Early Child Development and Care, 22,* 53–64.

Malmgren, K. W., & Meisel, S. M. (2004). Examining the link between child maltreatment and delinquency for youth with emotional and behavioral disorders. *Child Welfare League of America,* special issue, www.cwla.org/articles/cwjabstracts.htm.

Martorella, A. M. (1998). Prevention of sexual abuse in children with learning disabilities. *Child Abuse Review, 7,* 355–359.

Mayor's national housing forum fact sheet. (2001.). [On-line]. Available: www.usmayors.org/ uscm/news/press_releases/documents/housingfactsheet_052102.pdf.

McMurran, M. (1999). Alcohol and violence. *Child Abuse Review,* 8.

McPartland, J. M., & Slavin, R. E. (1990). *Increasing achievement of at-risk students at each grade level.* Office of Education Research and Improvement, Policy Perspectives, Washington, DC: U.S. Government Printing Office.

Meadows, K., & Walsh, M. (1996, January 21). Littlest victims: Why are there children dead? *The Birmingham News*, pp. 1–16.

Meier, J., & Sloan, M. (1984). The severely handicapped and child abuse. In J. Blacher (Ed.), *Severely handicapped young children and their families* (pp. 247–272). New York: Academic Press.

Menken, K., & Look, K. (2000). Making chances for linguistically and culturally diverse students. *Education Digest, 65* (8), 14–19.

Moll, L. C., Amanti, C., Neff, D., & Gonzales, N. (1992). Funds of knowledge for teaching. Using a qualitative approach to connect homes and classrooms. *Theory into Practice, 31* (2), 132–141.

National Center for Education Statistics. (2004). *Indicators of school crime and safety, executive summary.* [On-line]. Available: http://nces.ed.gov/pubs.2005/crime-safe04/.

National Clearinghouse on Child Abuse and Neglect Information. (1997). *What is child maltreatment?* [On-line]. Available: www.calib.com/nccanch/pubs/whatis.htm.

National Clearinghouse on Child Abuse and Neglect Information. (2005a). *Child maltreatment 2003: Summary of key findings.* [On-line]. Available: http://nccanch.acf.hhs.gov/.

National Clearinghouse on Child Abuse and Neglect Information. (2005b). LONGSCAN. [On-line]. Available: www.ndacan.cornell.edu/NDACAN/Datasets/Abstracts/DatasetAbstract_87.html.

National Coalition for the Homeless. (2005, June). *Employment and homelessness.* [On-line]. Available: www.nationalhomeless.org/publications/facts/employment.pdf.

National Coalition for the Homeless. (2001, June). *Homeless families with children. NCH Fact Sheet #7.* [On-line]. Available: www.nationalhomeless.org/numbers.html.

National Coalition for the Homeless. (1997; 2002, September). *How many people experience homelessness? NCH Fact Sheet #2.* [On-line]. Available: www.nationalhomeless.org/numbers.html.

National Committee to Prevent Child Abuse. (1998). *Prevent child abuse in America, fact sheet 2005* (2nd ed.) (November 1996). *National Incidence Study: Implications for prevention.* [On-line]. Available: www.childabuse.org/fs13.html.

Natriello, G., McDill, E. L., & Pallas, A. M. (1990). *Schooling disadvantaged children: Racing against catastrophe.* New York: Teachers College Press.

Newton, C. J. (2001a, April). *Child abuse and child care.* [On-line]. Available: www.therapistfinder.net/Child-Abuse/Child-Abuse-Effects.html.

Newton, C. J. (2001b, April). *Child abuse: An overview. Effects of child abuse on children: Abuse in general.* [On-line]. Available: www.therapistfinder.net/Child-Abuse/Child-Abuse-Effects.html.

Newton, C. J. (2001c). Child physical abuse and corporal punishment. *Mental Health Journal.* [On-line]. Available: www.therapistfinder.net/Child-Abuse/Corporal-Punishment.html.

Office for Victims of Crime. (1998, August). New directions from the field: Victims rights and services for the 21st century. Child Victims. [On-line]. Available: www.ojp.usdoj.gov/new/directions/pdftxt/bulletins/bltn18.pdf.

Oestereich, L. (1999, December). *Child abuse and child care.* Iowa State Extension. [On-line]. Available: www.extension.Iastate.edu/Publications/PM1810.pdf.

Palusci, V. J., Smith, E. G., & Paneth, N. (2004). Predicting and responding to physical abuse in young children using NCANDS. *Children and Youth Services Review, 27,* 667–682.

Parents and Teachers against Violence in Education (PTAVE). (1987). Contact info: 560 South Hartz Avenue, #408, Danville, CA 94526.

Peterson, N. (1987). *Early intervention for handicapped and at-risk children.* Denver CO: Love Publishing.

Phillips, S. (2004, May 31). *Choosing child poverty. Connect for kids, 1–5.* [On-line]. Available: www.connectforkids.org/node/577.

Preventing child abuse. (2005). [On-line]. Available: http://preventchildabuseny.org.

Price, L. (2001, August 20). Study: *Bullying rampant in U.S. middle schools.* Chicago: CNN. [On-line]. Available: www.cnn.com/ US/9908/20/bullies.

Puett, R. A. (2004). *Cheating: What do elementary school children think?* [On-line]. Available: http://clearinghouse.mwsc.edu/manuscripts/114.asp.

Radbill, S. (1974). A history of child abuse and infanticide. In R. Helfer & C. Kempe (Eds)., *The battered child* (pp. 3–21). Chicago, IL: University of Chicago Press.

Reach for the child. (1999). [On-line]. Available: www.wmpenn.edu/PennWeb/LTP/DOEMAT/ ReachVid.html.

Rosemond, J. (1995, May 14). U.N. treaty pushing child rights is outrage. *Charlotte Observer.*

Runyan, D. K., Cox, C. E., Dubowitz, H., Newton, R. R., Makund, U., Kotch, J. B., Leeb, R. T., Everson, M. D., & Knight, E. D. (2005). Describing maltreatment: Do child protective service reports and research definitions agree? *Child Abuse & Neglect, 29* (5), 461–477.

Sattler, J. M. (2001). *Assessment of children: Cognitive applications* (4th ed.). San Diego, CA: Author.

Scannapieco, M., & Connell-Carrick, K. (2005). Focus on the first years: Correlates of substantiation of child maltreatment for families with children 0 to 4. *Children and Youth Services Review.*

Schuck, A. M. (2005). Explaining black–white disparity in maltreatment: Poverty, female-headed families, and urbanization. *Journal of Marriage and Family, 67,* 543–551.

Sedlak, A., & Broadhurst, D. (1996). The Third National Incidence Study of Child Abuse and Neglect: NIS 3. U.S. Department of Health and Human Services, Washington, DC. [On-line]. Available: www.nhsa.org/announcements/anounce_childabuse.htm.

Segal, J. (1978). *A child's journey.* New York: McGraw Hill.

Shepard, L. A., & Smith, M. L. (Eds.). (1989). *Flunking grades: Research and policies on retention.* London: The Falmer Press.

Sher, K. J., Trull, T. J., Bartholow, B., & Vieth, A. (1999). Personality and alcoholism: Issues, methods and etiological processes. In H. Blane & K. Leonard (Eds.), *Psychological theories of drinking and alcoholism* (2nd ed., pp. 55–105). New York: Plenum Press.

Sherman, A. (1994). *Wasting America's future: The Children's Defense Fund report on the costs of child poverty.* Boston: Beacon Press.

Shinn, M., & Weitzman, B. (1996). Homeless families are different. In *Homelessness in America,* pp. 109–122. Washington, DC: National Coalition for the Homeless.

Skeels, H. (1966). Adult status of children with contrasting early life experiences: A follow-up study. *Monograph of the Society for Research in Child Development, 31,* 3.

Slavin, R. E. (1989). Students at risk of school failure: The problem and its dimensions. In R. E. Slavin, N. L. Karweit, & N. A. Madden (Eds.), *Effective programs for students at risk* (p. 319). Boston: Allyn & Bacon.

Sobsey, D. (1992). *Sexual offenses against people with developmental disabilities: An international comparison.* Paper presented at the 9th World Congress of the International Association for Scientific Study of Mental Deficiency, Gold Coast, Australia.

Sobsey, D., & Doe, T. (1991). Patterns of sexual abuse and assault. *The Journal of Sexuality and Disability, 9,* 243–259.

Sprague, J. R., Sugai, G., & Walker, H. (1998). Antisocial behavior in schools. In S. Watson & F. M. Gresham (Eds.), *Handbook of child behavior therapy* (pp. 451–474). Eugene: University of Oregon College of Education.

State and local profiles. (1997). [On-line]. Available: http://nch.ari.net/edsurvey97/profiles.html

Straus, M. A., & Kaufman Kantor, G. (1986). Corporal punishment of adolescents by parents: A risk factor in the epidemiology of depression, suicide, alcohol, abuse, child abuse, and wife beating. *Adolescence, 29,* 543–561.

Stimpson, L., & Best, M. (1991). *Courage above all: Sexual assault against women with disabilities.* Toronto: Disabled Women's Network.

Sullivan, P. M., & Knutson, J. F. (2000). Maltreatment and disabilities: A population-based epidemiological study. *Child Abuse and Neglect, 24,* 1257–1273.

Swadener, B., & Lubeck, S. (Eds.). (1995). *Children and families "at promise."* Albany, NY: SUNY Press.

Tokarski, P. (2001). *Abuse and religion.* Orlando, FL: Lexington Books.

UNICEF. (1999a). *Child labour: What do you know about child labour?* [On-line]. Available: www.unicef.org/.

UNICEF. (1999b). *The convention on the rights of the child.* [On-line]. Available: www.unicef.org/crc/.

UNICEF. (1999c). *Why make a special case for children?* [On-line]. Available: www.unicef.org/crc.htm.

U.S. Department of Education. (2002). *Digest of education statistics, 2001.* Washington, DC: National Center for Education Statistics.

U.S. Department of Health and Human Services. (2005). *Alternative responses to child maltreatment: Findings from the National Clearinghouse on Child Abuse and Neglect Information (NCCAN).* [On-line]. Available: http://nccanch.acf.hhs.gov/general/stats/index.cfm.

U.S. Department of Housing and Urban Development. (1998). *The crisis continues: 1998 report to Congress on worst-case housing needs.* Washington, DC: HUD User.

U.S. Senate. (1990, May 22). *Testimony of Kendrick Williams before Subcommittee on Employment and Productivity, Committee on Labor and Human Resources.* [On-line]. Available: www.nlchp.org/Pubs/index.cfm?startRow=6&FA=2&TAB=1.

Van Hook, J. (2003). *Poverty grows among children of immigrants in US.* Migration information source. [On-line]. Available: www.migrationinformation.org/US focus/display.cfm?ID=188.

Vissing, Y. (1996). *Out of sight: Out of mind.* Lexington, KY: The University Press of Kentucky.

Wang, C. T., & Daro, D. (1998). *Current trends in child abuse reporting and fatalitites: The reality of the 1997 annual fifty-state survey.* Chicago: The National Committee on Prevention of Child Abuse.

Wallace, L. B. (1994). *Violence and young children's development.* [On-line]. Available: http://ericeece.org/pubs/digests/1994/wallac94.html.

Walker, H., Horner, R., Sugai, G., Bullis, M., Sprague, J., Bricker, D., & Kaufman, I. (1996). Integrated approaches to preventing antisocial behavior patterns among school-age children and youth. *Journal of Emotional and Behavioral Disorders, 4,* 194–209.

Werner, E., & Smith, R. (1992). *Overcoming the odds: High-risk children from birth to adulthood.* Ithaca, NY: Cornell University Press.

Widom, C. S. (1999). Post-traumatic stress disorder in abused and neglected children. *Journal of Psychiatry, 156,* 1223–1229.

Williamson, D. E. (2002, June). Childhood immunization laws: A state perspective. Presentation conducted at The Public Health and the Law in the 21st Century, a meeting of the Centers for Disease Control and Prevention, Atlanta, GA.

Williamson, D. E. (2003). Montgomery, AL: The Alabama Child Death Review System.

Wolak, J., Mitchell, K. J., and Finkelhor, D. (2003). Escaping or connecting? Characteristics of youth who form close online relationships. *Journal of Adolescence, 26,* 105–119.

Zill, N., Moore, K., Smith, E., Stief, T., & Coiro, M. J. (1991). *The life circumstances and development of children in welfare families: A profile based on national survey data.* Washington, DC: Child Trends.

Zirpoli, T. (1986). Child abuse and children with handicaps. *Remedial and Special Education, 7* (2), 39–48.

CHAPTER 4

THEORETICAL SHIFTS IN OUR UNDERSTANDING OF CHILDREN

People living in the 21st century will experience more rapid changes than in any other period in human history. These changes have necessitated theoretical shifts in our understanding of children. This chapter explores the rapidly changing perspectives held about children and education. We will look at changing world-views; theories that inform our educational practices; problems with these theories; critical, modern, and postmodern conceptions of children; and, finally, what all of this means for education in the new millennium.

CHANGING WORLDVIEWS

We cannot fully address current issues in education without exploring major shifts in worldviews. Worldviews (sometimes called *paradigms* or *metatheories*) are the big picture. Paradigms are very general models of humankind. Although they are neither true nor false, they are used as reference points for interpreting the world around us (Vander Zanden, 1989). Such worldviews were first discussed in detail by Pepper (1942), and Kuhn (1970) provided an early explanation of para-digms and how they are adopted.

Three worldviews have significantly influenced practices in education and child development: the organismic worldview, the mechanistic worldview, and the contextualistic worldview (Miller, 1993). Table 4.1 provides an overview and comparison of these three worldviews and their influence on education.

As the table shows, there are some irreconcilable differences among the three worldviews—in defining the nature of children, the nature of development,

An earlier version of this chapter was published in *No Easy Answers: Helping Children with Attention and Activity Level Differences* by Jerry Aldridge, E. Anne Eddowes, and Patricia Kuby, Olney, MD: Association for Childhood Education International, 1998.

TABLE 4.1   A Comparison of Organicism, Mechanism, and Developmental Contextualism

	ORGANISMIC WORLDVIEW	MECHANISTIC WORLDVIEW	DEVELOPMENTAL CONTEXTUALISTIC WORLDVIEW
The nature of children	More active (passive environment)	More passive (active environment)	Interactive
Driving forces of development	Biological, predisposition, genetics, factors indigenous to the child	Environmental, adults, factors outside the child	A bidirectional interaction between the child and the environment
Nature of development	Qualitative changes, emphasizes stages or steplike development, big changes	Quantitative changes, emphasizes linear development, small changes	Both qualitative and quantitative changes, emphasizes both large and small changes
Humans are like . . . (metaphors used)	Growing plants	Machines	Multifaceted individual and social beings
How children learn	From the inside out	From the outside in	In many ways, based on numerous factors both within the child and between the child and context
Where the difficulty is when the child is not learning or developing as expected	Within the child	In the child's environment	Interactions between the child and the multiple contexts that influence the child
Examples of theorists	Gesell, Piaget, Freud	Watson, Skinner, Thorndike, Bijou	Vygotsky, Bronfenbrenner, Lerner

and solutions related to teaching and learning. During the past three decades, both organismic and mechanistic paradigms have been criticized (Bronfenbrenner, 1989; Ford & Lerner, 1992; Lerner, 1986, 2002; Overton, 2003; Thomas, 1999, 2005). Pelligrini and Horvat (1995) "argue against the simplistic dichotomizing of biology and experience" (p. 14) and favor a more developmental contextual view. Both organismic and mechanistic paradigms are unidirectional. By organismic paradigms, learning difficulties are described as problems *within* the child; whereas in mechanistic paradigms, the environment is considered a major unidirectional contributor. "In contrast, a transactional model posits that children and their environments influence each other (e.g., special children elicit different reactions from different teachers; the reactions/expectations of these different teachers feed back to affect individual children's behavior)" (Pelligrini & Horvat, 1995, p. 15). Responsibility for any differences in learning would be a result of the transaction between the two systems.

CHANGING THEORIES

Theories of development are much more specific than paradigms or worldviews (Miller, 1993). A theory of development deals with change over time and is usually concerned with three things. First, it should describe changes over time within an area or several areas of development. Second, it should describe changes among areas of development. Third, it should explain these changes.

No one theory has proved adequate to describe and explain learning or development. Numerous theories of development have influenced educational practices during the 20th century (Aldridge, Kuby, & Strevy, 1992), and currently a shift is affecting theories of child development and education. Some of the historical and current theories that have influenced education include Gesell's (1925) maturational theory, Skinner's (1974) behaviorist approach, Freud's (1935) psychoanalytic theory, Piaget's (1952) constructivist theory, Vygotsky's (1978) sociohistorical approach, Bronfenbrenner's (1989) ecological systems theory, and Gardner's (1983) multiple intelligences theory. More recently, critical theory (see Kessler & Swadener, 1992) has influenced education and child development practices, even though critical theory is not a theory of development. Finally, postmodern conceptions have changed the way we think of children and how to educate them (Elkind, 1995, 2000/2001).

Maturational Theory

The maturational theory of Arnold Gesell (1925) continues to affect what goes on in schools, particularly in early childhood classrooms in some parts of the United States. Gesell based his theory on three major assumptions: (a) development has a biological basis, (b) good and bad years alternate, and (c) body types (endomorph, ectomorph, mesomorph) are correlated with personality development (Thomas, 1992). Maturational theory strongly influenced the teaching of reading in the mid 1900s (Morphett & Washburne, 1931). Children were not thought to be ripe for reading until they had a mental age of six and a half years. Consequently, readiness activities were developed for children who were not yet ready to read. Some of this nonsense still occurs in preschool, kindergarten, and even primary-level classrooms. Today, maturational theory is partially responsible for the existence of prekindergartens and prefirst grades aimed at children who supposedly need the "gift of time," because of immaturity or a late birthday. These classrooms tend to have a ratio of boys to girls of anywhere from 7:1 to 10:1 (Aldridge, Eddowes, & Kuby, 1998).

Practitioners subscribing to maturational theory consider any difficulties a child experiences as being found *within* the child. This oversimplistic explanation for anything from reading problems to Attention Deficit (Hyperactivity) Disorder (AD[H]D) is extremely limiting to children and to those who work with them. If a problem lies within a child, then what value does a supportive (or, for that matter, a nonsupportive) environment have?

Another, perhaps unintentional consequence of maturational theory is the recently popular "late birthday" phenomenon. Children in classrooms who are the youngest and have a "late birthday" are often branded by the teacher as slower and less ready for instruction. Many teachers report other instructors as saying, "I knew the child would have problems. He has a late birthday."

Behaviorist Theory

The behavioral theories of Skinner (1974) and Bijou (1989) also continue to influence what goes on in schools, especially for some special education programs. The mechanistic theory of behaviorism emphasizes the role of the environment on an individual's development. Preparing the environment for appropriate reinforcement is a major goal.

Two examples of Skinner's (1974) contribution to education include behavior modification and programmed learning. Both of these rely heavily on immediate reinforcement, in which a child has to exhibit the "right" behavior or produce the "correct" answer in order to be positively reinforced.

Teachers using behavioral theory will consider any difficulties a child has as being found within the environment. As with Gesell's (1925) overemphasis on nature, Skinner's (1974) overemphasis on nurture limits our understanding of children and their differences. Applications of this theory have resulted in an overemphasis on isolated skills and drill, as well as a heavy reliance on teacher-directed and teacher-reinforced activities. Consequently, teachers often ignore children's curiosity and prior knowledge.

Chapter 6 of this book is concerned with the impact of No Child Left Behind. Many educators believe the theory behind No Child Left Behind is behaviorism. The methods reported to be scientifically based are rooted in the behaviorist tradition, and so the methodology recommended under No Child Left Behind is behavioral in nature.

Psychoanalytic Theory

Freud's (1935) psychoanalytic theory served as the theoretical basis for analysis of behavior disorders during the 1920s through the 1940s. "Behavior problems displayed by children were viewed as symbolic manifestations of unresolved conflict, often emanating from early caregiver–child interactions" (Hinshaw, 1994, p. 10). Problems with attention and activity levels were attributed to unconscious processes. Play therapy was the recommended form of intervention, with accompanying therapy for the child's parents. Psychodynamic models continue to have an effect on education and intervention for children with special needs.

One of the biggest problems with psychoanalytic theory is the inherent allocation of blame on parent–child interactions—more specifically, on the mother's actions. Fortunately, theoretical shifts have moved from a blame-the-parent model to more bidirectional, transactional, and interactional models of childhood differences.

Constructivist Theory

Although there are several "brands" of constructivism, Piaget's theory (1952) continues into the 21st century to affect what goes on in many classrooms. This theory relies heavily on logical–mathematical knowledge and universal invariant stages of development to the neglect of other forms of knowledge and the importance of context in a child's development. Even though knowledge is constructed from the "inside out" through interaction with the environment, the focus is more on the individual's coordination of relationships rather than on socially constructed knowledge.

Autonomy is the aim of education in constructivism (Kamii, 2000). Constructivist theory, however, has not adequately addressed either individual differences or cultural and contextual contributions to development and education (Delpit, 1988; Kessler & Swadener, 1992; Mallory & New, 1994). Thus, the needs of children who are different often are not met in constructivist classrooms.

The Sociohistorical Approach

The more cultural approach of Vygotsky (1978) affected learning and development through an emphasis on sociohistorical context, language and literacy learning, and the scaffolding of an adult or more able peer within a child's zone of proximal development. Although Vygotsky (1978) emphasized the salience of culture and language, the zone of proximal development concept probably has had the biggest effect on education.

The zone of proximal development is the instructional level of a child, the area in which the child can most benefit from instruction with the help from an adult or more knowledgeable peer. According to Vygotsky (1978), that which a child can do today with help from a teacher (or more able peer), the child can do tomorrow by herself. Trying to figure out a child's zone of proximal development, however, is somewhat nebulous and difficult. Vygotsky (1978) did not expound on the nature of the child's zone of proximal development, how to determine it, or how to work with a child within that zone. For children exhibiting attention and activity-level difficulties, the zone of proximal development may be even more difficult to determine and utilize.

Ecological Systems Theory

Another theory used to guide education in the late 20th century and early 21st century is Bronfenbrenner's (1989) ecological systems theory. Bronfenbrenner (1989) proposed that children are influenced by, and thus influence, the multiple systems in which they reside, either directly or peripherally. These systems include the microsystem, the mesosystem, the exosystem, and the macrosystem. Applications of this contextual theory focus on the seemingly endless variables within the child, and between the child and the numerous contexts affecting her. Although few people would quarrel with the importance of these influences, trying to account for all the endless interactions and variables affecting a child is exhausting and impractical. How would we ever have enough information about children's temperament, activity levels, attentional states, or learning capacities as they relate to the microsystem, mesosystem, exosystem, and macrosystem?

Multiple Intelligences Theory

The multiple intelligences theory of Howard Gardner (1983) is a more recent influence on education. Traditional views of intelligence favored particular cognitive processes, including certain types of problem solving (mathematical–logical intelligence) and language abilities (linguistic intelligence). According to Gardner (1983), however, these are just two types of intelligence. Five other intelligences— musical, visual–spatial, bodily kinesthetic, interpersonal, and intrapersonal—must be considered. Gardner (1983) has also added an eighth intelligence he calls *the naturalist*. A naturalist is someone who has the ability to recognize important distinctions in the natural world (Checkley, 1997).

Multiple intelligences theory shows promise in developing appropriate practices for children who do not fit the traditional mold or do not excel in the math or linguistic areas. Teachers can use children's types of intelligences to assist in planning and teaching in areas in which they are not as gifted. Schools and teachers, however, are not usually equipped equally to deal with multiple intelligences. For example, children from lower socioeconomic areas may not have many opportunities to explore music or visual–spatial intelligences, even if these are areas in which they might thrive. More efforts need to be made to understand multiple intelligences fully and to develop the resources necessary to support them.

PROBLEMS WITH TRADITIONAL PSYCHOLOGICAL THEORIES

All the theories just mentioned are still influencing what happens in education today—some more than others. However, there are several issues with the psychological theories we have chosen to adopt as foundations for educating children and adolescents. Three of the most important follow.

1. Most of our theories come from dead, white, Western men.
2. Discussions of our theories leave out significant details that, if known, would make us reconsider their usefulness.
3. The psychological theories we use to support our curriculum and instruction have neglected feminist, critical, and postmodern perspectives (see Overton, 2003).

WHAT SHALL WE DO WITH DEAD, WHITE, WESTERN MEN?

Why is it that more than 95 percent of the individuals who take care of our children are women—many of them women of color—and yet more than 95 percent of the people we use to inform our practice are dead, white, Western men (Bee, 2000)? Most of these men have never taught children. Even if they had, their conceptions of children were formed at another time, place, and context from the complex world in which we now live. Neither Gesell, Skinner, Freud, Piaget, nor Vygotsky have taught in a multicultural elementary or secondary school. None of them majored in education; most were psychologists or in professions related to psychology. Some made more money for an hour's lecture than child care workers or public school teachers make in two months. Have we really considered why we are using these men and their theories to inform how we teach in the 21st century? The issue here is not to throw the baby out with the bathwater. That is, we don't have to dispose of everything we have learned from Piaget or Vygotsky or Freud. However, in light of their backgrounds and the current state of education, we need to be constantly questioning the relevance of their theories in a postmodern world. Furthermore, if we subscribe to their theories, we need to look more closely at the details of their work that is often left out of textbook discussions.

WHAT DID THESE DEAD, WHITE, WESTERN MEN REALLY SAY?

Textbooks can be very dangerous things—often not because of what is said in them, but because of what is left out. An example of this is how G. Stanley Hall (1844–1924), the inventor of the term *adolescence* (Hall, 1899), has been recognized in human development and child development books as the "father of developmental psychology" (Turner & Helms, 1983, p. 19). However, what the authors fail to discuss are his views concerning women. He believed that girls should go to all-female schools where they could "metaphorically be turned out to grass and lie fallow so far as strenuous intellectual effort goes" (Hall, 1908, p. 589). He also pointed out that it was important for girls to "keep the purely mental back and by every method . . . bring the intuitions to the front" (Hall, 1899, p. 640). In discussing Hall's contributions to child development and education, authors have failed to point out his other ideas and the fact that his writing discriminates against women and limits their opportunities for full participation in education and society (Sadker & Sadker, 1994).

A second example of relevant omission is the work of Jean Piaget (1896–1980). Piaget believed in universal, invariant stages. In a series of interviews with Jean-Claude Bringuier, Piaget discusses these stages. Bringuier asks Piaget if all children go through the same stages in the same order. Piaget responds, "Yes, of course. . . . Children in Martinique are in the French school system. . . . They do get through, but in my studies of operations and conversations they are four years behind" (Bringuier, 1980, p. 34).

Bringuier was curious as to why this happens. Piaget tells him, "Their society, which is lazy. The father of one of these children had just built a house. When it was finished, he realized he had forgotten to put in the stairs" (Bringuier, 1980, p. 34).

Piaget does not take into account that many of the inhabitants of Martinique were brought there as slaves and did not intentionally adopt the French system. The French system was imposed on them. He does not consider that their ways of thinking and operating may be different from his white, upper middle-class way of thinking. Very few texts adequately discuss this when discussing Piaget's universal, invariant stages.

A third example of glaring omission is in the work of Lawrence Kohlberg (1969). Kohlberg proposed a theory of moral development that was highlighted in virtually every child and human development text in the 1970s and 1980s. However, these sources failed to report that Kohlberg's original sample was male (see Turner & Helms, 1983; Vander Zanden, 1989).

During the past 30 years, theories have been proposed to counter many of the psychological theories used in education. These theories have included critical, postmodern, and feminist perspectives (Wink, 2005).

Critical Theory

Although critical theory is more a social or political theory than a developmental one, its influence on education has gained momentum during the past two decades. There are, in fact, many critical theories that have several things in common. Critical theories "examine the way in which philosophies and practices have determined what is taught in school and have served the 'state' to reproduce class lines and economic relationships" (Bloch, 1992, p. 6). Critical theories also "examine interrelationships among cultural, ideological, and economic relationships and race, class, and gender-related oppression" (p. 6).

Most critical theorists believe that certain forms of knowledge are valued over other forms. For example, when cutbacks occur in the schools, it is likely the arts will go, whereas the math and science curricula are likely to be increased. They further believe that school knowledge belongs to a certain group, and that group remains in charge of school knowledge, often keeping it from other groups.

The bottom line is that knowledge is unequally distributed and those in power use that knowledge to maintain their dominant position in society (Bloch, 1992).

Modern and Postmodern Theories

Perhaps one of the biggest and most recent shifts in our understanding of children took place with the advent of postmodernity. Elkind (1995) defines postmodernism as "not a revolt against the beliefs of modernity. Rather, it is perhaps best regarded as a set of attitudes and efforts designed to modify and correct modern ideas that have been perverted and modern beliefs that have proved to be too broad or too narrow" (p. 9). Table 4.2 shows a comparison of modern beliefs and practices versus postmodern beliefs and practices.

Both modernity and postmodernity currently exist simultaneously. Some families' beliefs and practices are more representative of the modern world. Others clearly live with postmodern values. It is not the purpose of this chapter to make a value judgment regarding whether modernity or postmodernity is best. Clearly, both have their strengths and weaknesses. Because we currently live in both a modern and postmodern world, however, conflicting conceptions of children and schooling abound.

One example of this conflict can be seen in a conversation between a mother and daughter talking about the daughter's son who was recently diagnosed with AD(H)D. The grandmother said, "No wonder Mark has AD(H)D. You and his father work all the time. You never eat together as a family. Everyone is always going their own way. Since you hurry all the time and go here and there, I'm not surprised at all" (Aldridge, Eddowes, & Kuby, 1998).

The daughter replied, "Mother, you don't understand. I work and go to school. Mark takes tennis and piano lessons. Although we are all busy, we are happy. It doesn't matter that we eat together. I take Mark to tennis and piano, and his father or a sitter are with him when I have to work or go to class."

The mother and daughter have different ideas about what families should be like. The mother appears to have more modern values, whereas her daughter seems to subscribe to her own postmodern reality. As for Mark, although we do not know all the contributing factors to his diagnosed AD(H)D, we do know that he is being raised in a basically postmodern family. Anyone working with Mark and his family will need to take this into consideration.

Currently, the problem of modern versus postmodern conceptions of education is not resolved. Postmodernism to many appears to be an "opposite reaction" to modernism. Overton (2003) reports:

> [T]he proponents of the postmodern agenda have approached this ideal almost exclusively through attacks directed at modernity's rational quest for absolute certainty. This has left in place the splitting of categories. The effect of this continued splitting is that postmodern thought has tended to define itself in terms of categories

TABLE 4.2   A Comparison between Modern and Postmodern Beliefs and Practices

BELIEFS AND PRACTICES	MODERNITY	POSTMODERNITY
1. General beliefs and practices	*Progress and reason*—Humans are gradually improving	*Ascendancy of language over reason*—Humans are embedded social, cultural and historical contexts
	Universals—Creative and rational thought can transcend social and historical boundaries in the arts and sciences	*Particulars*—Humans are more concerned with specific cultural issues than with grand universals
	Regularity—Humans value a search for natural laws that govern the physical and social worlds	*Irregularity*—Humans value differences and irregularities in language, culture, science, the arts, industry, family, and school
2. General beliefs about the family	*Romantic love*—There is only one person in the world who is your other half	*Consensual love*—One person cannot fulfill all your needs; divorce is a real possibility
	Maternal love—Mothers instinctively love and care for their children	*Shared parenting*—Mothers, fathers, extended family, and other caregivers share responsibility for children
	Togetherness—Family is placed before self (family eats together at mealtime)	*Autonomy*—Self is placed before family (family does not eat together; each person is "doing own thing")
3. General beliefs about school and children	Education for progress, universality and regularity	Education for diversity, pluralism, and autonomy
	Personal adjustment	Self-esteem
	Childhood innocence and adolescent maturity	The competent child

Adapted from Elkind, D. (1995). School and family in the postmodern world. *Phi Delta Kappan, 76,* 8–14.

that reflect the opposite of those that defined modernity. Thus, if modernity was *rational*, the postmodern celebrated the *emotional*; if modernity was objectivist *observational*, the postmodern celebrated subjectivist *interpretation*; and if modernity aimed for the *universal*, the postmodern argued for the *particular*. (p. 21)

Education has historically relied heavily on modern psychological theories. Postmodern, critical, and feminist theories turn modern theories upside down and reject such notions as universals, stage theories, and even objective reality. By relying too heavily on theories, either modern or postmodern, education is left with either/or-ism that is counterproductive to developing quality educational practices.

Still, there are those who deny the constructs of modernism and postmodernism (Overton, 2003). Latour (1993) has suggested that this split can be resolved by a relational metatheory or an *amodern* approach. Amodernism rejects the dichotomy or either/or-ism of modernity versus postmodernity. This "approach" has promise for educators. Because most people have beliefs and practices that reside in both the modern and postmodern worlds, a new way of looking at the world is needed to address or resolve these conflicts and move us to developing educational approaches that do not fall into "we do either this or that" categories.

In the real world, or on a practical level, educators must move beyond modernism and postmodernism to develop appropriate hybrid theories. In other words, we must develop our own theories and stop relying on other disciplines to inform our profession. For example, modernism relies too heavily on universals and stage theories to the exclusion of context and particulars. However, there are some universals—maybe not as many as modernists believe. Still, most people have two eyes, two ears, and a nose. On the other hand, not everything is particular as postmodernists would have us believe. If there is no standard on which to base instruction, then everything is relative. A major issue in theory, then, is for educators to move beyond the arguments of universals versus particulars and cautiously recognize the value of both. At this time, no modern or postmodern theory has been able to address this dilemma fully when it comes down to the curriculum and instruction.

QUESTIONS

1. Which theory do you believe impacts educational practice in today's classrooms the most? Why?

2. What beliefs do you hold that are modern? Postmodern? Are these beliefs irreconcilable? Why? Why not?

3. Do you believe educational practice relies too heavily on the theories of "dead white men"? If so, why do you believe this has happened? If not, what theories do you believe influence education today?

REFERENCES

Aldridge, J., Eddowes, E. A., & Kuby, P. (1998). *No easy answers: Helping children with attention and activity level differences.* Olney, MD: Association for Childhood Education International.

Aldridge, J., Kuby, P., & Strevy, D. (1992). Developing a metatheory of education. *Psychological Reports, 70,* 683–687.

Bee, H. (2000). *The developing child* (9th ed.). Boston: Allyn & Bacon.

Bijou, S. W. (1989). Behaviorism. In R. Vasta (Ed.), *Annals of child development* (pp. 61–83). Greenwich, CT: JAI Press.

Bloch, M. (1992). Critical perspectives on the historical relationship between child development and early childhood education research. In S. Kessler & B. B. Swadener (Eds.), *Reconceptualizing the early childhood curriculum: Beginning the dialogue* (pp. 3–20). New York: Teachers College Press.

Bringuier, J. (1980). *Conversations with Piaget.* Chicago: University of Chicago Press.

Bronfenbrenner, U. (1989). Ecological systems theory. In R. Vasta (Ed.), *Annals of child development* (Vol. 6, pp. 187–250). Greenwich, CT: JAI Press.

Checkley, K. (1997). The first seven . . . and the eighth: A conversation with Howard Gardner. *Educational Leadership, 55* (1), 8–13.

Delpit, L. (1988). The silenced dialogue: Power and pedagogy in educating other people's children. *Harvard Educational Review, 55* (3), 280–298.

Elkind, D. (1995). School and family in the postmodern world. *Phi Delta Kappan, 76,* 8–14.

Elkind, D. (2000/2001). The cosmopolitan school. *Educational Leadership, 5* (4), 12–17.

Ford, D. H., & Lerner, R. M. (1992). *Developmental systems theory.* Newbury Park, CA: Sage.

Freud, S. (1935). *New introductory lectures on psychoanalysis.* New York: Norton.

Gardner, H. (1983). *Frames of mind: The theory of multiple intelligences.* New York: Basic Books.

Gesell, A. (1925). *The mental growth of the pre-school child.* New York: Macmillan.

Hall, G. S. (1899). *Adolescence.* New York: Appleton.

Hall, G. S. (1908). The question of coeducation, *Muncey's Magazine, 35,* 589.

Hinshaw, S. P. (1994). *Attention deficit hyperactivity in children.* Thousand Oaks, CA: Sage.

Kamii, C. (2000). *Young children reinvent arithmetic: Implications of Piaget's theory* (2nd ed.). New York: Teachers College Press.

Kessler, S., & Swadener, B. B. (Eds.). (1992). *Reconceptualizing the early childhood curriculum: Beginning the dialogue.* New York: Teachers College Press.

Kohlberg, L. (1969). Stage and sequence: The cognitive–developmental approach to socialization. In D. A. Goslin (Ed.), *Handbook of socialization theory and research.* Chicago: Rand McNally.

Kuhn, T. S. (1970). *The structure of scientific revolutions* (2nd ed.). Chicago: University of Chicago Press.

Latour, B. (1993). *We have never been modern.* Cambridge, MA: Harvard University Press.

Lerner, R. M. (1986). *Concepts and theories of human development* (2nd ed.). New York: Random House.

Lerner, R. M. (2002). *Concepts and theories of human development* (3rd ed.). New York: Random House.

Mallory, B. L., & New, R. S. (Eds.). (1994). *Diversity and developmentally appropriate practice: Challenges for early childhood education.* New York: Teachers College Press.

Miller, P. (1993). Theories of developmental psychology (3rd ed.). San Francisco: W. H. Freeman.

Morphett, M. V., & Washburne, C. (1931). When should children begin to read? *Elementary School Journal, 31,* 496–503.

Overton, W. F. (2003). Development across the life span. In R. M. Lerner, M. A. Easterbrooks, & J. Mistry (Eds.), *Handbook of psychology: Volume 6, developmental psychology.* Hoboken, NJ: John Wiley & Sons.

Pelligrini, A. D., & Horvat, M. (1995). A developmental contextualist critique of attention deficit hyperactivity disorder. *Educational Research, 24* (1), 13–19.

Pepper, S. C. (1942). *World hypotheses: A study in evidence.* Berkeley, CA: University of California Press.

Piaget, J. (1952). *The child's conception of number.* London: Routiedge & Kegan Paul.

Sadker, M., & Sadker, D. (1994). *Failing at fairness: How our schools cheat girls.* New York: Houghton Mifflin.

Skinner, B. F. (1974). *About behaviorism.* New York: Knopf.

Thomas, R. M. (1992). *Comparing theories of child development* (4th ed.) Belmont, CA: Wadsworth.

Thomas, R. M. (1999). *Human development theories: Windows on culture.* Thousand Oaks, CA: Sage.

Thomas, R. M. (2005). *Comparing theories of child development* (6th ed.). Belmont, CA: Wadsworth.

Turner, J. S., & Helms, D. B. (1983). *Lifespan development* (2nd ed.). New York: Holt, Rinehart and Winston.

Vander Zanden, J. W. (1989). *Human development* (4th ed.). New York: Random House.

Vygotsky, L. S. (1978). *Mind in society: The development of higher psychological processes.* Cambridge, MA: Harvard University Press.

Wink, J. (2005). *Critical pedagogy: Notes from the real world* (2nd ed.). Boston: Allyn & Bacon.

CHAPTER 5

CHANGING CURRICULAR PRACTICES

This chapter is a particularly short one for a very important reason. How we teach and how students learn are arguably the most salient topics we could possibly consider in education. Because teaching and learning practices are changing, we want you to consider and discuss this topic carefully. The daily, lived experiences of teachers and children are discussed in this chapter. How do students learn? How should we teach?

Most people reading this book are probably veteran teachers, new teachers, or prospective teachers. So, most of you have beliefs about what good teachers do and what takes place in an exemplary classroom. What do you believe about curriculum and instruction? If we combine Heald-Taylor's (1996) description of curriculum models and Jungck and Marshall's (1992), we can formulate four basic models of teaching that are practiced today: (1) curriculum as transmission, (2) curriculum as transaction, (3) curriculum as inquiry, and (4) curriculum as transformation. Although all four models are used in the 21st century, many would argue that curriculum as transmission is still the prevailing practice—especially in light of No Child Left Behind and standardized testing.

TEACHING AS TRANSMISSION

Anyone who has attended school has experienced the transmission model at one time or another. Straight rows, worksheets, textbooks, and scripted lessons are all popular in transmission classrooms. When teaching as transmission, the curriculum is clearly prescribed by the "experts" and is measured as a commodity or product. This is traditional teaching. The teacher's role is that of a technician who utilizes the prescribed curriculum, such as basal readers or curriculum guides, and makes few real decisions. She simply follows the preformed lesson plans. Students work individually to complete the tasks. Usually, the tasks involve getting the correct answers. Decisions are made by outside experts and all meaning resides within either the materials or with the experts (Heald-Taylor, 1996).

Most schools of education discourage teaching as transmission. Many instructors believe it maintains the status quo and students are not expected to do any real or higher level thinking. However, as we will see in Chapter 6, the federal government appears to promote transmission as the preferred model—especially when it comes to teaching reading (see McCardle & Chhabra, 2004).

One of the most heated debates in education today revolves around teaching as transmission. However, does teaching and learning always have to be either/or? Let's look at a few situations when transmission may or may not be appropriate.

Piaget (1952) described three types of knowledge: (a) *physical knowledge*—knowledge gained from interacting with objects, (b) *social knowledge*—knowledge derived from other people, and (c) *logical–mathematical knowledge*—knowledge that is constructed from the "inside out" by creating and coordinating relationships. So, both physical knowledge and logical–mathematical knowledge are *not* dependent upon other people. However, social knowledge is. Reading is social, or arbitrary, knowledge. For example, the letter "a" and the sounds of "a" are something we have socially agreed upon. To learn the name and sound of the letter "a," we have to rely on other people. We cannot learn this on a desert island, no matter how smart we are. Social knowledge is transmitted. Many things we learn in school are social knowledge. The pledge of allegiance, the names of colors, the names of the 50 states, and the former presidents are all social knowledge. This knowledge relies originally on transmission.

A main issue related to *teaching as transmission* is *how* information is transmitted and what we expect students to do with it once it is transmitted. If we expect students to get the right answer but do not expect any understanding of what they are "learning," then a lot of pseudolearning or "false" learning is taking place. True learning involves prior knowledge or being able to relate new knowledge to something we already know. For example, if a teacher holds an object in front of the class and says, "Class, this is a ziggledebot. What is it? That's right. It is a ziggledebot." The next time the teacher shows the object, many of her students will recognize and name the object as a ziggledebot. But, what is a ziggledebot? What does this mean? What does it do? How do we use it?

Are teachers who use transmission the vast majority of the time not interested in understanding or meaning? Have you ever heard a teacher say, "Don't try to understand it. Just learn it. Just memorize it." If so, we can probably assume the facts were more important to the teacher than meaning or understanding. Transmission teachers believe the facts come first and the meaning comes later. This is not so with teachers who prefer the second curriculum framework—teaching as transaction.

TEACHING AS TRANSACTION

Curriculum as transaction is different from teaching as transmission. In transaction, "knowledge is seen as constructed and reconstructed by those participating in the teaching–learning act" (Jungck & Marshall, 1992, p. 94). Although teachers still use curriculum guides, they make decisions about selections and activities for students. Although students usually study the prescribed curriculum, they work in groups. Activities are more open-ended and promote higher level thinking. Students can choose among various ways to represent what they have learned. Decisions still are made primarily by the teacher, with student input, but meaning is guided by the teacher and constructed by the students (Heald-Taylor, 1996). Teaching as transaction has also been referred to as the *generative model* (Wink, 2005). Constructivists also subscribe to most of the tenets of this framework (Kamii, 2000).

The following is one example of teaching as transaction. Ms. Nissen's fifth grade students are studying Native American nations. This is part of the prescribed curriculum. However, she divides the class into groups of four and gives each group a native Nation in which the group is to become experts. Students in each group research their tribe. They share power and information. One student collects books from the library. Two others in the group search the Internet for information. Another student in the group coordinates resources that the teacher has provided. After sharing information with one another, the group decides how best to represent the information they have learned. One group decides to do a mural. Another group plans a fact sheet, and another group decides to perform a skit or play.

This is transaction. A significant amount of higher level thinking is involved because students have to determine how to represent and share the material. The teacher guides students' interpretations of the material and expresses what is most important. In other words, the teacher guides activities and meaning, but the students construct their own knowledge.

Teachers who prefer transmission have some problems with transaction. In today's classrooms, teachers are often expected to hurry through the curriculum. Transaction takes time. Students often cover less surface information but go more in depth with other information. If the instructor is concerned about transmitting a lot of facts in a short amount of time, then transaction is less likely to be used.

TEACHING AS INQUIRY

A third model is *curriculum as inquiry*. Similar to curriculum as transaction, inquiry classrooms encourage a considerable amount of student interaction in groups. The same group skills a teacher would encourage and develop in transaction are also taught in inquiry classrooms.

Curriculum as inquiry is often used in developmentally appropriate classrooms. Teachers who use this type of curriculum create an inquiring environment that encourages children to explore and learn more about topics of their own interest. The students play an active role in determining what the class, in general, and what they, in particular, will study. If a hurricane or earthquake recently hit the community, the students may express an interest in learning more about hurricanes or earthquakes. The topic becomes the theme or unit of study. Such decisions are made by the students, who are encouraged to explore and construct their own meaning. Meaning in these classrooms does not rest with some outside expert.

Teachers often use the project approach as a vehicle for inquiry. With projects, students come up or invent their own questions for investigation. The teacher's role is to make sure that what children are interested in is something that can be investigated or studied. With younger children, projects should be investigated using a hands-on approach. Older children may end up using the Internet or secondary resources more for exploring the topic. (For a full explanation of how the project approach works, see Katz & Chard, 2000.)

General management of an inquiry classroom takes a tremendously resourceful and skilled teacher. Any instructor who does not have such abilities will surely risk havoc in the classroom from students who are inattentive or overactive. In inquiry classrooms, the curriculum is less crucial than the teacher's ability to be a good resource guide and classroom manager. When instructors have the skills and resources to run an inquiry class effectively, children who would otherwise be inattentive or overactive may actually thrive.

Teachers who prefer inquiry to transmission or transaction are more concerned with or tend to focus on the process more than the content. Most people have heard the adage, "Give a person a fish and you feed him for the day. Teach a person to fish and you feed him for life." With inquiry, teachers teach students how to investigate and how and where to find information. When students know how to do this, then they will, at least theoretically, know how to find the content they need.

Inquiry is viewed by some teachers and administrators as an enemy of content-driven curriculum guides and standardized testing. If students are off investigating topics for which they are interested, then the prescribed content such as state courses of study may be somewhat neglected. Still, inquiry and transmission or transaction are not mutually exclusive. According to Katz and Chard (2000), *transmission* is necessary for *learning* content and skills. *Inquiry* is used for *applying* the skills learned.

TEACHING AS TRANSFORMATION

A fourth model, *curriculum as transformation*, appears at first glance to be identical to the curriculum-as-inquiry model. There is, however, one important difference. In transformation classrooms, the curriculum is designed so that students can study how people or other living creatures make a difference in the world. In an inquiry classroom, if students express an interest in studying bats, a study on bats may be developed. In transformation classrooms, however, this study of bats would go a step further. Students' interest in bats would lead to the study of how bats make a difference in the world. How are bats helpful? How can humans and bats live together in the same community? In these classrooms, curriculum takes on a whole new meaning. We study things so that we can make a difference on the planet (Jungck & Marshall, 1992).

An example of transformational learning took place in Mr. Cutro's classroom. One of the students in his sixth grade class is from Kenya. Jepkembao explained that many of the people from his country were dying of AIDS and there are many orphans whose parents have died. Mr. Cutro and the class jointly decided to study AIDS and its impact on Kenya and the African continent. Mr. Cutro, always looking for ways to make the curriculum more transformative, asks the class if they can think of a project that would make a difference. Students decide they want to have a "pocket change" campaign to help the orphans of Kenya.

Although transformation sounds ideal to many teachers, there are many problems and issues involved in implementing a transformational curriculum. In Mr. Cutro's class, there are also children of poverty. They do not have pocket change. How will they contribute to the project? Furthermore, the community in which he teaches is quite conservative. Many of the parents object to the students studying AIDS and believe that parents should be the ones to discuss such issues with their children.

Another example of how transformation is challenging occurred in Ms. Capp's third grade classroom in the Pacific Northwest. The vast majority of the economy in the small community in which she teaches involves the logging industry. However, conservationists are concerned that logging is destroying the owl's habitat. Ms. Capp would meet great resistance among the community if her class decided to develop a "Save the Owl" study or transformational project.

Important questions to ask before using a transformational model are these: Whose transformation is it? For what purpose? Colonialism is a form of transformation. And Hitler's notion of making a certain type of world certainly involved a severely off-track notion of some type of "transformation." Still, what type of education do we want for our students? Do we not want them to grow up to make a better world?

QUESTIONS

1. Some teacher–educators say that instructors teach like they were taught—not like they were taught to teach. Do you agree with this statement? Why or why not?

2. The four models presented in this chapter are not mutually exclusive. When do you believe it is appropriate to use transmission? Transaction? Inquiry? Transformation?

3. Which of the frameworks presented here do you believe the federal government most supports? Parents most support? Principals? Professors of education? Why?

REFERENCES

Heald-Taylor, B. G. (1996). Three paradigms for literature instruction in grades 3 to 6. *Reading Teacher, 49* (6), 456–466.

Kamii, C. (2000). *Young children reinvent arithmetic: Implications of Piaget's theory* (2nd ed.). New York: Teachers College Press.

Katz, L., & Chard, S. (2000). *Engaging children's minds: The project approach* (2nd ed.). Stamford, CT: Ablex.

Jungck, S., & Marshall, J. D. (1992). Curricular perspectives on one great debate. In S. Kessler & B. B. Swadener (Eds.), *Reconceptualizing the early childhood curriculum: Beginning the dialogue* (pp. 19–37). New York: Teachers College Press.

McCardle, P., & Chhabra, V. (Eds.). (2004). *The voice of evidence in reading research.* Baltimore, MD: Paul H. Brookes.

Piaget, J. (1952). *The child's conception of number.* London: Routledge & Kegan Paul.

Wink, J. (2005). *Critical pedagogy: Notes from the real world* (3rd ed.). Boston: Allyn & Bacon.

CHAPTER 6

NO CHILD LEFT BEHIND?

Unless you have been living under a rock for the past five years, no doubt you have heard of the No Child Left Behind Act of 2001. But what is it? According to the U.S. Department of Education, Office of Elementary and Secondary Education, *No Child Left Behind: A Desktop Reference* (2002), "the No Child Left Behind Act of 2001 is a landmark in education reform designed to improve student achievement and change the culture of America's schools" (p. 9). But what does that mean? This chapter is designed to answer that question. It is divided into two major sections. The first section explains the 10 major sections (titles) of No Child Left Behind. The second part describes nine major issues related to the document.

AN OVERVIEW OF NO CHILD LEFT BEHIND

No Child Left Behind is based on four key principles: "(1) stronger accountability for results; (2) greater flexibility for states, school districts, and schools in the use of federal funds; (3) more choices for parents of children from disadvantaged backgrounds; and (4) an emphasis on teaching methods that have been demonstrated to work" (U.S. Department of Education, 2002, p. 9).

In more specific terms, No Child Left Behind was intended to

1. Give greater control and flexibility to schools and local districts
2. Require scientifically based teaching methods
3. Make states and local school districts accountable for their results

States and U.S. territories are required to test students in reading and math in grades 3 through 8, with science testing required for grades 3 through 8 by 2007. However, each state and territory determines, with federal government approval, what tests are used for accountability.

No Child Left Behind is divided into 10 "titles." For a complete explanation of each provision under Titles I through X, we recommend you consult the *No Child Left Behind: A Desktop Reference* (U.S. Department of Education, 2002). However, a brief summary of Titles I through X are provided here.

Title I. Improving the Academic Achievement of the Disadvantaged

Title I deals with improving how programs are operated by local education agencies. Two new early childhood initiatives were also added to Title I: *Early Reading First* and *Reading First*. Early Reading First was designed to prepare young children for success in kindergarten with regard to cognitive skills, language development, and early reading skills. Early Reading First is a preventative program. Public or private organizations within eligible school districts can apply for funds individually or collaboratively with other agencies.

Reading First is different from *Early Reading First*. Reading First is designed to improve literacy in kindergarten through third grade for those districts that qualify. Unlike Early Reading First, Reading First money flows from the federal government through the state departments of education. Reading First increases accountability for student performance, with the goal of closing the achievement gap between disadvantaged students and middle-class children. Of course, reading methods must be based on scientifically based research. The result of this has been a major emphasis on five areas of early reading instruction: (a) phonemic awareness, (b) phonics, (c) fluency, (d) vocabulary, and (e) comprehension (Ehri, 2004; Kamil, 2004; Stahl, 2004).

Title I also includes a number of other programs and provisions. These include the Even Start family literacy programs, improving school libraries, education of migrant children, a strong parental involvement component, programs for children who are neglected or at risk, comprehensive school reform advanced placement, and school dropout prevention (U.S. Department of Education, 2002).

Title II. Preparing, Training, and Recruiting High-Quality Teachers and Principals

Title II deals with the recruitment, education, and professional development of highly qualified teachers and administrators. Under Title II, requirements for school leaders are discussed as well as advanced certification and credentialing. Although certification of teachers is left up to each individual state or territory, No Child Left Behind requires certain standards be met in the development of these standards. Other provisions in Title II include the Troops-to-Teachers Program, the National Writing Project, civic education, and enhancing teaching and learning through the use of technology.

Title III. Language Instruction for Limited English Proficient and Immigrant Students

The entire focus of Title III is on English language learners. Teachers who are certified to teach English language learners must be proficient in English. Once again, the teaching methods used in language instruction for limited English proficient (LEP) and immigrant students must be based on scientifically based research. Students enrolled in these programs must meet adequate yearly progress and results must be reported to the U.S. Department of Education. The report should include program activities and their effectiveness.

Title IV. Twenty-first Century Schools

Title IV begins with safety issues. Requirements include guarantees that schools be free of environmental tobacco smoke as well as be both drug free and gun free. Provisions are made for reporting unsafe schools. However, each state determines the definition of an unsafe school. This makes comparisons among the states virtually impossible because of the lack of standard definition.

Perhaps the most important provision under Title IV involves after-school services that promote students' academic performance. This, however, is not limited to public schools. Local governments, faith-based organizations, and community centers may apply for funds under Title IV.

Title V. Promoting Informed Parental Choice and Innovative Programs

A wide range of innovative programs are described under Title V of No Child Left Behind. Everything from physical education to community technology centers to foreign language assistance falls under Title V. School configurations are also addressed in Title V. These include everything from public charter schools to magnet schools to smaller learning communities. The book distribution program, known as Reading Is Fundamental, is also addressed through Title V.

Parental choice is a major theme explained in Title V. Parental information centers are one example. Grantees of parental information centers must spend 30 percent of their award money to develop or expand some early childhood parent education program. Centers are also to assist schools in meeting the Title I parental involvement component.

Title VI. Flexibility and Accountability

As you have probably figured out by now, *accountability* is a major word associated with No Child Left Behind. Under Title VI, grants for state assessments are provided. Rural education initiatives are also part of Title VI, which include rural school achievement and rural and low-income school incentives.

A general provision of Title VI is the National Assessment of Education Progress. "The National Assessment of Educational Progress (NAEP) provides high-quality data on the achievement of elementary and secondary school students in reading, mathematics, science, and other subjects" (U.S. Department of Education, 2002, p. 161). NAEP is considered the Nation's Report Card and is the only report of its kind. While it has been given since the late 1960s only a few schools from each state are chosen to participate.

Titles VII–X—Other Requirements under No Child Left Behind

No Child Left Behind includes information about Native American, Native Hawaiian, and Alaskan Native education (Title VII), as well as impact aid related to schools on federal property (Title VIII) and general provisions that impact all programs under No Child Left Behind (Title IX). Repeals, redesignations, and amendments to other statutes (Title X) complete the federal guidelines under No Child Left Behind.

NINE ISSUES RELATED TO NO CHILD LEFT BEHIND

Since the beginning of No Child Left Behind there have been numerous issues. Nine of the most salient follow.

1. *Funding*—The federal government promised to provide extensive funding to implement all the requirements of No Child Left Behind. However, the federal government has not provided all the funds necessary for implementing the law and now expects states to pick up some of the slack. "A court challenge to the controversial No Child Left Behind education reform law brought by school districts in Michigan, Texas, Vermont and the National Education Association was thrown out today by a federal judge. . . . The suit claimed the U.S. Department of Education has imposed massive unfunded mandates on the states and local school districts" (Shepardson, 2005, p. 1). U.S. District Judge Bernard Friedman dismissed the lawsuit. However, the president of the NEA promised to appeal the ruling.

2. *Diversity of definitions and tests used by the states and territories*—The United States was originally organized with the notion that states were responsible for education. Each state has its own definition of highly qualified teacher. Each state has its own battery of tests used for adequate yearly progress. Each state has its own notion of what a safe school is. At least theoretically, a state could have a stringent definition of what constitutes safe schools whereas another state would have a much looser requirement. No real comparisons can be made because of these variations in definitions.

3. *Conflicting requirements with IDEA*—Questions have been raised by many educators about conflicts between No Child Left Behind and the Individuals with Disabilities Education Act (IDEA). The National Conference of State Legislatures conducted a study that identified problems with No Child Left Behind. One of the problems involved conflicts with the Individuals with Disabilities Education Act. "Utah State Representative Kory Holdaway, a member of the committee and a special education teacher, said the No Child Left Behind Act conflicts with a previous law designed to help students with disabilities, the Individuals with Disabilities Education Act" (National Conference of State Legislatures, 2005, p. 2). According to Holdaway, "ignoring the contradictions between IDEA and No Child Left Behind is one of the act's worst weaknesses" (p. 2). IDEA requires modifications for students with an established disability. However, only a certain percentage of students in a school district can receive modifications for adequate yearly progress testing according to No Child Left Behind.

4. *Adequate yearly progress and student attendance on test day*—According to the Florida Department of Education (2005) Website:

> Adequate Yearly Progress (AYP) measures the progress of all public schools, and school districts toward enabling all students to meet the state's academic achievement standards. AYP measurements target the performance and participation of various subgroups based on race or ethnicity, socioeconomic status, disability, and English proficiency. The goal of NCLB is to have 100 percent of students proficient by 2013–14. (p. 1)

To meet adequate yearly progress, a school must have a minimum average of 95 percent attendance over a three-year period. Otherwise, the school will not meet adequate yearly progress based on attendance alone. Schools in poverty areas have lower attendance rates than middle- or upper middle-class schools. This penalizes poor schools and students who need the most support.

5. *Highly qualified teachers*—Some teachers in some states who were highly qualified before No Child Left Behind find themselves not highly qualified today. This means they must go back to school for course work that may not be helpful. For example, in one state, "highly qualified" for early childhood, elementary, and special education teachers is defined by several possibilities. For teachers who only have a bachelor's degree, the definition includes what is known as a $4 \times 4 \times 4 \times 4$ plan. This means a teacher must have 4 courses in science, 4 courses in social science, 4 courses in language arts, and 4 courses in math. Most teachers meet the requirement for all except math. Some teachers who were certified more than 10 years ago only had one math course. At that time, only one math course was required in teacher education. So, kindergarten teachers may have to go back and take an advanced math class to be highly qualified. How will this help them teach kindergarten?

On the other hand, the federal government Website reports new flexibility with regard to "highly qualified." This source specifically addresses issues related to highly qualified status in rural areas, plus science and multisubject teachers, as well as middle school and special education teachers. According to *New No Child Left Behind Flexibility: Highly Qualified Teachers Fact Sheet* (U.S. Department of Education, 2004), "No Child Left Behind does not require current teachers to return to school or get a degree in every subject they teach to demonstrate that they are highly qualified" (p. 1). States may create alternative methods for teachers who have been teaching several years to measure their subject matter competence. Still, many people believe there is not enough flexibility with the requirement for highly qualified teachers.

6. *Deprofessionalization of teachers*—According to Ken Goodman (2004), "one avowed purpose of NCLB is to eliminate the gaps between white middle-class and minority children in school achievement. But NCLB thinks that is to be accomplished by treating all children alike" (p. 198). One way that children are all treated alike is through the use of scripted reading instruction. This destroys the professionalism of teaching. According to Bredekamp and Copple (1997) teachers should be reflective decision makers. However, NCLB "deprofessionalizes" the teaching profession by encouraging teachers to use scientifically proven methods, which in many cases results in scripted instruction (Aerni, 2004). No real decision making is necessary when scripted instruction is required. Where is the decision making when teachers are expected to follow the teacher's manual verbatim? "Say to the children_____. Now say_____."

7. *Unrealistic expectations for students of low income, special needs populations and English language learner students in adequate yearly progress*—Very few educators would argue that we should have high standards and expectations for all students regardless of race, ethnicity, gender, disability, primary language, or immigration status. But, is it appropriate to expect "all students to meet the same standards at the same pace when no other aspect of their lives treats them equally? Regardless of these concerns, AYP mandates that schools separate the achievement levels for each group and make those levels known to the public" (Shannon, 2004, p. 35). Shannon (2004) suggests that if the federal government is serious about exceptional expectations for students from exceptional populations, there should also be high standards that all children should be "well-fed, well-housed, well-cared-for, and secure in this standard of living" (p. 38).

8. *Management of No Child Left Behind at the federal level*—The federal government received great criticism for its response after Hurricane Katrina. Some questioned Michael Brown's qualifications and experience to lead the disaster relief. Similarly, some educators have questioned the credentials of Margaret

Spellings, the current Secretary of Education, to administer No Child Left Behind (Kirylo, 2005). Spellings has a bachelor's degree in political science. Ironically, she would not be highly qualified to teach in many states and territories. Yet, she is the one who is responsible for interpreting the policies and makes major decisions related to No Child Left Behind.

9. *Finally, 2014—the impossible dream!*—Again, nobody questions the need for high standards and rigorous expectations for students in our public schools. But what about the year 2014? In 2014, every child in the United States is expected to meet the standards of No Child Left Behind. We are talking about students in special education, English language learners, and all other students in the United States. Should we have high standards for all students? Of course. But is it realistic to expect every student to be on grade level?

In this chapter we presented a thumbnail sketch of No Child Left Behind and looked at nine concerns related to implementing it. Consider some of the following questions as you ponder the pros and cons of No Child Left Behind.

QUESTIONS

1. What does it mean to be a highly qualified teacher in your state or territory? How does this differ from other states?

2. If you were asked to write a letter to President Bush or Margaret Spellings regarding No Child Left Behind, what would you say? Why?

3. In this chapter we considered some of the issues or concerns educators have about No Child Left Behind. What are some of the good points of No Child Left Behind?

4. If you could change one thing about No Child Left Behind, what would it be? Why?

5. Interview a current public school teacher regarding No Child Left Behind. Discuss what he believes are the pros and cons of No Child Left Behind.

REFERENCES

Aerni, J. C. (2004). There is no one-plan-fits-all in education. In K. Goodman, P. Shannon, Y. Goodman, & R. Rapoport (Eds.), *Saving our schools—Saying no to "No Child Left Behind"* (pp. 125–128). Berkeley, CA: RDR Books.

Bredekamp, S., & Copple, C. (Eds.). (1997). *Developmentally appropriate practice in early childhood programs* (Rev. ed.). Washington, DC: NAEYC.

Ehri, L. C. (2004). Teaching phonemic awareness and phonics: An explanation of the National Reading Panel meta-analyses. In P. McCardle & V. Chhabra (Eds.), *The voice of evidence in reading research* (pp. 153–186). Baltimore, MD: Paul H. Brookes.

Florida Department of Education. (2005). *No Child Left Behind—fact sheet: NCLB and adequate yearly progress.* [On-line]. Available: www.fldoe.org/NCLB/.

Goodman, K. (2004). Reading and the federal laws. In K. Goodman, P. Shannon, Y. Goodman, & R. Rapoport (Eds.), *Saving our schools: The case for public education—Saying no to "No Child Left Behind"* (pp. 198–209). Berkeley, CA: RDR Books.

Kamil, M. L. (2004). Vocabulary and comprehension instruction: Summary and implications of the National Reading Panel findings. In P. McCardle & V. Chhabra (Eds.), *The voice of evidence in reading research* (pp. 213–234). Baltimore, MD: Paul H. Brookes.

Kirylo, J. (2005). Commentary. *Focus on Teacher Education, 5* (3), 1.

National Conference of State Legislatures (NCLS) News. (2005, February 23). *State legislators offer formula for improving No Child Left Behind Act.* [On-line]. Available: www.ncsl.org/programs/press/2005/pr050223.htm.

Shepardson, D. (2005, November 24). Judge dismisses challenge to No Child Left Behind funding. *Detroit News.* [On-line]. Available: www.detnews.com/apps/pbcs/dll/article?AID=/20051124/SCHOOLS/511240315/1.

Shannon, P. (2004). Adequate yearly progress. In K. Goodman, P. Shannon, Y. Goodman, & R. Rapoport (Eds.), *Saving our schools: The case for public education—Saying no to "No Child Left Behind"* (pp. 33–38). Berkeley, CA: RDR Books.

Stahl, S. A. (2004). What do we know about fluency? Findings of the National Reading Panel. In P. McCardle & V. Chhabra (Eds.), *The voice of evidence in reading research* (pp. 187–212). Baltimore, MD: Paul H. Brookes.

U.S. Department of Education, Office of Elementary and Secondary Education. (2002). *No Child Left Behind: A desktop reference.* Washington, DC: Author.

U.S. Department of Education. (2004, March). *New No Child Left Behind Flexibility: Highly Qualified Teachers Fact Sheet.* [On-line]. Available: www.ed.gov/nclb/methods/teachers/hqtflexibility.html.

CHAPTER 7

DEVELOPMENTALLY APPROPRIATE PRACTICE

BEST PRACTICE FOR ALL STUDENTS

Every day Ms. Latham's third graders are expected to sit quietly at their desks from 8:30 to 11:00, completing worksheets and workbook pages. No talking is allowed. If children need assistance, they are expected to raise their hands and wait patiently until Ms. Latham calls them to her desk. Expectations are similar in the afternoon as well. The students complete math problems that have been written on the blackboard. Then Ms. Latham lectures the whole class in either a social studies or a science lesson. Ms. Latham uses a reinforcement system in which students who have successfully completed all their work at the end of the week receive a prize.

Down the hall, Mr. Brunson's fourth grade class is quite different. Students are actively engaged all morning in collaborative groups. Each group of four students is discussing the subtopic that they have chosen from the theme "Elections in a Democratic Society." In fact, students work in groups or individually most of the day. Mr. Brunson has established learning stations at which students experience hands-on learning. Mr. Brunson expects students to feel passionate about their work because they have helped select the topics they will study. Rewards are rarely given because learning should be its own reward.

These two examples indicate two teachers with vastly different philosophies. Is one teacher involved in more developmentally appropriate practice or is it just a difference of styles? Just what is *developmentally appropriate practice?* This chapter is designed to answer six important questions. What is developmentally appropriate practice? What is the history of developmentally appropriate practice? What is the research base for developmentally appropriate practice? How has developmentally appropriate practice influenced educational practice? What are the criticisms of developmentally appropriate practice? What is the future of developmentally appropriate practice?

WHAT IS DEVELOPMENTALLY APPROPRIATE PRACTICE?

The original developmentally appropriate practice guidelines, published in 1986 (Bredekamp, 1986) and 1987 (Bredekamp, 1987) by the National Association for the Education of Young Children (NAEYC), were written "to provide guidance to program personnel seeking accreditation; the accreditation criteria call for developmentally appropriate activities, materials, and expectations" (Bredekamp, 1997, p. 35). A second purpose was to respond to the trend of pushing academic learning further and further down to the preschool level. The original guidelines had two dimensions that included both age appropriateness and individual appropriateness (Bredekamp, 1987).

In 1997, the guidelines were revised to emphasize the teacher as a reflective decision maker, planning for children based on three important dimensions: (a) what is known about child development and learning, (b) what is known about the individual child in the group, and (c) what is known about the cultural and social contexts of the students we teach (Bredekamp, 1997; Bredekamp & Copple, 1997). Essentially, the revised guidelines added *culturally appropriate practice to the existing age-appropriate practice and individually appropriate practice.*

Special educators have also determined recommended practices, especially for early intervention and early childhood special education (Sandall, Hemmeter, Smith, & McLean, 2005; Sandall, McLean, & Smith, 2000). Recommended practices are divided into direct services and indirect supports. Recommended practices for direct services include assessment, child-focused practices, family-based practices, interdisciplinary models, and technology applications. Indirect supports include recommendations concerning policies, procedures, and systems change, as well as personnel preparation issues (Sandall et al., 2005).

But what about older children? Extending the trend of developmentally appropriate practice upward, the Association for Childhood Education International (ACEI) published *Developmentally Appropriate Middle Level Schools* (Manning, 1993, 2002). Recognizing early adolescence as a legitimate developmental period between childhood and adolescence, these guidelines were provided to address specifically preadolescence or children from roughly 10 to 14 years of age. According to Manning (2002), developmentally appropriate practice for preadolescents can be defined as both organizational and curricular provisions "designed to meet 10- to 14-year-olds' developmental needs while acknowledging their tremendous diversity" (p. 7). The second edition of *Developmentally Appropriate Middle Level Schools* (Manning, 2002) defines *developmentally appropriate* as "educational experiences that are appropriate for individuals' physical, psychosocial, and cognitive developmental needs and interests" (p. 8).

But what about high school? Interestingly enough, the older a child becomes, the less we talk about developmentally appropriate practice. In fact, there are no specific guidelines endorsed by a professional organization that directly address developmentally appropriate practice for students older than 14 years. However, there are guidelines for "best practice" that include secondary schools (Daniels & Bizar, 2005; Zemelman, Daniels, & Hyde, 1998). Still, the emphasis of best practice recommendations in these sources tends to focus more on early childhood, elementary, and middle school students. But should there be developmentally appropriate practice guidelines for high school students? What would that mean?

WHAT IS THE HISTORY OF DEVELOPMENTALLY APPROPRIATE PRACTICE?

The roots for developmentally appropriate practice extend back to the early 1900s, when the International Kindergarten Union appointed a panel of 19 experts to determine how children should be taught in kindergarten. From this group, three separate reports were issued—one advocating highly structured, teacher-directed instruction; another, a play-based, child-initiated emphasis; and a third that was a compromise of the other two (Bredekamp, 1997). In the mid 1920s the National Association for Nursery Education (NANE), which later became the NAEYC, published *Minimum Essentials for Nursery School Education* (NANE, 1930). By the 1980s there were a large number of daycare programs that were unregulated, with a staggering number of untrained workers. The NAEYC once again began to develop criteria for high-quality preschools and early childhood programs by developing a national voluntary accreditation system in 1985 (Bredekamp & Glowacki, 1996). This resulted in the publishing of the 1986 and 1987 versions of developmentally appropriate practice (Charlesworth, 1998). During the next decade, criticisms and concerns of the document were published (see Bloch, 1991; Delpit, 1988; Katz, 1996; Kessler & Swadener, 1992; Mallory & New, 1994).

The roots of developmentally appropriate practice for middle school students also go back 100 years. In 1899, G. Stanley Hall published a two-volume source entitled *Adolescence*, coining the term *adolescence*. By 1944, preadolescence was proposed as a developmental stage (Redl, 1944); by 1951, a text on the psychology of the preadolescent was available (Blair & Burton, 1951). During the next 50 years, numerous sources described the development and needs of preadolescents (see Dorman, 1984; Eichhorn, 1966; Havighurst, 1968; Kagan & Coles, 1972; Lipsitz, 1984), and the *Journal of Early Adolescence* was founded by Thornburg in 1981 (Manning, 1993). Organizations such as the ACEI began publishing articles focusing on preadolescence. In fact, ACEI began a new publication known as *Focus on Later Childhood/Adolescence*.

WHAT IS THE RESEARCH BASE FOR DEVELOPMENTALLY APPROPRIATE PRACTICE?

Not surprisingly, developmentally appropriate practice spurred numerous research agendas, many of them originating at Louisiana State University (Charlesworth,

Hart, Burts, Mosley, & Fleege, 1993; Charlesworth, 1998). A summary of some of the findings, related to early childhood education, are described here:

■ Children in less developmentally appropriate classrooms exhibit almost twice the levels of stress behaviors compared with children in developmentally appropriate practice programs (Burts, Hart, Charlesworth, Fleege, Mosley, & Thomasson, 1992; Love, Ryer, & Faddis, 1992)

■ Students in inappropriate preschool programs have poorer academic achievement once they get to elementary school (Bryant, Burchinal, Lau, & Sparling, 1994).

■ Children in developmentally appropriate classrooms rank higher on behavioral evaluations (Marcon, 1994).

■ Students in developmentally appropriate programs score higher on measures of work–study habits (Marcon, 1992).

■ Students in developmentally inappropriate classrooms are more distractible (Charlesworth, 1998).

■ Children in developmentally appropriate programs are more prosocial during the early elementary years (Charlesworth, 1998).

■ Boys, children from low-socioeconomic-status homes, and blacks are the most "adversely affected by [developmentally inappropriate practice] DIP programs" (Charlesworth, 1998, p. 276).

■ Children in [developmentally appropriate practice] DAP classrooms do better than those in DIP classrooms on the California Achievement Test (Charlesworth, 1998).

However, since the first edition of *Current Issues and Trends* was published in 2002, psychologists and educators have looked more closely at the studies just summarized. Van Horn, Karlin, Ramey, Aldridge, and Snyder (2005) reported:

> [A]fter reviewing 17 empirical studies comparing the effects of DAP and DIP, there are no clear conclusions about the effects of DAP. For academic and cognitive outcomes these studies found a mix of positive, neutral, and negative effects of DAP. For psychosocial outcomes, especially stress, the results have been more consistently positive in favor of DAP classrooms. However, the measurement of DAP, use of teacher-rated outcomes, and inadequate statistical modeling in many of these studies further limit the conclusions that can be drawn. (p. 342)

Few studies have directly addressed developmentally appropriate practice in middle schools (Manning, 1993, 2002). Again, interest and research on developmentally appropriate practice appear to be centered in early childhood education.

HOW HAS DEVELOPMENTALLY APPROPRIATE PRACTICE INFLUENCED EDUCATIONAL PRACTICE?

Developmentally appropriate practice has influenced education in a number of ways. The following are 10 examples of how developmentally appropriate practice has made an impact on educational philosophy and practice.

Accreditation

The development of standards for accreditation has been remarkably influenced by developmentally appropriate practice. NAEYC launched an accreditation system in 1985. Today, early childhood programs that are accredited by NAEYC have followed developmentally appropriate practice guidelines (Bredekamp, 1997; Bredekamp & Glowacki, 1996). Furthermore, NAEYC is one of the largest professional education organizations in the world, with more than 100,000 members (Gestwicki, 1999). Many of the members have been involved in accreditation and have subscribed to many of the tenets of developmentally appropriate practice (Bredekamp, 1997).

An Emphasis on the Whole Child

Most teachers who subscribe to developmentally appropriate practice believe that physical, social, emotional, and cognitive development are closely related, interact, and strongly influence one another. "All learning experiences are recognized as integrated opportunities for growth, instead of separate skill or content entities" (Gestwicki, 1999, p. 9). The use of integrated teaching using thematic units and projects that cut across developmental domains has been used more because of developmentally appropriate practice.

Individualized Instruction

All children learn at varying rates in different areas of development. There are interindividual differences, or differences *among* children, and intraindividual differences, or differences *within* the same child, in areas of development. Teachers who recognize these differences are more likely to individualize instruction to the unique needs of each child (Charlesworth, 1998).

The Acceptance and Use of Children's Prior Knowledge

All education builds on previous experiences. The developers of developmentally appropriate practice guidelines encourage teachers to take into consideration children's previous experiences when planning instruction. Learning is influenced by multiple cultural and social contexts. All children develop in these multiple contexts. These contexts should be valued and used in instruction, rather than ignored (Gestwicki, 1999).

Active Learning

Particularly with younger children, hands-on materials and movement are necessary for optimal learning and development. Children construct knowledge through interaction with the environment. Knowledge, whether it is physical, social, or mathematical, is constructed from inside the child through activity (Kamii, 2000). Developmentally appropriate practice supports a constructivist approach to education (Kamii, 2000; Manning, 1993).

More In-Depth Study of a Topic

Children learn more when their day in school is less fragmented and they have opportunities to study fewer topics, but study these in greater depth (Chard, 1997; Katz & Chard, 1989; Manning & Manning, 1981). Just as constructivism has been encouraged by developmentally appropriate practice advocates, so has the project approach (Chard, 1997; Katz & Chard, 1989).

The Importance of Play

Play is an important way children learn. It strongly affects not only cognitive development, but also social, emotional, and language development. According to Gestwicki (1999), "teacher-supported play is an essential component of developmentally appropriate practice" (p. 10). Teachers who use developmentally appropriate practice guidelines incorporate play as an integral part of the curriculum.

Multiage Grouping

The implementation of multiage classrooms has increased as a result of developmentally appropriate practice guidelines (Gestwicki, 1999). Traditional same-age-group classrooms do not go well with developmentally appropriate practice, nor does retention. Children learn from others, both younger and older. The use of multiage classrooms has increased during the past 10 years, partly because of developmentally appropriate practice (Gestwicki, 1999).

The Teacher as Reflective Decision Maker

A strong addition to the revised developmentally appropriate practice text (Bredekamp & Copple, 1997) was an emphasis on teachers making informed decisions and on their becoming reflective practitioners. Bredekamp and Copple acknowledged that although guidelines can inform teachers, they must use their knowledge of children and the multiple contexts in which both teachers and children operate to make informed decisions.

Parent Involvement

A major component of developmentally appropriate practice (DAP) is working in concert with families. Parents and guardians are encouraged to be active participants and co-operators in developing the best education for their children. The increase in parent involvement in schools can be partially attributed to DAP (Wien, 1995).

WHAT ARE THE CRITICISMS OF DEVELOPMENTALLY APPROPRIATE PRACTICE?

During the past 15 years, numerous criticisms have been wielded at developmentally appropriate practice. These criticisms can be divided into three major categories that include (a) problems related to children with disabilities, (b) criticisms related to context, and (c) issues related to theory.

Problems Related to Children with Disabilities

Some special educators have suggested that developmentally appropriate practice can be equally beneficial for children with disabilities (Charlesworth, 1998), but others have called into question the applicability of DAP guidelines to children with special needs (Jipson, 1991). Some have even suggested that developmentally appropriate practice is necessary for children with special needs but not sufficient. Donna Dugger–Wadsworth (1997) sees limited problems in using DAP with children with disabilities. Charlesworth (1998) agrees. She suggests, ". . . teachers need to learn how to modify materials and activities so that special needs children can be included in regular classroom activities" (p. 280). Still, children with special needs may need more direct instruction and intensive one-on-one attention to achieve their full potential. Bredekamp and Copple (1997) see no problem in using DAP with children with diverse abilities because the teacher is expected to be a reflective decision maker. However, Lubeck (1998) questions the use of DAP guidelines with not only children with special needs but with children from various backgrounds.

Criticisms Related to Context

One of the biggest problems with DAP, according to the critics, is the fact that it does not work in certain contexts. There are problems in implementing DAP with black children (see Phillips, 1994), Native American individuals (see Williams, 1994), children in school who use English as a second language (see Genishi,

Dyson, & Fassler, 1994), and children from other cultural contexts, including those from a lower socioeconomic environment (see Bowman & Stott, 1994).

Developmentally appropriate practice reflects liberal middle-class values and is often very different from the real-world practice, beliefs, and prior experiences of parents and teachers who do not share these assumptions. In subtle ways, those who do not subscribe to DAP are often seen as uncaring people who do not attempt educational practices that are in the best interest of children. For example, Meredith, who is a teacher of young children, does not subscribe to DAP guidelines. She is currently taking a child development class in which developmentally appropriate practice assumptions guide class discussions. In her reflections, she is questioning her own beliefs as well as the DAP guidelines. Here she writes about her ideas on the hurried child:

> This issue has brought to my attention some important factors that pertain to my daily life—as a teacher and as a parent. Every day in my classroom, my students do many of the things that the experts warn against. We do many pencil-and-paper tasks, we have interactive Bible lessons, which last at least 30 minutes, we have homogeneous reading groups, and the children memorize many things such as the Lord's Prayer and A through Z in Bible verses. All of these things are taboo according to developmentally appropriate practice.
>
> I have to say there have been times when I have asked the questions: Is this really the best program for the children? Was it better when I was in kindergarten and all we did was socialize, play, and do hands-on activities? My opinions are still uncertain. I have been teaching this same curriculum for two years now and it seems to have worked well for the majority of the children. None of the students seem to be experiencing high stress. In fact, they cannot wait to return to school from day to day. My own daughter is in my class and she loves it. She is a normal five-year-old who enjoys being a child like any other. I also try to help the children understand everything they are learning. I am the kind of teacher, though, who allows much time for socialization, imaginative play, experimental learning, and just being a kid. I use reflective teaching in my class and am constantly aware of what is and what is not working with the children. If things do not seem to be going well, I change to find a more suitable method for the setting.
>
> On the other hand, I do worry about the children in today's society growing up too quickly. I also understand the fact that by fourth grade, you cannot determine those children who went to preschool or those who entered school in first grade. As a parent, it is very important that my child does not grow up too quickly.
>
> My main goal right now, as a parent and as a kindergarten teacher, is to provide children with a strong foundation that will give them a love and hunger for learning that will last a lifetime. It is my personal belief that I cannot do this on my own. I want to make positive, lasting impressions on those around me that will show them love and lead them down the right path. I hope what I am doing is giving the children the best of both worlds by allowing them to gain self-esteem, create lasting childhood memories, and ignite a passion for learning success.

Meredith lives, works, and rears her daughter in a community that does not generally support developmentally appropriate practice. Does Meredith exhibit developmentally appropriate practice in her classroom? Some would say yes. In fact, Bredekamp and Copple (1997) would probably say yes. Meredith is a reflective practitioner. She thoughtfully prepares her teaching and tries to balance teacher-directed with child-initiated activities. However, she does use worksheets, memorization, has children sit and listen for long periods of time, and utilizes homogeneous grouping—all of which are not recommended as developmentally appropriate practice.

Another student in the child development class believes she did not experience developmentally appropriate practice when she was a young child but believes her learning experiences were good for her, even though they may not be classified as DAP. Lakennia writes,

> I was placed in a preschool at the age of two. I was introduced to a lot of new things and places at a very young age. I believe I was in a rushed environment because I was expected to do many things that my mother did not require of me at such a young age. I was told to clean up after myself, write my name, and trace things. I was also taught to tie my own shoelaces and many other difficult tasks. The more of these tasks that I could accomplish, the more pleased I was, and this encouraged me to learn more. I enjoyed the attention given by my parents when I could do something other children who stayed at home could not do. I enjoyed the feeling of success when I finally learned how to do something that the others in my class could do. I was hurried, but some of it was of my own doing and it has made me into the self-assertive person I am today.

Lakennia, like Meredith, is questioning developmentally appropriate practice. The waters of developmentally appropriate practice have been muddied even more since the revised edition was published (Bredekamp & Copple, 1997). With the addition of an entire chapter devoted to the teacher as reflective decision maker, and the incorporation of context and culture as being important considerations in developmentally appropriate practice, practitioners are less certain of exactly what developmentally appropriate practice is. Sally Lubeck (1998) suggests that by including voices critical of DAP, the guidelines have become an attempt to be all things to all people. But she believes there are multiple points of view and that DAP is based on specific assumptions and a highly selective theoretical background that cannot absorb many dissenting voices.

Issues Related to Theory

Developmentally appropriate practice is clearly based on the theories of Piaget, Vygotsky, and Erikson (see Bredekamp & Rosegrant, 1992). In defense of Piaget, Vygotsky, and Erikson, it should be noted that these three theorists were not really interested in their work shaping educational practice. They wanted, instead, to contribute to other fields, especially psychology.

Although other theorists are mentioned, virtually all of them are modern (as opposed to postmodern) theorists who are also dead, white, Western men

(Hsue & Aldridge, 1995). All the theories on which DAP guidelines are based are Euro-American, masculine, psychologically based theories, yet the majority of the people who teach are women—many of them women of color. Although this might seem amusing but not important at first glance, let's take a look at some of the statements these men have made about women and minorities.

As pointed out in Chapter 4, G. Stanley Hall, the father of developmental psychology, indicated that women should not go to college with men, but to a separate college where they can rest their brains and use their intuition (Sadker & Sadker, 1994). Piaget indicated that the children of Martinique were four years behind in their progression through the stages of cognitive development because their families were lazy (see Bringuier, 1980). He did not seem to take into consideration the fact that the children who were tested using his theory in France, Switzerland, or French Canada were white, upper middle-class children whose families chose to be a part of the French education system. The children of Martinique were children of color whose families were taken against their will as slaves. Their historical ways of thinking and their educational system were quite different from the one imposed on them by the French. Kohlberg, a follower of Piaget, based his theory of moral development on a male sample, yet the child development texts of the 1970s and 1980s rarely reported this important fact (see Turner & Helms, 1983; Vander Zanden, 1989).

Another issue is the fact that DAP guidelines have virtually ignored postmodern, critical, and feminist thinking. There is probably a good reason for this. Developmentally appropriate practice is based on universal principles of child development, whereas postmodern and critical theories focus on the context, the particular, and refrain from the belief of universal ideas constructed by dead, white, Western men. With the decidedly biased framework, what will become of developmentally appropriate practice?

Problems Related to No Child Left Behind

Can developmentally appropriate practice survive No Child Left Behind? Liberals are quite concerned about this (see Goodman, Shannon, Goodman, & Rapoport, 2004). Conservatives tend to ignore the issue or discuss DAP using another label (see McCardle & Chhabra, 2004). The definition of scientifically based research used by the federal government in implementing No Child Left Behind appears, to some educators, to be in direct conflict with developmentally appropriate practice. For example, Robert Sweet (2004) suggests, "teaching a child to read, however, is not a complicated process and does not require years to accomplish. The findings of decades of careful research . . . provide reading teachers with a rock-solid foundation upon which to build their instructional practices. There are many problems in life for which there appear to be no answers, but teaching a child to read is not one of them" (p. 36).

Developmentally appropriate practitioners do not believe that "one size fits all" (Aerni, 2004; Parks, 2004). However, scripted reading programs that are teacherproof are much more likely to meet the federal government's definition of reading than early reading programs that are considered to be developmentally appropriate.

There are also major differences in what constitutes appropriate assessment. One example is Dynamic Indicators of Basic Early Literacy Skills (or DIBELS) (Good & Kaminski, 2002). Proponents of developmentally appropriate practice believe qualitative and authentic reading assessments are salient. However, the federal government does not support early reading research based on portfolio assessments and considers instruments such as DIBELS quite appropriate, even though many educators believe it is developmentally inappropriate (Houk–Cerna, 2004; Torgensen, 2004).

WHAT IS THE FUTURE OF DEVELOPMENTALLY APPROPRIATE PRACTICE?

Similar to what occurred at the turn of the 20th century, at the beginning of the 21st century we cannot accurately predict what will happen with regard to educational issues in the next 100 years. That doesn't keep us from asking: What is the future of developmentally appropriate practice? Aldridge (1996) suggests five questions that need to be addressed to predict the future of DAP:

1. Is DAP a dynamic, ever-changing construct or is Developmentally Appropriate Practice considered the bible for educational practice?
2. Can DAP incorporate critics' voices?
3. Can DAP support a more family-centered focus with regard to very young children?
4. Can DAP be more culturally sensitive?
5. Will DAP advocates become more politically active in working for the rights of children and minorities?

Developmentally appropriate practice will always be an issue in education because the notion of DAP takes a particular perspective that is not shared by everyone. Developmentally appropriate practice guidelines rely heavily on universal principles, which reflect modern values that are not embraced by most postmodern thinkers. According to Lubeck (1998), modern ideas "must be tempered with a postmodern appreciation for the oral, particular, local, and timely— the practical concerns of people in specific situations" (p. 287).

QUESTIONS

1. Why are professional organization guidelines sometimes in conflict with recommendations made by federal, state, and local administrators?

2. What should you be learning in college or graduate school? What is currently happening in our public schools and how to teach in the culture of public schools? Or, should you be learning what is best practice or developmentally appropriate practice? Are these in conflict? If so, explain.

3. Is developmentally appropriate practice in conflict with No Child Left Behind? If so, in what ways? In what ways are they alike? Different?

4. Was developmentally appropriate practice used when you were in school? If so, how?

5. What are the pros and cons of developmentally appropriate practice?

REFERENCES

Aerni, J. C. (2004). There is no one-plan-fits-all in education. In K. Goodman, P. Shannon, Y. Goodman, & R. Rapoport (Eds.), *Saving our schools: The case for public education—saying no to "No Child Left Behind"* (pp. 125–128). Berkeley, CA: RDR Books.

Aldridge, J. (1996). Is developmentally appropriate practice for everyone? *ACEI Focus on Infancy, 9* (1), 1–2.

Aldridge, J., & Goldman, R. (2002). *Current issues and trends in education.* Boston: Allyn & Bacon.

Blair, A. W., & Burton, W. H. (1951). *Growth and development of the preadolescent.* New York: Appleton-Century-Crofts.

Bloch, M. (1991). Critical science and the history of child development's influence on early education research. *Early Education and Development, 2* (2), 95–108.

Bowman, B., & Stott, F. (1994). Understanding development in a cultural context: The challenge for teachers. In B. L. Mallory & R. S. New (Eds.), *Diversity and developmentally appropriate practice: Challenges for early childhood education* (pp. 119–134). New York: Teachers College Press.

Bredekamp, S. (1986). *Developmentally appropriate practice in early childhood programs serving children from birth through age 5.* Washington, DC: NAEYC.

Bredekamp, S. (Ed.). (1987). *Developmentally appropriate practice in early childhood programs serving children from birth through age 8* (Exp. ed.). Washington, DC: NAEYC.

Bredekamp, S. (1997). NAEYC issues revised position statement on developmentally appropriate practice in early childhood programs. *Young Children, 52* (2), 34–40.

Bredekamp, S., & Copple, C. (Eds.). (1997). *Developmentally appropriate practice in early childhood programs* (Rev. ed.). Washington, DC: NAEYC.

Bredekamp, S., & Glowacki, G. (1996). The first decade of NAEYC accreditation: Growth and impact on the field. In S. Bredekamp & B. Wilier (Eds.), *NAEYC accreditation: A decade of learning and the years ahead* (pp. 1–10). Washington, DC: NAEYC.

Bredekamp, S., & Rosegrant, T. (Eds.). (1992). *Reaching potentials: Appropriate curriculum and assessment for young children* (Vol. 1). Washington, DC: NAEYC.

Bringuier, J. (1980). *Conversations with Piaget.* Chicago: University of Chicago Press.

Bryant, D. M., Burchinal, M., Lau, L. B., & Sparling, J. J. (1994). Family and classroom correlates of Head Start children's developmental outcomes. *Early Childhood Research Quarterly, 9,* 289–309.

Burts, D. C., Hart, C. H., Charlesworth, R., Fleege, P. O., Mosley, J., & Thomasson, R. H. (1992). Observed activities and stress behaviors of children in developmentally appropriate and inappropriate kindergarten classrooms. *Early Childhood Research Quarterly, 7,* 297–318.

Chard, S. (1997). *The project approach.* New York: Scholastic.

Charlesworth, R. (1998). Developmentally appropriate practice is for everyone. *Childhood Education, 74* (5), 274–282.

Charlesworth, R., Hart, C. H., Burts, D. C., Mosley, J., & Fleege, P. O. (1993). Measuring the developmental appropriateness of kindergarten teachers' beliefs and practices. *Early Childhood Research Quarterly, 8,* 255–276.

Daniels, H. D., & Bizar, M. (2005). *Teaching the best practice way: Methods that matter, K–12.* Portland, ME: Stenhouse.

Delpit, L. (1988). The silenced dialogue: Power and pedagogy in educating other people's children. *Harvard Educational Review, 58* (3), 280–298.

Dorman, G. (1984). *Middle grades assessment program.* Chapel Hill, NC: Center for Early Adolescence, UNC.

Dugger–Wadsworth, D. (1997). The integrated curriculum and students with disabilities. In C. H. Hart, D. C. Burts, & R. Charlesworth (Eds.), *Integrated curriculum and developmentally appropriate practice: Birth to age eight* (pp. 335–362). Albany, NY: SUNY Press.

Eichhorn, D. (1966). *The middle school.* New York: Center for Applied Research in Education.

Genishi, C., Dyson, A., & Fassler, R. (1994). Language and diversity in early childhood: Whose voices are appropriate? In B. L. Mallory & R. S. New (Eds.), *Diversity and developmentally appropriate practice* (pp. 250–268). New York: Teachers College Press.

Gestwicki, C. (1999). *Developmentally appropriate practice: Curriculum and development in early education* (2nd ed.). Albany, NY: Delmar Publishers.

Good, R. H., & Kaminski, R. A. (Eds.). (2002). *Dynamic indicators of basic early literacy skills* (6th ed.). Eugene, OR: Institute for Development of Educational Achievement.

Goodman, K., Shannon, P., Goodman, Y., & Rapoport, R. (Eds.). (2004). *Saving our schools: The case for public education—Saying no to "No Child Left Behind."* Berkeley, CA: RDR Books.

Hall, G. S. (1899). *Adolescence.* New York: Appleton.

Havighurst, R. J. (1968). The middle school child in contemporary society. *Theory into Practice, 7,* 120–122.

Houk–Cerna, F. (2004). What the DIBELS is that? In K. Goodman, P. Shannon, Y. Goodman, & R. Rapoport (Eds.), *Saving our schools: The case for public education—Saying no to "No Child Left Behind"* (pp. 129–131). Berkeley, CA: RDR Books.

Hsue, Y., & Aldridge, J. (1995). Developmentally appropriate practice and traditional Taiwanese culture. *Journal of Instructional Psychology, 22* (4), 320–323.

Jipson, J. (1991). Developmentally appropriate practice: Culture, curriculum, connections. *Early Education and Development, 2,* 120–136.

Kagan, J., & Coles, R. (Eds.). (1972). *Twelve to sixteen: Early adolescence.* New York: Norton.

Kamii, C. (2000). *Young children reinvent arithmetic: Implications of Piaget's theory* (2nd ed.). New York: Teachers College Press.

Katz, L. (1996). Child development knowledge and teacher preparation: Confronting assumptions. *Early Childhood Research Quarterly, 11* (2), 135–146.

Katz, L. G., & Chard, S. C. (1989). *Engaging children's minds: The project approach.* Norwood, NJ: Ablex.

Kessler, S., & Swadener, B. (Eds.). (1992). *Reconceptualizing the early childhood curriculum: Beginning the dialogue.* New York: Teachers College Press.

Lipsitz, J. (1984). *Successful schools for young adolescents.* New Brunswick, NJ: Transaction.

Love, J., Ryer, P., & Faddis, B. (1992). *Caring environments: Program quality in California's publicly funded child development programs.* Portsmouth, NH: RMC Research.

Lubeck, S. (1998). Is developmentally appropriate practice for everyone? *Childhood Education 74* (5), 283–292.

Mallory, B. L., & New, R. S. (Eds.). (1994). *Diversity and developmentally appropriate practices: Challenges for early childhood education.* New York: Teachers College Press.

Manning, M. L. (1993). *Developmentally appropriate middle level schools.* Olney, MD: ACEI.

Manning, M. L. (2002). *Developmentally appropriate middle level schools* (2nd ed.). Olney, MD: ACEI.

Manning, M., & Manning, G. (1981). The school's assault on childhood. *Childhood Education, 58* (2), 84–87.

Marcon, R. A. (1992). Differential effects of three preschool models on inner-city 4-year-olds. *Early Childhood Research Quarterly, 7,* 517–530.

Marcon, R. A. (1994). Doing the right thing for children: Linking research and policy reform in the District of Columbia public schools. *Young Children, 50* (8), 8.

McCardle, P., & Chhabra, V. (Eds.). (2004). *The voice of evidence in reading research.* Baltimore, MD: Paul H. Brookes.

NANE (National Association for Nursery Education). (1930). *Minimum essentials for nursery school education.* Washington, DC: Author.

Parks, J. (2004). No illusion left behind: "High standards" meet the real world. In K. Goodman, P. Shannon, Y. Goodman, & R. Rapoport (Eds.), *Saving our schools: The case for public education—Saying no to "No Child Left Behind"* (pp. 123–124). Berkeley, CA: RDR Books.

Phillips, C. B. (1994). The movement of African-American children through sociocultural contexts: A case of conflict resolution. In B. L. Mallory & R. S. New (Eds.), *Diversity and developmentally appropriate practice: Challenges for early childhood education* (pp. 137–154). New York: Teachers College Press.

Redl, F. (1944). Preadolescents: What makes them tick? *Child Study, 21,* 44–48.

Sadker, M., & Sadker, D. (1994). *Failing at fairness: How schools shortchange girls.* New York: Houghton Mifflin.

Sandall, S., Hemmeter, M. L., Smith, B. J., & McLean, M. E. (2005). *DEC recommended practices: A comprehensive guide for practical application in early intervention/early childhood special education* (2nd ed.). Longmont, CO: Sopris West.

Sandall, S., McLean, M. E., & Smith, B. J. (2000). *DEC recommended practices: A comprehensive guide for practical application in early intervention/early childhood special education.* Longmont, CO: Sopris West.

Sweet, R. W. (2004). The big picture: Where we are nationally on the reading front and how we got here. In P. McCardle & V. Chhabra (Eds.), *The voice of evidence in reading research* (pp. 13–44). Baltimore, MD: Paul H. Brookes.

Torgensen, J. K. (2004). Lessons learned from research on interventions for students who have difficulty learning to read. In P. McCardle & V. Chhabra (Eds.), *The voice of evidence in reading research* (pp. 355–382). Baltimore, MD: Paul H. Brookes.

Turner, J. S., & Helms, D. B. (1983). *Lifespan development* (2nd ed.). New York: Holt, Rinehart and Winston.

Vander Zanden, J. W. (1989). *Human development* (4th ed.). New York: Random House.

Van Horn, M. L., Karlin, E. O., Ramey, S. L., Aldridge, J., & Snyder, S. W. (2005). Effects of developmentally appropriate practices on children's development: A review of research and discussion of methodological and analytic issues. *The Elementary School Journal, 105* (4), 325–352.

Wien, C. A. (1995). *Developmentally appropriate practice in real life. Stories of teacher practical knowledge.* New York: Teachers College Press.

Williams, L. (1994). Developmentally appropriate practice and cultural values: A case in point. In B. L. Mallory & R. S. New (Eds.), *Diversity and developmentally appropriate practice: Challenges for early childhood education* (pp. 155–165). New York: Teachers College Press.

Zemelman, S., Daniels, H., & Hyde, A. (1998). *Best practice: New standards for teaching and learning in America's schools* (2nd ed.). Portsmouth, NH: Heinemann.

CHAPTER 8

SOCIAL PROMOTION, RETENTION, AND ALTERNATIVE POSSIBILITIES

JANICE N. COTTON

Thousands of children each year fail to acquire the skills necessary to experience success in the next grade. Some are retained with the intent of providing more time and opportunities to master needed concepts. Others are *socially* promoted in the belief that retention may possibly do more harm than help. Which is more effective in promoting immediate and long-term academic success—grade retention or social promotion? A review of the research indicates that neither is an appropriate course of action for students who are failing academically (Alexander, Entwisle, & Dauber, 1994; Shepard & Smith, 1989; Thompson, 1999). Ironically, the evidence against the effectiveness of retention and social promotion continues to mount as more states develop rigorous promotion and graduation standards. If neither is effective, what course of action should schools take with struggling students? The purpose of this chapter is to present the research on retention and social promotion, and then detail proven alternatives to these practices.

SOCIAL PROMOTION

Prevalence of Social Promotion

Social promotion is the practice of promoting students to the next grade even though they have not acquired minimum competencies expected of that grade. The number of students socially promoted each year is unknown because few school districts report these data and other districts have only limited data (U.S. Department of Education, 1999). This practice appears to be fairly widespread, however, according to a 1997 survey conducted by the American Federation of Teachers (AFT). Results from the AFT (1997) survey showed that 85 large urban school districts do not have a policy endorsing social promotion. Even though social promotion is not officially endorsed in these districts, more than half the teachers surveyed indicated that they had promoted unprepared students the previous year. Reasons given for these social promotions were fear that high failure rates would reflect poorly on the school and school personnel, pressure exerted by principals and parents to promote unready students, knowledge that retention is ineffective, and the absence or insufficiency of effective educational alternatives to social promotion.

Negative Effects of Social Promotion

Educational leaders, governmental officials, and policymakers are clearly concerned about the prevalence of social promotion. In February 1998, President Clinton recommended that the U.S. Department of Education (USDOE) (1999) put an end to social promotion. In the past 15 years, 15 states have established specific standards for grade promotion, and others are planning such policies (Northwest Regional Educational Laboratory [NWREL], 1999).

Social promotion is problematic for students, teachers, and parents. Social promotion gives some students the false sense that they have mastered skills necessary for later success. It sends a message to other students that their effort and achievement do not count. Having socially promoted students in the classroom is challenging, because teachers must plan for and teach to a group of children with widely divergent skills and knowledge. Furthermore, it creates frustration among teachers who feel powerless to expect hard work from all students. Social promotion sends parents the false message that their children are adequately prepared to be successful in school and in the labor force (AFT, 1997; National Association of State Boards of Education [NASBE], 1999).

Colleges, universities, and businesses also encounter negative side effects from the practice of social promotion. Data from the NCES showed in 1995 that about one in three freshmen had to take a remedial class in math, science, or writing (NCES, 1996). In addition, college professors are finding that they must lower their standards to assist students who are not prepared for college work. The business community is now investing substantial funds to reeducate students who lack skills needed to be successful in the labor force (AFT, 1997; NASBE, 1999; Thompson, 1999).

Implications and Findings from Local Social Promotion Policies

An increasing number of state and local school districts have created promotion policies that guide decisions regarding students' advancement to the next grade level. The long-term results of these promotion policies are unknown. Recent events with the Los Angeles Unified School District provide an interesting case study of the possible fallout from implementing such standards.

The Los Angeles Unified School District reported on January 31, 2000, that if they retained all the students who had not met grade-level standards, two-thirds of all eighth graders and 40 to 60 percent of second through eighth graders would flunk. Therefore, the district redefined or loosened their standards and it now appears that 6,000 second graders and 4,000 eighth graders will not be promoted. Even though the number is substantially reduced, Los Angeles still faces several significant problems. School officials plan to tailor a curriculum for these students rather than have them repeat the same material. However, they have no place to house the retainees, so they are investigating leasing space from hospitals and setting up bungalows in school parking lots. In addition, they have not identified teachers to work with these students nor have they provided training to give them the skills they need to be successful. Teachers, administrators, and parents are all questioning why the district did not adequately prepare for the possible consequences of the tougher promotion standards (Sahagun & Sauerwein, 2000).

A research study examining Chicago's promotion standards also provides information on the effect of promotion standards on student academic achievement. In 1997, Chicago established promotion standards for grades 3, 6, and 8. Students who do not meet the standards are required to attend a summer program and retake the promotion test. Those who fail in the summer are retained, promoted, or sent to an alternative school. The Consortium on Chicago Research completed a study examining the efficacy of the 1997 to 1998 promotion standards on student achievement (Roderick, Byrk, Jacob, Easton, & Allensworth, 1999). Results from this study showed that the summer program was successful in raising students' performance, but these students remained at risk because the gains were not sustained the following academic year. The students who were retained fared poorly. Only about one in three retained students were able to meet the test cutoff score after two years in the same grade. Furthermore, the retained students did no better than comparable children who had been socially promoted.

Conclusions about Social Promotion

Social promotion is a widespread practice that is being questioned by school personnel and the community at large. Districts are implementing policies to eliminate or severely curtail the practice because of the negative short- and long-term effects. Even though this practice is not in the best interest of students, schools, businesses, colleges, or the community, school officials are struggling with how best to eliminate social promotion and at the same time provide manageable, cost-effective programs that promote positive student achievement.

GRADE RETENTION

Educators and researchers have examined the effectiveness of grade retention for decades. From the early 1980s to the present, opinions regarding the merit of grade retention have varied from being positive for some students and in some circumstances, to being overwhelmingly negative and of little value in promoting academic achievement in others. Several conclusions regarding the helpfulness and harmfulness of retention can be drawn from the wealth of research that has been conducted. Overall, one point is clear—retention is not effective in producing significant gains in student achievement or in having lasting benefits for struggling students (Alexander et al., 1994; Shepard & Smith, 1989; Thompson, 1999).

Prevalence and Cost of Grade Retention

The prevalence of grade retention, much like social promotion, is unknown, because school districts rarely keep records of how many children are retained each year. Estimates can be derived, however, from census data. These estimates show that the number of grade-retained children ranges from six to nine percent annually (Association of California School Administrators, 1999; Center for Policy and Research in Education [CPRE], 1990). For students in urban school districts, the retention rate has been estimated to be approximately 50 percent (AFT, 1997). The cost of retaining or reeducating U.S. students for at least one year is staggering. For example, in 1996 to 1997 there were about 46 million children enrolled in public schools in the United States with an average cost per pupil expenditure of $5,923 (NCES, 1999b). Using these figures, this means that at least 3.2 million children (7 percent) were retained in grade at a cost of almost $19 billion.

Retention and Academic Achievement

Retention can help some students and in certain circumstances, but there are serious risks associated with it (Thompson, 1999). The majority of studies show that retention is not effective in promoting positive academic achievement, especially in the long run. Holmes (1989) conducted a meta-analysis of 63 empirical studies that examined the effectiveness of retention. Fifty-four of the 63 studies showed that at-risk children who were promoted achieved at the same or higher levels than comparable peers who were retained and spent two years rather than one in a grade. Other studies have also confirmed these findings and found that when retained and promoted students of like ability were compared, the promoted students outperformed the retained students the next year (Norton, 1990; Walters & Borgers, 1995).

Children are often retained in kindergarten or first grade in the belief that if a student must be retained, it is best to do so very early in a child's school career. Several well-designed studies show, however, that retaining children in kindergarten and first grade ultimately can be ineffective and harmful. A large study in the Chicago public schools showed that retained children, especially in first grade, did not improve over time (Reynolds, Temple, & McCoy, 1997). Alexander and colleagues (1994) followed 775 students in Baltimore city schools for eight years. They found that children retained in first grade improved their achievement test scores the year they were retained. However, these same retainees achieved in second grade and every grade thereafter at the same relative level as their first year in first grade. Researchers speculate first grade retention may be especially difficult for young children because of the difficulty they experience transitioning into a formal school environment. Being removed from peers with whom they have formed a relationship appears to hinder their development rather than foster positive growth (Entwisle & Alexander, 1993).

There is a considerable amount of research that also shows that kindergarten retention and use of transition grades (such as two-year kindergarten programs) have no lasting academic advantage over other children who were never retained but were also equally unready because of immaturity or low achievement. Children who spent the extra year in kindergarten were just as likely as their promoted counterparts to be at the bottom of the third grade class (Gredler, 1984; Holmes, 1989; Meisels, 1992; Nason, 1991; Rose, Medway, Cantrell, & Marus, 1983; Shepard & Smith, 1986, 1989).

Retention and Social and Health Implications

Children who are retained tend to feel more poorly about their capabilities, score lower on measures of personal and psychological adjustment, and display more discipline problems. Clinical interviews with students show that they felt angry or sad about the retention and feared the reaction of family and friends. Some were teased by neighbors and reported having a difficult time adjusting to school (Byrnes, 1989; Holmes, 1989; Norton, 1990; Shepard & Smith, 1989).

Being retained in a grade has also been strongly correlated with dropping out of school. Children who are retained one year are five times more likely to drop out of school than those who have never been retained. Children who are retained two or more years have almost a 100 percent probability of becoming dropouts compared with similar low performers who are promoted (CPRE, 1990).

School failure has also been linked to participation in health-risk behaviors (cigarette use, alcohol use, and weapons-related violence) for adolescents, according to data from the National Longitudinal Study of Adolescent Health (Blum, Beuhring, Shew, Bearing, Sieving, & Resnick, 2000). In-home interviews with a nationally representative sample of about 10,000 students ages 12 to 17 and their families showed that school failure is more likely to predict participation in violent activities, use of alcohol, and involvement in sexual activity than is poverty, race, or family structure. The researchers concluded that school failure should be viewed as a public health problem (Blum et al., 2000).

Conclusions about Retention

Even though a few studies have found that retention can have a positive short-term benefit (Alexander et al., 1994; Holmes, 1989), the vast majority have shown either no long-term advantage, harm, or a consistent "washout" effect (Gredler, 1984; Holmes, 1989; Mantizicopoulos & Morrison, 1992; Meisels, 1992; Nason,

1991; Reynolds et al., 1997; Rose et al., 1983; Shepard & Smith, 1986, 1989). This indicates that the potential benefit does not warrant the risk. Even researchers who otherwise support retention do not view it as a tool for helping children succeed in school (Alexander et al., 1994).

ALTERNATIVES TO SOCIAL PROMOTION AND GRADE RETENTION

In 1998, the U.S. Secretary of Education urged school districts to find alternatives to social promotion and retention. The White House Press Office stated that promoting unprepared students and retaining students in the same grade are not appropriate responses to low student achievement because these practices presume that academic failure is unavoidable and acceptable. Instead, they recommended that schools should implement research-based practices that help students meet standards the first time they are exposed to them (NWREL, 1999).

As schools create plans to prevent school failure, two key points should be emphasized. Schools must

1. be proactive and attempt to prevent failure, and
2. identify at-risk children as soon as possible and immediately take action to implement best practices.

One of the best means to ensure student success is to provide a program that strives to prevent school failure and provides intervention at the first indication of a problem (USDOE, 1999). Yet all too often, intervention is provided too late to be truly effective. Often schools step in to help children after an academic problem has escalated out of control, rather than identifying and providing assistance in preschool, kindergarten, or first grade. Many children who enter school with insufficient skills, especially those two or more years behind their peers, are never able to meet grade-level standards and fall further and further behind their peers. A longitudinal study with about 800 students found that children retained in elementary or middle school were those who were having significant problems in first grade or had insufficient skills upon entering school (Alexander et al., 1994). It is incumbent on schools to identify and provide remediation with proven practices early in a child's school career.

The following research-based strategies have proved to be effective in preventing school failure and in curtailing potential academic failure. Each should be considered in a total plan to reduce or eliminate grade retention and social promotion.

1. *Provide high-quality preschool programs, especially for children at greatest risk for academic failure due largely to starting "way behind" in kindergarten.*

A number of longitudinal research studies have demonstrated that early intervention programs can provide immediate and long-term benefits for children at risk for failure and special education placement. Programs that are intensive and individualized are more likely to improve the developmental outcomes for children (Ramey & Ramey, 1999).

Two long-term research studies demonstrate the efficacy of early intervention programs for children at greatest risk. The Abecedarian Project studied the potential benefits of early childhood education for economically disadvantaged children. It provided intensive, individualized full-day preschool education five days a week for children from six weeks to five years of age. Long-term findings from this study revealed participating children scored higher on reading and math tests through age 15 and had lower rates of special education placement and grade retention (Campbell & Ramey, 1995). At age 21, these children continued to have higher cognitive test scores and higher academic achievement in both reading and math. These individuals were more likely to postpone parenthood until their young adult years. In addition, they were more likely to attend a four-year college (Frank Porter Graham Child Development Center, 1999).

The Perry Preschool Project focused on three- and four-year-old children with low IQ scores and tracked these children to age 27. It was found they were less likely to be placed in special education, had fewer grade retentions, attained greater academic achievement, had lower teen pregnancy rates, and had lower juvenile crime rates (Schweinhart, Barnes, Weikart, Barnett, & Epstein, 1993). A cost–benefit analysis completed in 1985 showed that for every dollar invested in this early intervention program, seven dollars were saved in the costs associated with additional or special schooling, juvenile crime, and welfare (Barnett, 1985).

2. *Provide teachers with intensive, quality professional development opportunities focused on (a) raising student achievement and (b) meeting the diverse needs of struggling students.*

One of the most effective remedies for school failure is skillful teaching. Skillful teachers are those who know their students' strengths and needs, are familiar with and utilize a wide range of successful teaching strategies, and continuously adapt strategies to meet their students' needs. Not surprisingly, studies conducted in several states showed that good teaching makes a positive difference in academic performance that is sustained over time (Education Trust, 1998). Specifically, a Tennessee study showed that students who have highly effective teachers for three straight years score about 50 percentile points higher than those who had ineffective teachers for three years (Sanders & Rivers, 1996). A 1991 study involving more than 900 Texas school districts shows, after controlling for socioeconomic status of students, that teacher qualifications and expertise accounted for more than 40 percent of the difference in student academic achievement (Ferguson, 1991). These studies provide convincing evidence that teacher expertise is a significant predictor of student academic success.

Such expertise and knowledge typically do not come naturally. "One-shot" workshops are the most frequently used format for professional development and have consistently been shown to be highly ineffective (Fullan & Stiegelbauer, 1991). Professional development opportunities that are intensive and sustained over time are more likely to produce skillful teachers. Research findings and practices of exemplary schools show that effective professional development practices (a) reflect best research and practices in teaching, (b) engage teachers in continuous study, (c) create networks for them to plan collaboratively, (d) encourage professional inquiry and exchange, and (e) require substantial time and resources (Office of Educational Research and Improvement, 1997). Well-prepared teachers who are engaged in continuous, high-quality professional development opportunities can prevent student failure.

3. *Provide research-based intervention strategies that meet the individual needs of struggling students.*

The U.S. Department of Education (1999) recommends that schools utilize different approaches if students are not responding to traditional methods. A number of intervention strategies have proved to be successful in remediating academic difficulties:

a. Looping—Looping is a practice by which the teacher works with the same group of children for more than one year. Looping supports academic success because the teacher develops long-term relationships with students. Because teachers spend less instructional time becoming acquainted with students and their needs, they are able to focus more of their time on instruction (U.S. Department of Education, 1999; Yang, 1997).

b. Class size reduction—A large four-year study conducted in Tennessee evaluated the effect of small class size on student performance in kindergarten through third grade. This study showed that classes with 13 to 17 students made significantly greater gains than classes with 21 to 25 students, with and without a classroom aide. The small class size advantage was evident in all four grades, but especially in kindergarten and first grades (Word et al., 1990).

c. One-on-One Tutoring—One-on-one tutoring has consistently been highly effective in preventing early reading failure. A synthesis of research studies that meet stringent criteria found that one-on-one instruction by adults produced large educationally significant gains. In addition, the use of certified teachers, compared with paraprofessionals, produced significantly larger educational gains. The studies that evaluated the lasting effects of one-on-one tutoring during the early grades found that the initial positive effects continued to grow into second and third grades (Wasik & Slavin, 1994).

d. Extended Learning Time—Providing extra time after school or in the summer in and of itself is not enough to make a difference in the lives of struggling students (Karweit, 1989). Programs that have the greatest likelihood of improving student achievement are after-school and summer programs that build on the regular curriculum and address students' specific needs. The use of appropriate techniques and the quality of teacher instruction are also critical elements in producing positive gains, especially for children at risk (Leinhardt & Pallay, 1989).

4. *Actively address the social needs and provide social support as well as academic assistance for struggling students.*

Young people who are struggling academically need not only effective intervention strategies focused on academic deficiencies, they also need the support that comes from teachers, peers, family, and other interested individuals. Personal relationships, or social support, motivates students to learn, builds confidence that academic success is possible, and instills a sense of trust and safety that allows them to be risk takers and "bounce back" when they experience failure (Lee, Smith, Perry, & Smylie, 1999; Wehlage, Rutter, Smith, Lesko, & Fernandez, 1999).

One study with more than 28,000 sixth and eighth graders showed that students who experienced a strong emphasis on academic success and had high social support achieved significantly higher levels than students who experienced only a strong emphasis on academic standards (Lee et al., 1999). An in-depth study of 14 schools showed that the provision of social support is critical in preventing school failure and school dropout (Wehlage et al., 1989). This social support is found in schools in which personnel actively create positive and respectful relationships with students and address students' personal problems through communication and direct support. It is likely that training on how to provide social support to students is needed.

5. *Develop rigorous, specific, grade-by-grade standards that provide direction for curriculum development and help teachers assess individual learning needs.*

Grade standards provide multiple benefits. Overall, standards provide a means for teachers, parents, and the community at large to judge adequate student performance consistently. This consistency will help ensure that teachers from school to school are judging performance by the same criteria. Standards also serve as the foundation for curriculum development and student assessment, and can demonstrate the need for additional educational services. They give parents and students an overview of the academic focus and expectations (AFT, 1997; NASBE, 1999). A study with more than 28,000 students showed that conformity to academic standards produces greater academic gains (Lee et al., 1999).

Grade standards should encompass more than simply designating a standardized test score as an indicator for student achievement. The AFT (1997) recommends a number of criteria when developing or critiquing existing standards.

They believe standards should be based on the core disciplines, that they reflect the essential components of the academic curriculum, and that they be rigorous and comparable with standards of other high-achieving countries. In addition, they believe standards should delineate different levels of student performance and include content and performance standards.

6. *Involve parents as team members in improving student performance.*

Teachers should be prepared and willing to work jointly with parents on supporting students' educational progress. Studies have shown that regardless of parental income, level of education, or work status, it is the schools' efforts and the teachers' practices that determine the success of parent involvement programs (Epstein, 1988; Funkhouser & Gonzales, 1997; USDOE, 1997). Parents need teachers to provide direction. In addition, excellent parent involvement programs include teacher training as an essential component to ensure that teachers are adequately prepared to support parent involvement activities (Decker, Gregg, & Decker, 1996; Shartrand, Weiss, Kreider, & Lopez, 1997). Parents are more likely to be involved when schools welcome parents, make it easy for them to be involved, and when parents and teachers respect each other (NCES, 1999a).

7. *Continue to monitor and provide assistance on an "as-needed" basis to students who graduate from intervention programs.*

Unfortunately, numerous studies have shown that the academic gains made in most intervention programs for at-risk students fade or "wash out" over time (Alexander et al., 1994; Gredler, 1984; Holmes, 1989; Mantizicopoulos & Morrison, 1992; Meisels, 1992; Nason, 1991; Reynolds et al., 1997; Shepard & Smith, 1986, 1989). Continuing intervention is needed to address new and different challenges that children face at various points in their school career (Karweit, 1994). Therefore, it is essential that schools continue to monitor children who have participated in intervention programs and provide assistance if problems reoccur. This assistance should come as soon as possible to prevent accelerated deterioration of academic performance.

THE BOTTOM LINE

Current systems for preventing school failure and social promotion in most schools do not work and will require comprehensive reform to provide equity and excellence in education. Implementing proven practices will require, in some situations, a total restructuring of schools and reeducation of school personnel. School systems must be informed of current research and must be provided opportunities to explore and adopt strategies that have the greatest potential of enhancing student development and achievement. Adopted strategies should be consistently evaluated to determine their effectiveness in enhancing student achievement. A total commitment on the part of teachers, administrators, parents, and school board members is needed to identify and implement effective strategies that will dramatically reduce the incidence of social promotion and retention, and at the same time help students attain their academic potential.

QUESTIONS

1. Ask three educators what they believe about retention. Then, ask them what they base their beliefs on. (It has been our experience that many teachers base their beliefs on anecdotal information that cannot be verified.)

2. What alternative to retention or social promotion do you believe is the most appropriate? For what circumstance?

3. What impact will No Child Left Behind have on retention? Why?

REFERENCES

Alexander, K. L., Entwisle, D. R., & Dauber, S. L. (1994). *On success or failure: A reassessment of the effects of retention in the primary grades.* Cambridge: Cambridge University Press.

American Federation of Teachers. (1997). *Passing on failure: District promotion policies and practices.* Washington, DC: Author.

Association of California School Administrators. (1999). *Student success in a standards based system: Moving beyond social promotion and retention.* [On-line]. Available: www.222.acsa.org/publications/EDCAL/EDCALJ_5_24_1999/master_plan.html.

Barnett, W. S. (1985). Benefit–cost analysis of the Perry Preschool Program and its long-term effects. *Education Evaluation and Policy Analysis, 7,* 387–414.

Blum, R. W., Beuhring, T., Shew, M. L., Bearing, L. H., Sieving, R. E., & Resnick, M. D. (2000). The effects of race/ethnicity, income and family structure on adolescent risk behaviors. *American Journal of Public Health, 90* (12), 202–235.

Byrnes, D. A. (1989). Attitudes of students, parents, and educators toward repeating a grade. In L. A. Shepard & M. L. Smith (Eds.), *Flunking grades: Research and policies on retention* (pp. 108–131). London: The Falmer Press.

Campbell, F. A., & Ramey, C. T. (1995). Cognitive and school outcomes for high risk students at middle adolescence: Positive effects of early intervention. *American Educational Research Journal, 32,* 743–772.

Center for Policy Research in Education. (1990). *Repeating grades in school: Current practices and research evidence* (CPRE publication no. RB-04-1/90). Brunswick, NJ: Author.

Decker, L., Gregg, G., & Decker, V. (1996). *Teacher's manual for parent and community involvement.* Alexandria, VA: National Community Education Association.

Education Trust. (1998). *Thinking K–16 report: Good teaching matters. How well qualified teachers close the gap.* [On-line]. Available: www.edtrust.org/pubs-online.htnu.

Entwisle, D. R., & Alexander, K. L. (1993). Entry into schools: The beginning of school transition and educational stratification in the United States. *Annual Review of Sociology, 19,* 58–59.

Epstein, J. (1988). How do we improve programs for parent involvement? *Educational Horizons, 66* (2), 58–59.

Ferguson, R. F. (1991). Paying for public education: New evidence of how and why money matters. *Harvard Journal on Legislation, 28,* 465–498.

Frank Porter Graham Child Development Center. (1999). *Early learning, later success. The Abecedarian Study.* [On-line]. Available: www.fpg.unc.edu/~abc.

Fullan, M. G., & Stiegelbauer, S. (1991). *The new meaning of educational change.* New York: Teachers College Press.

Funkhouser, J. E., & Gonzales, M. R. (1997). *Family involvement in children's education: Successful local approaches.* [On-line]. Available: www.ed.gov/pubs/FamInvolve/title.html.

Gredler, G. R. (1984). Transition classes: A viable alternative for the at-risk child? *Psychology in the Schools, 27,* 463–470.

Holmes, C. T. (1989). Grade-level retention effects: A meta-analysis of research studies. In L. A. Shepard & M. L. Smith (Eds.), *Flunking grades: Research and policies on retention* (pp. 16–33). London: Falmer Press.

Karweit, N. L. (1989). Time and learning: A review. In R. Slavin (Ed.), *School and classroom organization* (pp. 69–95). Hillsdale, NJ: Erlbaum.

Karweit, N. L. (1994). Can preschool alone prevent early learning failure? In R. E. Slavin, N. L. Karweit, & B. A. Wasik (Eds.), *Preventing early school failure: Research, policy, and practice* (pp. 58–77). Boston: Allyn & Bacon.

Lee, V. E., Smith, J. B., Perry, T. E., & Smylie, M. A. (October 1999). *Social support, academic press, and student achievement: A view from the middle grades in Chicago.* [On-line]. Available: www.consortium-chicago.org/acrobat/social%20support.pdf.

Leinhardt, B., & Pallay, A. (1989). Instruction's the thing wherein to catch the mind that falls behind. In R. E. Slavin (Ed.), *School and classroom organization* (pp. 197–226). Hillsdale, NJ: Erlbaum.

Mantizicopoulos, P., & Morrison, D. C. (1992). Kindergarten retention: Academic and behavioral outcomes through the end of second grade. *American Educational Research Journal, 29* (1), 182–198.

Meisels, S. J. (1992). Doing harm by doing good: Iatrogenic effects of early childhood enrollment and promotion policies. *Early Childhood Research Quarterly, 7,* 155–174.

Nason, R. B. (1991). Retaining children: Is it the right decision? *Childhood Education, 67* (5), 300–304.

National Association of State Boards of Education. (1999). *Policy update: Social promotion and retention of students.* Alexandria, VA: Policy Information Clearinghouse.

National Center for Education Statistics. (October 1996). *Statistical analysis report: Remedial education at higher education institutions in fall 1995* (NCES publication no. 97-584). [On-line]. Available: www.nces.ed.gov/pubs/97584.html.

National Center for Education Statistics. (April 1999a). *Statistics in brief: Public school student, staff, and graduate counts by state, school year 1997–1998* (NCES publication no. 1999327). [On-line]. Available: www.nces.ed.gov/pubs99/1999326.pdf.

National Center for Education Statistics. (June 1999b). *Statistics in brief: Revenues and expenditures for public elementary and secondary education: School year 1996–1997.* [On-line]. Available: www.nces.ed.gov/pubs99/!999301.

Northwest Regional Educational Laboratory. (July 1999). *When students don't succeed: Shedding light on grade retention.* [On-line]. Available: www.nwrel.org/request/july99/index.html.

Norton, M. S. (1990). Practical alternatives to student retention. *Contemporary Education 61* (4), 204–208.

Office of Educational Research and Improvement. (1997). *National awards program for model professional development 1998 application.* Washington, DC: Author.

Ramey, S. L., & Ramey, C. T. (1999). Early experience and early intervention for children "at risk" for developmental delay and mental retardation. *Mental Retardation and Developmental Disabilities Research Reviews, 5* (1), 1–10.

Reynolds, A., Temple, J., & McCoy, A. (1997). Grade retention doesn't work: Three reasons why and what should be tried instead. *Education Week, 17* (3), 37.

Roderick, M., Byrk, A. S., Jacob, B., Easton, J. Q., & Allensworth, E. (December 1999). *Finding social promotion: Results from the first two years.* [On-line]. Available: www.consortium-chicago.org/Html_web_store_3.0/Html/end_social_promo.html.

Rose, J. S., Medway, F. J., Cantrell, V. L., & Marus, S. H. (1983). A fresh look at the retention–promotion controversy. *Journal of School Psychology, 21* (3), 201–211.

Sahagun, L., & Sauerwein, K. (2000, January 31). L.A. schools brace for task of holding back thousands. Education get-tough policy on promotions could bring campus crowding, confrontations with parents. *The Los Angeles Times*, p. Al.

Sanders, W. L., & Rivers, J. C. (1996). *Cumulative and residual effects of teachers on future student academic achievement.* Knoxville, TN: University of Tennessee.

Schweinhart, L. J., Barnes, H. V., Weikart, D. P., Barnett, W. S., & Epstein, A. S. (1993). *Significant benefits: The High-Scope Perry Preschool Study through age 27.* Ypsilanti, MI: High Scope Press.

Shartrand, A., Weiss, H., Kreider, H., & Lopez, M. (1997). *New skills for new schools: Preparing teachers in family involvement.* Cambridge, MA: Harvard Family Research Project.

Shepard, L. A., & Smith, M. L. (1986). Synthesis of research on school readiness and kindergarten retention. *Educational Leadership, 44* (3), 786–788.

Shepard, L. A., & Smith, M. L. (Eds.). (1989). *Flunking grades: Research and policies on retention.* London: Falmer Press.

Thompson, C. L. (1999). *Research on retention and social promotion: Synthesis and implications for policy.* Chapel Hill: The North Carolina Education Research Council.

U.S. Department of Education. (1997). *Parent involvement and participation.* Washington, DC: Author.

U.S. Department of Education. (1999). *Taking responsibility for ending social promotion.* Washington, DC: Author.

Walters, D. M., & Borgers, S. B. (1995). Student retention: Is it effective? *School Counselor, 42* (4), 300–310.

Wasik, B. A., & Slavin, R. E. (1994). Preventing early reading failure with one-to-one tutoring: A review of five programs. In R. E. Slavin, N. L. Karweit, & B. A. Wasik (Eds.), *Preventing early school failure: Research, policy, and practice* (pp. 143–174). Boston: Allyn & Bacon.

Wehlage, G., Rutter, R., Smith, G., Lesko, N., & Fernandez, R. (1989). *Reducing the risk: Schools as communities of support.* Philadelphia: Falmer Press.

Word, E., Johnston, J., Bain, H., Fulton, B., Zaharias, J., Lintz, N., Achilles, G. M., Folger, J., & Breda, C. (1990). *Student/teacher achievement ratio: Tennessee's K–3 class size study. Final report and final report summary.* Nashville, TN: Tennessee State Department of Education.

Yang, X. (February 1997). *Educational benefits in elementary school through looping and Friday in-services, part 2: Benefits of looping.* Paper presented at the annual seminar of the National Association for Year-Round Education, San Diego, CA.

CHAPTER 9

TEACHING IN INCLUSIVE SETTINGS

THE CHALLENGE AND THE OPPORTUNITY TO ENGAGE IN INCLUSIVE STRATEGIES

We all live with the objective of being happy;
our lives are all different and yet the same.

—Anne Frank

Consider the following perspectives:

"Why should students with disabilities be excluded? Why not exclude children with red hair, children with dimples, or kids who play basketball?"

"Don't talk to me about inclusion if you are just considering children with disabilities. There are a lot of children who are excluded within regular classrooms for a variety of reasons such as gender, race, ethnicity, weight, height, looks, and who knows what else."

"I'm against inclusion, especially full inclusion, because neither regular education nor special education teachers are prepared for it. It won't work."

"Theoretically I'm for full inclusion, but it doesn't work for two reasons—money and time. For full inclusion to work, more personnel are needed to support regular education teachers who teach students with special needs. No one is going to pay for that. So, it takes too much extra time for a regular teacher to modify instruction and help those children who would have been in special education. Regular education students should have rights. With full inclusion, too much time is spent with special kids."

"Special education has been just another way to marginalize those who do not fit the traditional mold. This has been true for many years. More minority students and more boys have been labeled as mentally retarded. This is not true for giftedness. Categories such as mental retardation are not characteristics of specific individuals. These labels are social constructions used to discriminate against those who are different. It's time all people were included in regular education and the labels reconsidered and probably thrown out."

Need we say more about inclusion being a hot topic in the 21st century? This chapter poses several questions about inclusion. First, we consider what inclusion is, then we address how we got to inclusion. The following difficult questions will also be addressed: Is inclusion better than full inclusion? What are the advantages of inclusive schools? What are the barriers? What would make full inclusion work? Finally, are there any results that support or refute inclusion?

WHAT IS INCLUSION?

As with most educational trends and issues, the debate over inclusion often begins with "What are we talking about?" What is *inclusion*? To begin with, inclusion is not the same thing as mainstreaming. Mainstreaming is defined as integrating children with special needs into the regular classroom with the understanding that there is a resource room or special education class to which they can go to receive assistance. Mainstreaming is still part of a pullout model in which students can go to another class for the help they need. Inclusion, on the other hand, is a movement that was designed to bring special education services into the general classroom. In such settings, children with disabilities are "considered as rail members of the classroom learning community, with their special needs met there" (Friend & Bursuck, 1996, p. 4). This movement is a significant change from the traditional practice of having students "pulled out" of regular education to receive special services in a resource room or self-contained special education classroom (Henley, Ramsey, & Algozzine, 1999).

An inclusive program has a "zero reject philosophy"; no one is turned away because of the presence of a disability (Thousand & Villa, 1989). Unlike mainstreaming, inclusion maintains an open door to all students regardless of abilities. Inclusive schools reflect the heterogeneous makeup of society. Instruction is designed around individual strengths and concerns, rather than placement of students in programs in which instruction is based on the type or severity of the students' disabilities. Inclusion assumes a positive attitude in which all students are accepted as members of the school and classroom environment (Bradley, King–Sears, & Tessier–Switlick, 1997).

Support for inclusion has been based on the ethical, legal, and educational benefits to members. Educators, parents, and legislators continue to question existing separateness between regular and special education (Sailor, 1991; Stainback & Stainback, 1992; Willis, 1994).

HOW DID WE GET HERE?

The purpose of this section is not to provide a full review of the history of special education, but to describe the general events that led up to inclusive practices. (For a historical review of special education, see Winzer, 1986, 1993.)

At the beginning of the 21st century, special education has had quite a colorful history. The historical route of students with disabilities started with neglect. It progressed to institutionalization, residential schooling, and other isolated schools and classes. This can be described as full segregation. Students who were different were placed in institutions or entirely separate schools. Later, pullout programs and eventually mainstreaming became the fashion. Today, inclusion is the trend. However, *how much* inclusion is quite an issue.

SHOULD WE HAVE INCLUSION
OR FULL INCLUSION?

In the early 1800s, pioneers such as Thomas H. Gallaudet and Louis Braille established special schools and communication that assisted children who were hearing impaired or blind. The first organized arrangements in the United States for the education of students with disabilities were copied from European asylums that had been established for the purpose of providing custodial care and "protecting persons with disabilities from the outside world" (Halvorsen & Sailor, 1990, p. 114). After it was proved that students with various disabilities were educable, residential schools were established.

Many states by the late 19th century were demonstrating public acceptance for the education of people with disabilities. Even some residential institutions began to train specialized teachers for special programs in some local schools. It was not, however, until the middle of the 20th century that parents of children with disabilities organized for political action. State and federal governments began to show support for special education in the form of research, training, and legislation (Turnbull, 1990).

The past three decades have witnessed dramatic changes in legal, social, and economic forces that have affected both regular and special education. Educational practices have been continually refined to reflect changes that should benefit a wide variety of learners.

In 1975, Congress passed Public Law 94-142, the Education of All Handicapped Children Act. Among the requirements of this law were the guarantees of a free appropriate public education for children and youth with disabilities. The law also stipulated that these students be educated in the "least restrictive environment." This meant that these students be educated to the maximum extent possible along with their peers without disabilities in the school they would have attended if they did not have a disability. However, the law did not specify how this was to occur. To meet the intent of this law, many school systems responded by creating segregated programs rather than by providing services to students *within* general education classrooms. Today, many of these programs continue to provide service in segregated programs (Bradley et al., 1997).

The results of the continued segregation of students with disabilities are fragmentation promoted by separate training, administration, labels, and buildings that increasingly isolate special education from general education. Many separate categories of students with special needs have been created to form the creation of many categorical programs, such as Tide I programs, bilingual programs, programs for students with mental retardation, programs for students with emotional disturbances, and so on. This fragmentation encourages competition between special needs groups for resources such as money, materials, and personnel.

Mainstreaming

The 1980s saw progressive moves toward inclusion in the general education of students with challenging learning and behavioral needs. Additional federal legislation passed, such as Public Law 99-457 in 1986, which extended services toward a younger population with special needs. Public Law 101-476, passed in 1990, required students with disabilities to be educated in general education to the maximum extent possible. The response of the educational community to these laws was to mainstream students whenever possible.

The Regular Education Initiative

The regular education initiative is founded on the premise that students with mild disabilities should be viewed as the shared responsibility of all educators, rather than the sole responsibility of special educators (Will, 1986). General education classes are adapted to meet the needs of a variety of individual learners (Semmel, Abernathy, Butera, & Lesar, 1991).

Regular inclusion completely changes the way all students are educated. Rather than having pullout special education services, special education teachers work collaboratively alongside regular educators in the same setting. This significantly restructures service delivery. All teachers and support personnel have a new and different role than previously conceived. A fourth grade teacher is no longer a person with her own classroom, separate from the rest of the school. She must share her room and students with a collaborative special educator, a Title I teacher, and other professionals and paraprofessionals, which might include speech therapists, physical therapists, and occupational therapists. However, neither special educators nor regular educators have been prepared for this (Fuchs & Fuchs, 1998).

IS INCLUSION BETTER THAN FULL INCLUSION?

Regular classrooms typically have a large number of children, ranging from 25 to 45. Although it has been shown that students' academic performance improved when their class size ranged from 13 to 17 (Viadero, 1998), inclusionists wonder whether such small classes are possible in the foreseeable future (Fuchs & Fuchs, 1998). In addition, the 25 to 45 students are not all performing on grade level. For example, a typical fifth grade class includes a few students reading below second grade level, a handful of students reading above the sixth grade level, and the majority of students reading somewhere in between. Even in traditional, noninclusive classrooms, few teachers differentiate their instruction to address this broad variety of academic achievements (Baker & Zigmond, 1990; McIntosh, Vaughn, Schumm, Haager, & Lee, 1993). Many teachers present the same lesson and instructional materials to all students. A reason for this is that not all teachers use best practices such as cooperative learning and classwide peer tutoring. About 30 percent of children with disabilities typically fail to respond to these best practices, suggesting that even very knowledgeable and devoted teachers using effective practices are not responsive to *all* children (Fuchs & Fuchs, 1998).

Willis Walter (personal communication, March 13, 2000), a principal of an urban elementary school serving children from kindergarten through fifth grade, describes his views on inclusion versus full inclusion:

> I am against full inclusion because I believe some students can benefit from smaller class settings and more one-on-one interaction with a special education teacher. I am for inclusion and mainstreaming for the majority of our students because children learn as much from one another as they do from the teacher. This is especially true for social habits in dealing with differences. This learning would not usually occur in a sterilized classroom. The teachers in my school are uncomfortable with full inclusion for several reasons. One of their biggest complaints is that professional development has lagged behind a lot of the issues they face—particularly [for] inclusion. Many of the teachers in my school believe [inclusion for] some special education students hinder[s] the learning community of the other students more than it helps their disability. This is particularly true of emotionally disturbed students—those who act out on a regular basis. These students do not have an aide or one-on-one support.

Kathy Blackwell (personal communication, April 25, 2000), a veteran fourth grade teacher who also teaches in an urban setting, echoes Walter's remarks:

> I don't have a problem with full inclusion if you get true support. I don't think that will ever happen. I believe the regular child in the classroom has rights also. There is so much emphasis placed on students with special needs we forget about the others—the average, normal child. Special education students take a lot of time. If we had full support, that would be different. But what is full support? If I had an aide in every classroom and 17 children, I don't think I would have a problem. This will never happen. It's purely a money issue.
>
> I would love for the resource teacher to come to my room. I would have no problem with that. The three students with special needs I teach this year are wonderful children. I personally don't have enough time to devote to them. It's a mat-

ter of time. So, time, money, and help are the big issues for me with regard to full inclusion.

When we consider the large numbers of students per class, the wide variability of academic accomplishment among students without disabilities, and the significant number of students with disabilities who are not helped by best practices, we must conclude that full placement in regular classes will not service the academic needs of some children with disabilities. Instead, they need to be placed in special education settings where they are more likely to benefit (Fuchs & Fuchs, 1998).

The differences between inclusionists' and full inclusionists' positions are threefold. First, inclusionists stress that the primary objective of schooling is to help children master skills and knowledge necessary for future successes in and out of school. Full inclusionists believe schools are most important to provide opportunities for friendship making, changing stereotypical thinking about disabilities, and strengthening socialization skills. Second, inclusionists maintain that the continuum of special education placement is vital. Full inclusionists insist that the proper place for all children is in the regular classroom. Third, inclusionists believe that although regular classrooms can and should be made more accommodating of special needs, there is a limit to what one realistically can expect of such settings. In contrast, full inclusionists believe all things are possible (Fuchs & Fuchs, 1998).

How can these fundamental differences between inclusionists and full inclusionists exist? The answer is fairly simple if one considers that inclusionists and full inclusionists advocate for different children with different needs. Most inclusionists speak for children with high-incidence disabilities such as children with behavior disorders, learning disabilities, and mild mental retardation. Many full inclusionists represent children with severe mental retardation. Their major concern is more with socialization opportunities than academic or vocational development (Fuchs & Fuchs, 1998).

What about Full Inclusion and the Law?

Special education services and the rights of children with disabilities are topics that constitute the fastest growing areas of school law. Most of the controversies center around the interpretations of the Individuals with Disabilities Education Act (IDEA). Although the term *inclusion* is not mentioned in the federal law, courts in the 1990s have interpreted IDEA as entailing a strong preference for inclusion (McCarthy, 1998). They have, accordingly, placed the burden on school personnel to establish that regular education placement is not appropriate for a given child with disabilities. Courts consider some of the following criteria in making this determination: the educational benefits of the inclusive versus segregated settings, the noneducational (for example, social) benefits of both placements, the costs of the respective placements, and the impact of the inclusive placement on other children in the class (McCarthy, 1998).

School authorities do not necessarily support the more restrictive environment. In several court cases, it was the parents who contested the school district's proposed inclusive placement. Parents have requested, instead, residential or other segregated settings for their children.

Courts are not requiring inclusive placements under all circumstances, although they are interpreting IDEA as entailing a presumption that children with disabilities should be placed in regular education. The court will review the specific circumstances for each case. Certainly, it is not impossible for school authorities to substantiate that the welfare of the child or classmates would be jeopardized in the regular classroom.

In several cases involving students with hearing impairments, courts have upheld centralized programs, some of which are in segregated settings. The courts believed that the language needs of these children would be served most appropriately in these more restrictive placements where the services are superior to what could be provided in a regular classroom (McCarthy, 1998).

Should We Prepare for Full Inclusion or Just Inclusion?

The underlying philosophy that embraces inclusion of students into regular education is based on welcoming all neighborhood students into the community school. It also is based on meeting these students' needs in that educational system. Several critical goals need to be considered when making the transition from a "segregated" to an inclusive school:

1. to promote a school philosophy and create an atmosphere based on egalitarianism and democracy
2. to win the support and value the ideas of all who will be involved
3. to integrate students, personnel, and resources so that regular and special educators can work together
4. to incorporate *best practices* of education throughout the school.

In order for inclusion to operate at its best, several best practices of education have been identified (Bradley, 1993; Fox, 1987). Students with or without special needs benefit from the following:

1. Students with special needs are to be included for at least part of the day in the regular program with peers who do not have disabilities.
2. Whenever possible, heterogeneous grouping should take place.
3. Technical expertise and equipment should be utilized.
4. Adaptations in the curriculum should be made when necessary.
5. Assessments should be curriculum based and should focus on how students learn instead of what is wrong with them.
6. Techniques for behavioral management may need to be used.
7. A curriculum based on social skills may be used.

8. Students should feel empowerment through the use of such techniques as peer teaching, cooperative learning, and self-developed rules.
9. The staff should engage in ongoing development (Bradley & Switlick, 1997).

Preparing the System

The current directions of school reform for the 21st century emphasize not only improvement in general education, but also improved performance for more challenging populations. We should use the opportunities that now exist in educational reorganization to merge the goals of regular and special education to work toward a "shared educational agenda" (Sailor, 1991, p. 8).

Preparing Teachers

Stainback and Stainback (1990) pointed out that although regular educators cannot educate students with disabilities alone, neither can special educators. Teachers in the past saw students who were not successful in the mainstream as needing special education programs. The problems were attributed to the student. A new paradigm is emerging that says that all students can learn if instruction and materials meet their needs (Bradley & Fisher, 1995). This shift in thinking requires both special and regular educators to work together for each student.

General and special educators must work collaboratively to gain understanding about how the best teaching and learning takes place. Materials and teacher expertise need to be shared. To help both teachers and students who require specialized instruction, Miller (1990) recommends a merger of (a) material, (b) knowledge, (c) skills, (d) personnel, (e) resources, and (f) categorical programs such as Title I or bilingual programs (Bradley et al., 1997).

Preparing Families

Families play a critical role in creating an inclusive school philosophy. They need to be included in all decisions that affect the instructional program of their children. Families are being asked to think differently about what is best for their children. Previously they were told that a self-contained classroom was the best setting for quality instruction. Now they are being told that the general education classroom with modifications and services will be best for their child's education. Offering families information about inclusion can help make a smoother transition to inclusive practices.

Preparing Students

The inclusion process needs to be explained to students *before* it is put into practice. Students should be asked to make suggestions. When students believe that their input is valued, they are more likely to feel vested and support the program (Bradley & Fisher, 1995). All students should have the opportunity to discuss their questions, fears, and concerns. They need to know how, when, and why to aid students with disabilities.

Students with disabilities need to be notified about what changes to expect and what new responsibilities come with inclusion. Students who receive special education services may need extra time to adjust to the changes. They may need more help to prepare them for the physical move to the regular education setting, such as learning how to follow schedules, finding locations in the school, and using lockers. Establishing networks of peer support can address many of these changes and help in making a smooth transition from a special education setting to a general education setting (Bradley et al., 1997).

WHAT ARE THE ADVANTAGES OF FULL INCLUSION?

Academic Advantages

A major purpose of academics is to prepare students for the world of work. Unfortunately, follow-up studies of special education students show that graduates of self-contained programs are employed less and often have lower self-esteem than those who received their education in the mainstream (Lipsky & Gartner, 1996).

Discipline Problems

When students are in inclusive programs, the number of IEP objectives that are accomplished increases, according to Halvorsen and Sailor (1990). In another study (Peterson, 1989), results indicated that students who have been placed in heterogeneously grouped programs showed significantly more improvement than those who were grouped by ability levels. In addition, students with special needs who were placed in mixed-ability groups participated more in class activities and presented fewer problems in the classroom.

When special education moves away from labeling and toward instruction, more of the special education teacher's time can be spent in direct service to students, rather than in attending meetings or administering tests. Also, continuity with grade-level academic programs more likely will take place. Students' time for instruction is better spent because they are not moving from class to class to receive special services (Bradley & Switlick, 1997).

Gains in Socialization

When special needs students are placed in inclusive settings, they have greater opportunities for normalization—exposure to the norms and cultural patterns of society in general (Halvorsen & Sailor, 1990). Special needs students also should be provided with opportunities for participation in programs to facilitate the acquisition of skills that will enhance their functioning in the general environment (Halvorsen & Sailor, 1990). When planned programs of interaction are made possible, both students with and without special needs can learn to interact, communicate, develop friendships, work together, and help one another. This interaction assists both groups to develop understanding, respect, sensitivity, and comfort with individual similarities and differences.

Inclusive settings allow students with special needs to have access to a range of learning opportunities and social models. With these opportunities, more appropriate social development can take place. The stigma and isolation that come with segregated programs decrease.

Benefits to Regular Education Students

Regular education teachers express concern that having students with disabilities, particularly severe disabilities, will adversely affect students without disabilities (Bradley & Switlick, 1997). Results of a study (Hollowood, Salisbury, Rainforth, & Palombaro, 1995) showed that the regular education students did not suffer detrimental effects. It was shown that no losses of instructional time were incurred when students with severe disabilities were included in classrooms. In addition, in inclusive settings, no significant differences existed for the two groups—students with or without disabilities—in either academic or behavioral performance.

Students without disabilities gain skills and insights that are beneficial to them, such as developing increased tolerance and appreciating human differences (Willis, 1994). "The greatest gain for students without disabilities who are educated with peers who have disabilities is that they develop values that enable them to support the inclusion of all citizens in the various aspects of community life" (Bradley & Switlick, 1997, p. 15).

WHAT ARE THE BARRIERS TO INCLUSION?

Changing Roles for Educators

Currently we do not have good data on the attitudes of regular education teachers toward inclusive schools (Bradley & West, 1994). For more than 20 years, regular education teachers were told that they do not know how to teach students with disabilities. Now they are told that because good teaching is good teaching, they will be able to do a good job. Regular teachers, therefore, are "skeptical and scared" (Miller, 1990, p. 32). They also feel caught between inclusion and test score accountability. Changes in instructional preparation, delivery, and assessment will be required of them to meet the needs of such a diverse group—from students who are gifted to those with severe physical, academic, and emotional challenges. Regular educators are concerned with the more comprehensive record-keeping systems that special education requires. They sometimes anticipate that inclusion will require them to do more with less. They fear a lack of support from special educators and have expressed the fear that these supports may likely be eliminated altogether (Bradley & Switlick, 1997).

Special educators may also experience some disadvantages as a result of the inclusion model. Confusion may occur regarding who is responsible for what—the implementation of IEP goals, for example, as well as the behavior and general achievement of students with disabilities (Bradley & Fisher, 1995). Special educators often run highly structured classrooms with a strong behavior management system in place. When classrooms are open to students without disabilities, this system may not be easy for them to follow.

Funding formulas encourage separateness between special and general education. These formulas encourage restrictive placements and reward systems for labeling and placing students in special education (Bergan, 1995; Katsiyannis, Conderman, & Franks, 1995). Schools housing students with disabilities for the first time face space and accessibility limitations. In sparsely populated areas, service delivery can be very difficult and may require cooperative agreements between school systems.

Adverse Effects on Students

Some parents who in the past have had their children served in special settings within small groups and with considerable individual attention wonder if programming in regular education settings is adequate to meet the needs of their children with disabilities. Sailor (1991) expresses concern that social discrimination can occur if students with disabilities enter an inclusive setting.

WHAT WOULD MAKE FULL INCLUSION WORK?

A meta-analysis of the research on inclusion identified seven factors that are necessary if inclusion is to succeed (Lipsky & Gartner, 1996):

1. Visionary Leadership—The comments of a Vermont special education director, who stated that several years ago his district came to view inclusion as a subset of the restructuring of the entire educational system, are illustrative of the kind of leadership necessary. He no longer viewed special education as a means to help students meet the demands of the classroom. Rather, he viewed special education as a part of the classroom services that must be available to accommodate the learning needs of *all* children in a restructured school.

2. Collaboration—No one teacher can or should be expected to have all the expertise required to meet the educational needs of all the students in the classroom. Support systems that provide collaborative assistance and enable teachers to engage in cooperative problem solving must be in place and available to teachers. Tools necessary for collaboration must be accessible and must include planning teams and scheduled time for teachers to work together.

3. A Redirected Use of Assessment—In the past, students' assessments have been used as screening devices to determine where students "fit." In special education, many studies have addressed the inadequacy of this screening. The inclusive movement has called for more authentic assessments, including the use of portfolios of students' work and performances.

4. Staff and Student Support—Systematic staff development and flexible planning time for regular and special education teachers to meet and work together are critical for inclusion to work successfully. Students need supplementary aides and support services available to them. School aides, needed therapy services that are integrated into the regular school program, peer support, buddy systems, effective use of computer-aided technology, and other assistive devices prove helpful to students.

5. Funding—Changes in funding are necessary because current special education funding formulas tend to encourage separation placements. Funds should follow the students. When this happens, inclusive education programs are no more costly overall than segregated models (McLaughlin & Warren, 1994).

6. Parental Involvement—Effective inclusive programs encourage and welcome parental participation through family support services and the development of educational programs that engage parents as colearners with their children.

7. Adaptation of Curricula and Adoption of Effective Instructional Practices—Inclusive programs should consider multilevel instruction, cooperative learning, activity-based learning, mastery learning, use of instructional technology, peer support, and tutoring programs.

Students with special needs have numerous legitimate needs that may go beyond the seven factors provided here. A simplistic, generalized agenda for success would make a mockery of the complexities concerning special education and inclusive practices. However, some delivery models have produced promising results so far.

Delivery Models That Work

Teachers, both regular and special educators, need to ask two questions: (1) How do kids learn best? (2) Does specialized instruction work to the extent we had hoped it would? The goal of setting up a program is to serve students most effectively. Teachers should ask which model is best for students' long-term needs, not what is most accommodating to teachers. For example, a pullout program is easier for all teachers involved to schedule and implement, but is not necessarily in the best interest of students (Elliot & McKenney, 1998).

Before choosing approaches to inclusion, teachers need to determine what attitudes staff members have about students with special needs. The school's approach to inclusion will depend heavily on staff beliefs. Because negative attitudes will impede inclusion, it is important to address these attitudes in the form of different delivery models. Ideally, we would like to adhere to one belief and therefore one model of inclusion. However, teachers, like students, work in an environment that accommodates their particular needs.

According to Elliot and McKenney (1998), as well as Rogers (1993), several approaches appear effective in including students with special needs in general classroom settings. These approaches include consultation, team teaching, aide services, and a limited pullout service. Elliot and McKenney (1998) describe four approaches that have been used successfully within their program to provide inclusive services for children with special needs and meet the belief systems of the teachers.

Consultation

Consultation in general involves no direct services to students in the classroom setting. The exceptions, however, include assessment, observation, and planning meetings. Special time allotments are granted to general and special educators to meet and discuss student needs and services. Adaptations and modifications are made as needed. The special educators may provide additional instructional materials based on individual needs.

With this model, the student's environment is modified to meet attention, visual, hearing, and behavioral needs. Academic adjustments are also modified. For example, teachers should alter classroom assignments. Teachers may provide materials to aid students with organizational difficulties. They may supply different writing tools, assignment formats, or a word processor.

To be successful, consultation requires strong trust and communication between two teachers—the regular and special education teachers—as well as the parents. Some regular education teachers may find inclusion very difficult to accept. They may have concerns that other students in the classroom may be neglected because of the considerable needs of students with special needs. They may feel ineffective working with students with disabilities. Other, less inclusive models, such as team teaching, may work for some teachers more effectively (Elliot & McKenney, 1998).

Team Teaching

Team teaching involves the general and special education teachers working together in the classroom and instructing the entire class. It can be done in a variety of ways. Coteaching is the least restrictive approach. Teachers teach together at the same time or switch subjects or days teaching. Other approaches involve small-group work as well as individual tutorial assistance. The team-teaching approach lends itself to flexibility in delivery. The advantage of team teaching over consultation is the ability to change, as needed, on the spot.

The problem with team teaching is the comfort level of the teachers involved. Coteachers may not hold the same belief systems and therefore are not working in a comfortable environment. In contrast, compatible teams have found team teaching to be successful and positive (Elliot & McKenney, 1998).

Aides' Services

The use of instructional aides in the classroom is one way to avoid tracking students by ability. Realistically, it is not possible for special education teachers to meet the needs of students placed in several different classrooms at different grade levels without the use of instructional assistance. It is important that the general education teacher also assume ownership. The success of this approach is dependent on the competency of the aides and the willingness of the school system to budget sufficiently. Furthermore, it is recommended that the special education teacher have direct contact at least monthly with the students in the classroom to observe and evaluate progress.

Aides typically work in the classroom where one to four students with disabilities are placed. Their responsibility is to check the students' progress, provide assistance on an individual or small-group basis, assist the classroom teacher, and report back to the special education teacher. Occasionally, the aide may take a small group of students out of the classroom to work on a test or project to avoid distractions. Most teachers value aide services as long as the aides are well trained and helpful to them. The problem with this service model is the inconsistency of personnel and funding from year to year (Elliot & McKenney, 1998).

Limited Pullout Service

The pullout service is the more traditional approach that special educators have used for years. It has relieved the regular educator from considerable responsibility involving students with disabilities. The special education teacher does not need to collaborate as frequently with the regular education teacher. Both teachers can independently direct their classroom and curriculum.

Although a pullout program often allows for more individualized instruction, it breaks apart the student's day and the student's learning. Students must leave the general classroom at certain times and travel to and from the resource room. Time is wasted gathering supplies and traveling the halls. Much of the material learned in the resource room is not transferred to the general classroom because the material is sometimes out of context. It is almost impossible to coordinate curriculum between regular and special education on a daily basis.

Stigmas are associated with pullout programs and students are often uncomfortable and do not feel part of the general class because they are not "smart enough" to remain the whole day.

Students with severe disabilities may need pullout services. For example, students may need to be pulled out to work on skills that are extremely low for their grade placement and cannot realistically be taught within the regular classroom. If the disability creates a distraction that prevents other students from learning or the teacher from teaching, the pullout program could be used.

Elliot and McKenney (1998) propose that a pullout program should be used only on a limited basis within an inclusion model. Their goal is to use the pullout program only when there is no way for students with disabilities to succeed in the classroom without the more individualized instruction and tutoring. They consider the pullout approach the most restrictive model within their program.

Peer Tutoring

Fischer, Schumaker, and Deshler (1996) reviewed the literature in search of validated inclusive practices. Peer tutoring is one of these. During peer tutoring, one student (the tutor) acts as a teacher, providing instruction to a peer (the tutee). The tutor helps the tutee master needed skills, providing instruction, opportunities for practice, clarification, and feedback by following a structured, teacher-developed lesson. Proponents of peer tutoring stress the importance of training tutors how to tutor. It is also essential that teachers interact with each group to keep students focused. The tutee's progress must be assessed continually and the sessions must be scheduled regularly (Jenkins & Jenkins, 1985).

Teaching Devices

In reviewing the literature on inclusive practices, researchers (Fischer et al., 1996) identified instructional tools teachers use that can be considered a part of inclusive practices. Many types of teaching devices (for example, mnemonic devices, role-play activities, and manipulatives) have been developed and described in both regular and special education literature. However, only two types of teaching devices met the criteria established for review by the researchers (Fischer et al., 1996). These were graphic organizers and study guides. Teachers use graphic organizers as visual displays to organize information in a manner that makes information easier to comprehend and learn. Synonyms for graphic organizers include *tree diagrams, semantic maps, flow charts,* and *webs.* Theoretically, graphic organizers allow students to consolidate information into a meaningful whole, rather than a set of unrelated terms and concepts. Horton, Lovitt, and Bergerud (1990) reported a series of studies undertaken to determine the effectiveness of graphic organizers as an inclusive practice.

ARE THERE ANY RESULTS THAT SUPPORT OR REFUTE INCLUSION?

Given that inclusive education programs have been implemented relatively recently, few full-scale evaluations of outcomes are available. Several studies are under way. We will consider some of the initial findings from studies of inclusion here:

1. Students with learning disabilities who were included in the regular classroom made academic gains, as reflected in their scores on criterion-referenced tests and report cards (Chase & Pope, 1993).

2. Students with significant disabilities experienced greater success in achieving IEP goals than did matched students in traditional programs (Ferguson, Meyer, Jeanchild, Juniper, & Zingo, 1992).

3. Benefits to students with disabilities happened without limiting the educational program available to students without disabilities (Michigan State Department of Education, 1991).

4. Gains were evidenced in student self-esteem, classmate acceptance, and social skills (Burrello & Wright, 1993).

QUESTIONS

As with any issue, where we go from here is debatable. Here are some questions to consider as we contemplate whether we can move into full inclusion or not.

1. Will the money be made available to support inclusive services? If so, where will it originate? Ideally, special education and regular education funding should merge.

2. How will educators be prepared for inclusion? (Remember, teachers who have been teaching for some time were trained in a different model.)

3. How can we assist children, teachers, and parents in becoming more tolerant of diversity?

4. Can class size in an inclusive setting be reduced to match the nature and needs of diverse children?

5. Will adequate support personnel be provided to assist in inclusive settings?

REFERENCES

Baker, J., & Zigmond, N. (1990). Are regular education classes equipped to accommodate students with learning disabilities? *Exceptional Children, 56,* 515–526.

Bergan, J. R. (1995). Evolution of problem-solving model of consultation. *Journal of Educational and Psychological Consultation, 6,* 125–144.

Bradley, D. F. (1993). Staff training for the inclusion of students with disabilities: Visions for educators. Unpublished doctoral dissertation. Walden University, Minneapolis, MN.

Bradley, D. F., & Fisher, J. F. (1995). The inclusion process: Role changes at the middle level. *The Middle School Journal, 26*, 13–19.

Bradley, D. F., King-Sears, M. E., & Tessier-Switlick, D. M. (Eds.). (1997). *Teaching students in inclusive settings.* Boston: Allyn & Bacon.

Bradley, D. F, & Switlick, D. M. (1997). The past and the future of special education. In D. F. Bradley, M. E. King-Sears, & D. M. Tessier-Switlick (Eds.), *Teaching students in inclusive settings.* Boston: Allyn & Bacon.

Bradley, D. F., & West, J. F. (1994). Staff training for the inclusion of students with disabilities: Visions from school-based educators. *Teacher Education and Special Education, 17,* 112–128.

Burrello, L. C., & Wright, P. T. (Eds.). (1993). Strategies for inclusion of behaviorally challenged students. *The Principal Letters, 10.*

Chase, V., & Pope, E. (1993, February 24). *Model for mainstreaming: The synergistic approach.* Paper presented at the Learning Disabilities of America Conference, San Francisco, CA.

Elliot, D., & McKenney, L. (1998). Four inclusion models that work. *Teaching Exceptional Children, V,* 54–57.

Ferguson, D., Meyer, G., Jeanchild, L., Juniper, L., & Zingo, J. (1992). Figuring out what to do with the grownups: How teachers make inclusion "work" for students with disabilities. *Journal of the Association for Persons with Severe Handicaps, 17,* 218–226.

Fischer, J. B., Schumaker, J. B., & Deshler, D. D. (1996). Searching for validated inclusive practices: A review of the literature. In E. Meyen, G. A. Vergason, & R. J. Whelan (Eds.), *Strategies for teaching exceptional children in inclusive settings* (pp. 123–154). Denver, CO: Love.

Fox, T. (1987). *Best practices guidelines.* Burlington, VT: Center for Developmental Disabilities.

Friend, M., & Bursuck, W. (1996). *Including students with special needs: A practical guide for classroom teachers.* Boston: Allyn & Bacon.

Fuchs, D., & Fuchs, L. S. (1998). Inclusion versus full inclusion. *Childhood Education,* 309–316.

Halvorsen, A. T., & Sailor, W. (1990). Integration of students with severe and profound disabilities: A review of research. In R. Gaylor–Ross (Ed.), *Issues and research in special education* (pp. 110–172). New York: Teachers College Press.

Henley, M., Ramsey, R. S., & Algozzine, R. F. (1999). *Characteristics of and strategies for teaching students with mild disabilities* (3rd ed.). Boston: Allyn & Bacon.

Hollowood, T. M., Salisbury, C. O., Rainforth, B., & Palombaro, M. M. (1995). Use of instructional time in classrooms serving students with and without severe disabilities. *Exceptional Children, 61,* 242–253.

Horton, S. V., Lovitt, T. C., & Bergerud, D. (1990). The effectiveness of graphic organizers for three classifications of secondary students in content area classes. *Journal of Learning Disabilities, 23,* 12–22.

Jenkins, J. R., & Jenkins, L. M. (1985). Peer tutoring in elementary and secondary programs. *Focus on Exceptional Children, 17,* 1–12.

Katsiyannis, A., Conderman, G., & Franks, D. J. (1995). State practices on inclusion: A national review. *Remedial and Special Education, 16,* 279–287.

Lipsky, D. K., & Gartner, A. (1996). Inclusive education and school restructuring. In W. Stainback & S. Stainback (Eds.), *Controversial issues confronting special education* (2nd ed., pp. 3–15). Boston: Allyn & Bacon.

McCarthy, M. M. (1998). Inclusion of children with disabilities: Seeking the appropriate balance. *Educational Horizons,* 116–118.

McIntosh, R., Vaughn, S., Schumm, J. S., Haager, D., & Lee, O. (1993). Observations of students with learning disabilities in general education classrooms. *Exceptional Children, 60,* 249–261.

McLaughlin, M. J., & Warren, S. H. (1994). *Resource implications of inclusion: Impressions of special education administrators at selected sites.* Palo Alto, CA: Center for Special Education Finance.

Michigan State Department of Education. (1991). *Co-teaching: Regular education/special education and co-teaching reference guide.* Lansing, MI: Author.

Miller, L. (1990). The regular education initiative and school reform: Lessons from the mainstream. *Remedial and Special Education, 11,* 17–22.

Peterson, J. M. (1989). Remediation is no remedy. *Educational Leadership, 6,* 24–25.

Rogers, J. (1993). The inclusion revolution. *Research Bulletin, 1,* 1–6.

Sailor, W. (1991). Special education in the restructured school. *Remedial and Special Education, 12,* 8–22.

Semmel, M. L., Abernathy, T. V., Butera, G., & Lesar, S. (1991). Teacher perceptions of the regular education initiative. *Exceptional Children, 58,* 9–24.

Stainback, S., & Stainback, W. (1992). Introduction. In J. Pearpoint, M. Forest, & J. Snow (Eds.), *The inclusion papers: Strategies to make inclusion work.* Toronto: Inclusion Press.

Stainback, S., & Stainback, W. (1990). *Support networks for inclusive schooling: Interdependent integrated education.* Baltimore: Paul H. Brookes.

Thousand, J. S., & Villa, R. A. (1989). Enhancing success in heterogeneous schools. In S. Stainback, W. Stainback, & M. Forest (Eds.), *Educating all students in the mainstream of regular education* (pp. 89–103). Baltimore: Paul H. Brookes.

Turnbull, H. R. (1990). *Free appropriate public education: The law and children with disabilities.* Denver, CO: Love.

Viadero, D. (1998). Small classes: Popular, but still unproven. *Education Week, 17* (23), 1–16.

Will, M. (1986). *Educating children with learning problems: A shared responsibility.* Washington, DC: Office of Special Education and Rehabilitative Services, U.S. Department of Education.

Willis, S. (1994). Making schools more inclusive. *Curriculum Update,* 1–8.

Winzer, M. A. (1986). Early developments in special education. Some aspects of enlightenment thought. *Remedial and Special Education, 7,* 42–49.

Winzer, M. A. (1993). *The history of special education: From isolation to integration.* Washington, DC: Gallaudet University Press.

CHAPTER 10

MULTICULTURAL EDUCATION AND THE CULTURAL CURRICULUM

Charlotte is a teacher of eighth grade social studies in a small Midwestern community. She uses the project approach because she believes that students should be able to relate what they study to their own personal lives. She is quite proud of the fact that her students are investigating the impact of the town's only traffic light on downtown congestion. Many of her students are actively engaged in this endeavor and take a personal interest because most have lived in this community all their lives and remember when there was not even a stop sign at the town's only major intersection. However, this is not true of all Charlotte's students. She has several in her classroom who moved to the area from a large urban area in Mexico only a few months ago. Their background knowledge and primary language are quite different from the mainstream students'. They are puzzled regarding the issue at hand, because, for most of their lives, they have dealt with congested traffic in one of the world's largest cities. Charlotte is doing the best she can, but how can she teach both process and content in such a way that she can reach all her students?

Teachers must be prepared to meet the needs of all children in their classrooms and this includes students from diverse backgrounds (Kirmani & Laster, 1999). According to Gollnick and Chinn (1990), multiculturalism challenges the traditional narratives of American history. Multicultural education "is not only more inclusive, but also more *accurate* to recognize this diversity. The intellectual purpose of multiculturalism is a more accurate understanding of who we are as Americans" (Halford, 1999, p. 9).

This chapter poses many questions related to cultural diversity and the curriculum. We will consider misconceptions about multicultural education, dilemmas teachers face in the 21st century, issues related to LEP students, and, finally, we will consider what and how we should teach. The issues are extremely complex. The goal of this chapter is to present numerous ideas for debate and discussion, rather than provide simplistic—and thus unrealistic—solutions.

MISCONCEPTIONS ABOUT CULTURAL DIVERSITY

As we begin to look at culture and what is taught in schools, let's consider some current misconceptions about multicultural education. According to Aldridge, Calhoun, and Aman (2000) there are at least 15 common misconceptions about cultural diversity in schools today:

1. *People from the same nation or geographical region, or those who speak the same language, share a common culture.* There are numerous examples across the planet that indicate this misconception is false. The people of Nicaragua, the Dominican Republic, and Chile may all have Spanish-speaking citizens, but their dialects and cultures are vastly different.

2. *Families from the same culture share the same values.* People from nondominant cultures live out their cultural pluralism in numerous ways. According to Lynch and Hanson (1998), there are at least four ways individuals from minorities express their cultural identities in the United States. These include "(a) mainstreamers, (b) bicultural individuals, (c) culturally different individuals, and (d) culturally marginal individuals" (p. 19). Grandparents might be culturally marginalized because they maintain their original culture and have limited participation in the dominant culture whereas their grandchildren may be either mainstreamers or bicultural (Aldridge et al., 2000).

3. *Children's books about another culture are usually authentic.* Texts and periodicals written about specific cultures may be inaccurate. This is particularly true in the 21st century, when virtually anything can be published on the Internet. However, there are published guidelines that help in selecting culturally appropriate and bias-free sources. These include Guidelines for Selecting Bias-Free Textbooks and Storybooks (see Derman–Sparks & The A.B.C. Task Force, 1989) and *Teaching Multicultural Literature in Grades K–8* (Bishop, 1993).

4. *Multicultural education includes only ethnic and racial issues.* Gender and socioeconomic diversity are also important and should be included in multicultural explorations. Children come from many types of homes, including those headed by lesbian or gay parents. Furthermore, children from lower socioeconomic environments often have more in common with one another than those of similar ethnic or racial heritage from higher income levels (Strevy & Aldridge, 1994).

Gollnick and Chinn (1990) recommend considering other issues in multicultural education beyond ethnic and racial considerations. They advocate promotion of social justice and equity, the acceptance of alternative life choices for people, and an emphasis on equal distribution of power among marginalized groups.

5. *The tour and detour approach is appropriate for teaching multicultural education.* Merely visiting a culture would be considered tourist multiculturalism (Derman–Sparks & A.B.C. Task Force, 1989). There is also the detour approach in which many elementary teachers incorporate the study of Native Americans during Thanksgiving, or Martin Luther King during Black History Month without integrating these topics into the mainstream curriculum. According to Aldridge and colleagues (2000), "students come away from such teaching with even more biases" (p. 3).

6. *Multicultural education should be taught as a separate subject.* This would add something else to teachers' already full plates. James Banks (1994) recommends a transformative approach to teaching multicultural education. For example, in the past, history has been taught from one perspective. This is usually the perspective of the victor. Students who study the Alamo may only get the American perspective. What about the Mexican point of view? By presenting multiple viewpoints, teachers can infuse cultural issues into the mainstream curriculum.

7. *Multicultural education is already an accepted part of the curriculum.* This is simply not true. E. D. Hirsch (1996) and Rush Limbaugh (1994), among many others, are harsh critics of multicultural education. In fact, Limbaugh (1994) suggests multicultural education is really an excuse for people who have not made it in what he refers to as "the American way."

8. *Multiculturalism is divisive.* Some people believe that when ethnicity is turned into a defining characteristic, it promotes divisiveness rather than unity. Multiple diversities have always existed in the United States. A countersuggestion to this myth is to consider the United States as a salad bowl rather than a melting pot. With a melting pot, all people are put into the system and come out alike. There is no distinction in this metaphor. However, a salad is rich with diversity. The onions, tomatoes, and celery play an important part in the unity of the salad (Aldridge, 1993).

9. *In predominantly monocultural or bicultural societies, there is no need to study other cultures.* Monocultural or bicultural societies are fading fast. Increasingly, all students need to learn about the cultures to which they will live in close proximity in the near or immediate future (Greenfield & Cocking, 1994). With a major influx of Hispanic and Asian immigrants, many if not most public schools represent a variety of cultures, languages, and religions.

10. *Multicultural education should be reserved for older students who are less egocentric or ethnocentric.* Young children establish cultural understanding by the age of five and more easily adapt to and learn from new cultural patterns than adults (Lynch & Hanson, 1998). Young children are capable of learning likenesses and differences when presented in developmentally appropriate ways. One way to begin might be to look at pictures of children's families and discuss their similarities and diversities.

11. *When multicultural education is implemented, the commonality is lost.* As more and more diverse cultures enter the schools, conflicts may arise, as occurred during the Civil Rights Movement. However, multicultural education can assist in helping students become more tolerant, equitable, and inclusive (Ravitch, 1991/1992).

12. *We do not need multicultural education because America already acknowledges its cultural diversity.* Critics are quick to point out that we have Martin Luther King's birthday as a holiday in most states and celebrate Black History Month. As we have pointed out, this tour or detour approach can often be more divisive than transformative (Aldridge et al., 2000).

13. *Historical accuracy suffers in multicultural education.* Educators who subscribe to this viewpoint object to the notion that Cleopatra might have been black or that Western civilization may have started in Egypt (Africa) rather than Greece. However, if students are taught healthy skepticism, not cynicism, then they will seek out multiple sources to support and refute what they are learning in school.

14. *Most people identify with only one culture.* Increasingly, children and families are multiethnic. Take the following example. Alex is of Chinese heritage but was born and raised in Trinidad. He and his parents do not speak Chinese. Recently they moved to Buffalo, New York, where Alex is attending middle school. Alex has a multiethnic heritage that defies stereotyping.

15. *There are not enough resources about multicultural education.* Although this may have been a real issue 20 years ago, it is not true in the 21st century. At the end of this chapter we provide numerous references.

Although Aldridge and colleagues (2000) have identified these as misconceptions, several critics disagree. Strotsky (1999) believes, "today's version of multiculturalism has led to the suppression of the stories of most immigrant groups to this country" (p. 19). She suggests that historical accuracy suffers because few students today read about scientific and technological discoveries. They are too busy reading books in which they learn words in Spanish, Japanese, or Swahili, which will be of little use to them in the real world. Strotsky (1999) is even bold enough to assert, "the present version of multiculturalism may well be largely responsible, through its effect on classroom materials and instruction, for the growing gap between the scores of minority students and other students on the National Assessment of Educational Progress examinations in reading" (p. 21).

Criticisms also spill over into the issue of affirmative action in higher education. Clegg (2000) provides multiple arguments against affirmative action. He maintains, "skin color does not equal ideas, and ethnicity does not equal experiences. The position to the contrary used to be called stereotyping. Moreover, since the invention of the printing press, it has not been necessary to meet people in order to learn their perspectives" (p. 22). He goes on to say, "When we impose diversity upon an institution, we create resentment and stigmatization, break the law, compromise a college's mission, and tell some people that they aren't going to be admitted or hired or promoted, because they have the wrong melanin content or ancestry. Whatever the dubious benefits of diversity, is it worth all that?" (p. 23).

This might be a good time to examine your own personal beliefs about diversity and multicultural education. In doing so, it is important to note that everyone has prejudices, regardless of whether they admit it (Aldridge et al., 2000). Recognizing and acknowledging your own prejudices can sometimes open up a dialog and help make better communication among groups. For example, at a seminar in the early 1990s on diversity, Charles suggested that everyone has prejudices and that recognizing them is important. Jerry thought to himself, "Not me. Maybe other people do, but not me." However, one day while driving, Jerry began to notice that many people had what looked like a crown in the middle of their car dashboards. On closer examination, Jerry realized that most of these drivers were black. He commented to a black colleague about this, but she didn't seem to know what they were. Jerry thought she was being evasive, that this must be some secret Black Power sign. Maybe, he thought, it had something to do with Martin Luther King, Jr., because it was a crown. Later he found out it was just air freshener.

Jerry called Charles, who is black, and they had a good laugh about this. It didn't stop here, however. Charles told a relative, who also thought the story was most amusing. Without ever meeting Jerry, she went out and bought him an elaborate crown air freshener with blinking lights. Not all interactions turn out this positive. Still, a dialog and camaraderie were established in this instance because Jerry acknowledged his own misconceptions.

CULTURAL DILEMMAS TEACHERS FACE
IN THE 21ST CENTURY

Teachers in the 21st century will be faced with numerous cultural dilemmas and opportunities to make decisions about how and what they teach about these episodes. The following are examples of dilemmas that have actually happened in the real world. The only changes we have made are in names and, in some cases, the ethnicity to protect the students and teachers who experienced them. As you read, determine what you might do in these situations. What information do you need to make an informed choice? What is the context and nature of the community in which this occurred? What are the shared values of the dominant culture in that community? We do not have simple answers to the experiences described. The question is: How can you find the information needed to make an informed decision when such instances arise in your classroom? A brief commentary follows each dilemma. These commentaries are meant to enhance further discussion of each of the scenarios presented here.

A director of a preschool program with a diverse population decides to have an Easter egg hunt. Children are to assist in painting and decorating eggs. Do you believe this is appropriate? Why or why not?

Kirmani and Laster (1999) provide more information related to this situation. They describe a child named Mukesh who is Hindu and faced with a similar situation. He says, "I am 9 years old and in the fourth grade. I am a Hindu and I am a strict vegetarian. Strict vegetarians neither touch nor eat meat and eggs. We view them as life or as a source of life and believe they shouldn't be destroyed. I appreciate Easter celebrations, but in some ways they are difficult for me. I have a hard time handling eggs. Painting eggs and egg hunting can be fun, but I always feel I am doing something wrong" (p. 61).

What should a teacher do? Should students like Mukesh just not participate? Should the activity be adapted? For example, would it be appropriate for Mukesh to draw eggs on construction paper? Should he draw some other symbol of springtime? What about Mukesh's feelings related to socialization with the other children? Will he feel he's a part of the group if the activity is modified for him? Is there something Mukesh can share about his own background and religion with the class that will broaden their experiences? Should the teacher be having the Easter egg hunt in the first place? What do you believe and how would you handle this?

The PTA president has developed a parent education group and worked closely with them throughout the year. The president asks the parents to bring a present for exchange with another parent at the December PTA meeting. What are your thoughts about this? If you were a parent, how would you handle this if you disagreed or thought it was a bad idea? Also, what are some reasons a person might disagree with this practice?

Some parents may not have enough resources to provide their own children with presents. Furthermore, certain cultures and religions do not focus on material things but still want to participate in the PTA and other school activities. What would you do?

You have a child whose parents are Christian Scientists. The parents do not believe in traditional medicine. The child falls and breaks a leg and the parents cannot be reached. The child is in your care. What would you do?

Many schools have policies related to this. Teachers need to discuss this with the parents before an incident like this occurs. Parents may be willing to provide a signed document regarding what should occur in such an event. However, because teachers are not medical specialists, it is within their right and moral obligation to call the paramedics and let them decide the appropriate course of action. How would you handle this?

You notice Kham (a child of Hmong heritage) has red marks on his arms and back. What is happening here? How would you find out? What would you do?

According to Lynch and Hanson (1998) this may be a religious practice. The Hmong "practice animism as well as ancestor worship" (p. 284). They also use *coining*, rubbing the skin until it is red to get rid of evil spirits. If this is a religious practice, should you report it to social welfare agencies? If so, what about circumcision, which would certainly be more painful? Would you report this? What would you do?

A child in your class has parents who are Jehovah's Witnesses. The principal of your program has planned for the entire school to have a Valentine's Day celebration. The child from the Jehovah's Witness background is not allowed to participate. What would you do?

A key issue in this vignette is the fact that the principal has planned for the entire school to participate. Derman–Sparks and the A.B.C. Task Force (1989) suggests that schools not use a seasonal curriculum in which Halloween, Thanksgiving, Christmas, and Valentine's Day are emphasized. This would alleviate some of the problem. However, in this situation, the celebration has already been "mandated." A child in kindergarten or first grade might not be able to comprehend the reasons for not participating. How would you deal with this dilemma?

A boy in your class is being raised by his uncle, who belongs to a group that worships Satan. The boy has been told to poke his enemies in the eye with two fingers. The child has attempted this several times on the playground. What would you do?

In schools we generally have common rules. Three common rules include (a) you cannot hurt other people, (b) you cannot hurt yourself, and (c) you cannot destroy property. Would these be helpful in working with this child? How would you discuss or approach this with the uncle or guardian? What would you do?

You are a teacher in a middle school. You have a new student in your classroom. This child is originally from Nepal, but has just moved to your community. You ask the student to tell something about herself to her new classmates. She describes herself and indicates she is a Buddhist. Another child responds, "Well, you're going to hell." How would you handle this?

The community in which this happened is Southern, rural, conservative, and predominantly Protestant. Most of the children in this student's class have never seen or interacted with anyone from Nepal. Many of the children come from evangelical or fundamentalist backgrounds. They are probably echoing the beliefs of their parents and a large portion of the community. Considering this context, what actions would you take?

> *You are an elementary teacher and your volunteer room mother has been very helpful. You are Jewish but your spouse is Christian and you have chosen to incorporate both religious backgrounds into your home. In an interaction with your room mother, she states, "Wouldn't the world be better if everyone were white and evangelical Christian?" How would you respond?*

This might be an appropriate time to share your background with the parent. What would you tell this parent? What approach would you take to teaching diversity with the understanding that some of the students you teach may have parents who have beliefs like this parent?

> *During a special education placement meeting with a parent of Native American heritage, the transdisciplinary team is asking the mother lots of questions but she does not appear to respond. She does speak English. What is happening here? What would you do? What information do you need to make an informed decision?*

Different families within and among various cultures communicate in different ways. Without stereotyping the family, child, or culture, it would have been helpful to find out as much as possible about them before the special education placement meeting. In this particular situation, the mother was providing the team with answers by looking up and down. When she looked up, she meant yes; when she looked down, she meant no.

> *Javier is a kindergarten student from Nicaragua. His teacher is constantly scolding him for not looking at her when she calls his name. Why does Javier look down? If you were his teacher, what would you do?*

Javier has been told in his family to look down when your name is called. If you have done something wrong, it brings shame to the family and to show your respect, you look downward. Javier's kindergarten teacher has two options. She can honor Javier's home culture and allow him to look down when she calls his name. *Or,* she could teach him how to *code switch,* meaning that she would explain to him, "At home you look down when your name is called. When I call your name, please look at me." The issue here is one of teaching the child to survive in the dominant culture while respecting his family and culture. Which do you believe is more appropriate—following the cues from home or teaching Javier to code switch?

HOW CAN WE WORK WITH STUDENTS WHO ARE LIMITED ENGLISH PROFICIENT?

Every year more and more students who are LEP enter schools in the United States (Menken & Look, 2000). Who are LEP students? Who teaches them? How do students with limited English proficiency learn best in an English-speaking classroom? The issue of how best to work with children whose primary language is other than English is a growing concern for many educators.

Who Are Limited English Proficient Students?

According to Peregoy and Boyle (1993), "students who speak English as a non-native language live in all areas of the United States" (p. 3). Non-English-speaking students come from all over the world. "Many recent immigrants have left countries brutally torn by war or political strife in regions such as Southeast Asia, Central America, and Eastern Europe; others have immigrated for economic reasons. Still others come to be reunited with families who are already here or because of educational opportunities they may find in the United States" (p. 3). Besides these, there are many LEP children who were born in the United States. These include groups such as Native Americans and second or third generation immigrants (Peregoy & Boyle, 1993).

By 2003 there will be well more than four million students who have English as a second language. Currently about 1 in 10 children in the United States are not fluent in English. LEP students are the fastest growing group in our schools, with an increase of 104 percent during the past 10 years (Menken & Look, 2000).

Who Teaches Students with Limited English Proficiency?

In some schools, all the teachers in the school teach some children with limited English proficiency. Nationally, it can be said that half of all teachers will experience LEP students during their teaching careers (Menken & Look, 2000). Peregoy and Boyle (1993) describe the first day of class for a first grade teacher named Mr. Bertolucci. They report, "It may surprise you to learn that more than half of the children in Mr. Bertolucci's class are new to the English language, coming from homes in which languages such as Spanish, Cantonese, and Japanese are spoken. Such linguistic variety was not always the case, but changes in the neighborhood over the past ten years have been dramatic" (p. 2). Mr. Bertolucci's class is not unusual. First grades all over the United States have children from many cultural and linguistic backgrounds.

How Do Students with Limited English Proficiency Learn Best in an English-Speaking Classroom?

Although all children have individual learning styles, most LEP students learn best in classrooms that provide the following five things:

1. *Integrated instruction*—When students study topics around connected units or themes, they are better able to construct relationships among content areas. "By integrating language instruction and content instruction, language learners will not fall behind in developing grade-level content skills" (Menken & Look, 2000, p. 17).

2. *Meaningful communication*—When LEP students have many opportunities to use language, they learn English faster. Cooperative and collaborative learning, peer tutoring, and pupil pairs encourage meaningful communication (California State Department of Education, 1994; Menken & Look, 2000).

3. *An interactive hands-on approach*—We have always known that students learn by doing. This is even more important for LEP students. Experimenting with objects in science and exploring the environment in social studies is just good teaching. However, this is even more important for LEP students. They are able to construct their own knowledge before being able to communicate it in English (Menken & Look, 2000; Peregoy & Boyle, 1993).

4. *Clear classroom procedures and guidelines*—A consistent and clear classroom structure can help students travel through the maze of classroom activities. Although guidelines and procedures are crucial, making sure these are communicated to LEP students and they understand them are just as important (California State Department of Education, 1994).

5. *Cultural connections*—Teachers need to familiarize themselves thoroughly with each child's culture so that connections between the child's culture and classroom learning can be encouraged (Aldridge et al., 2000; Menken & Look, 2000).

WHAT SHOULD WE TEACH WITH REGARD TO CULTURE?

There are basically two types of cultural literacy—mainstream and marginalized. Many of us were taught mainstream literacy in school. For example, who discovered America? What we learned was Christopher Columbus in 1492. However, there were people who were already living here, and there are rumors that Leif Erikson came here before Columbus. If we consider this question from multiple viewpoints, we move into marginalized cultural literacy—different perspectives that are not addressed in mainstream literacy.

With regard to culture, both mainstream and marginalized literacy are not enough. Another option is *critical literacy*. If we teach students to consider multiple viewpoints from varying sources, then we also need to teach them how to evaluate these sources. Who said that? Who is served by this perspective? Who is marginalized? Who has been left out in telling their side of the story? All knowledge has political and cultural content. Absolutely no knowledge is value free. What we learn in school is highly political, social, and cultural in nature. This is a given. Isn't it our job as teachers to point this out to students and have them evaluate everything we ask them to read?

HOW SHOULD WE TEACH WITH REGARD TO CULTURE?

To answer this question we have to consider how the dominant culture emphasizes certain values whereas minority groups often share different ones. A big issue is *collectivism* versus *individualism*. "Collectivism is a cluster of interrelated values that emphasize the interdependence of family members. Within this value system, children are taught to be helpful to others and to contribute to the success of any group they belong to—beginning with the family" (Rothstein–Fisch, Greenfield, & Trumbull, 1999, p. 64). Individualism, on the other hand, is most often promoted in the dominant culture and in the schools, and promotes individual achievement, independence, and competition (Rothstein–Fisch, 1998; Triandis, 1989).

Many of the more recent arrivals from Mexico, Central America, South America, and Asia share more collectivist values (Lynch & Hanson, 1998). There are several ways teachers can incorporate teaching strategies that more effectively reach a wide variety of students from many different cultures. These include promoting collaborative learning and cooperation, encouraging helpfulness through such avenues as peer tutoring, and sharing group success as well as individual triumphs.

Although teachers often feel the frustration of not knowing enough about each of their children's cultures and home backgrounds, they can incorporate collectivist practices to reach more children from a broad range of cultural histories. Collectivism can be used "to understand the underlying motivation behind specific cultural practices, including those of the school" (Rothstein–Fisch et al., 1999, p. 66).

QUESTIONS

1. Go back and consider the cultural dilemmas described in this chapter that teachers face in the 21st century. How would you respond to these dilemmas? What information do you need to help you consider them?

2. What misconceptions about multicultural education described in this chapter do you believe are misconceptions? Which ones do you question? Why?

3. Search the professional education literature for other cultural dilemmas teachers face. Discuss them with the class.

4. What cultural dilemmas have you experienced during your own school experience? Were they resolved? If so, how? If not, why not?

REFERENCES

Aldridge, J. (1993). *Self-esteem: Loving yourself at every age.* Birmingham, AL: Doxa Books.

Aldridge, J., Calhoun, C., & Aman, R. (2000). 15 misconceptions about multicultural education. *ACEI Focus on Elementary, 12,* 1–6.

Banks, J. (1994). *An introduction to multicultural education.* Boston: Allyn & Bacon.

Bishop, R. S. (1993). Multicultural literature for children: Making informed choices. In V. J. Harris (Ed.), *Teaching multicultural literature in grades K–8* (pp. 37–53). Norwood, MA: Christopher-Gordon.

California State Department of Education. (1994). *Building bilingual instruction: Putting the pieces together.* Sacramento, CA: Bilingual Education Office.

Clegg, R. (2000). The perversity of "diversity." *Education Digest, 66* (1), 20–23.

Derman–Sparks, L., & The A.B.C. Task Force. (1989). *Anti-bias curriculum: Tools for empowering young children.* Washington, DC: National Association for the Education of Young Children.

Gollnick, D., & Chinn, P. (1990). *Multicultural education in a pluralistic society* (3rd ed.). New York: Macmillan.

Greenfield, P., & Cocking, R. (Eds.). (1994). *Cross cultural roots of minority child development.* Hillsdale, NJ: Lawrence Erlbaum.

Halford, J. M. (1999). A different mirror: A conversation with Ronald Takaki. *Educational Leadership, 56* (7), 8–13.

Hirsch, E. D. (1996). *The schools we need and why we don't have them.* New York: Doubleday.

Kirmani, M. H., & Laster, B. P. (1999). Responding to religious diversity in classrooms. *Educational Leadership, 56* (7), 61–63.

Limbaugh, R. (1994). *See, I told you so.* New York: Simon and Schuster.

Lynch, E., & Hanson, M. (Eds.). (1998). *Developing cross-cultural competence: A guide for working with children and their families* (2nd ed.). Baltimore: Paul H. Brookes.

Menken, K., & Look, K. (2000). Making chances for linguistically and culturally diverse students. *Education Digest, 65* (8), 14–19.

Peregoy, S. F., & Boyle, O. F. (1993). *Reading, writing, and learning in ESL: A resource book for K–12 teachers* (2nd ed.). New York: Longman.

Ravitch, D. (1991/1992). A culture in common. *Educational Leadership, 49* (4), 8–11.

Rothstein–Fisch, C. R. (1998). *Bridging cultures: A pre-service teacher training model.* San Francisco: WestEd.

Rothstein–Fisch, C. R., Greenfield, P. M., & Trumbull, E. (1999). Bridging cultures with classroom strategies. *Educational Leadership, 56* (7), 64–67.

Strevy, D., & Aldridge, J. (1994). Personal narrative themes of African American mothers. *Perceptual and Motor Skills, 78,* 1143–1146.

Strotsky, S. (1999). Is it really multicultural illiteracy? *Education Digest, 65* (4), 17–21.

Triandis, H. C. (1989). Cross-cultural studies of individualism and collectivism. *Nebraska Symposium on Motivation, 37,* 43–133.

CHAPTER 11

WORKING WITH FAMILIES

Thanks to cable television, many people are familiar with what was considered the traditional family of the 1950s through such TV shows as *Leave It to Beaver*, *Father Knows Best*, and the *Donna Reed Show*. Of course, teachers in the 21st century work with numerous family structures. Before we look at family structures, important questions that need answering are: What is a family? How do *you* define family? Are there any biases in your definition? How did you come up with your definition?

There are many definitions of family. These fall into two broad categories. Some definitions focus on what families look like, whereas others are based on what families do (Fuller & Olson, 2003). Families can be defined as those who live in the same dwelling to those who support and help one another. Throughout this chapter we ask you to consider and reconsider what you believe constitutes a family.

If you teach for any length of time, no doubt you will work with children who come from a wide variety of family structures. Try the following activity: *Name as many family structures as you can.*

According to Watts and Tutwiler (2003), family structures are changing rapidly. They describe the following family types:

- married-couple families
- grandparents as parents
- gay- and lesbian-headed households
- black families
- Asian American families
- Latino families
- Native American families
- families described by religious affiliation

There are other types of family structures. These include blended families, immigrant families, single-parent families, foster families, homeless families, biracial families, families with joint custody, and what we define as *hybrid fami-*

lies. Which family structures did you omit from your list? Consider the fact that those you did not mention are important too.

The purpose of this chapter is threefold. First, a major purpose is to describe briefly some of the family structures listed here. A more important purpose is to describe general guidelines for working with each family type. Lastly, we propose a scenario or vignette related to each family structure for problem solving.

MARRIED-COUPLE FAMILIES

The traditional *Leave It to Beaver* family, contrary to popular belief, is not the majority. "Slightly more than one-third of all family households consists of married couples with children" (Watts & Tutwiler, 2003, p. 46). Furthermore, more and more married couples are choosing not to have children. Today there are more married couples who have never had children than those who have them (Outtz, 1993).

Married couples with children are by no means a homogeneous group. Differences include one parent who works outside the home while the other's primary responsibility resides inside the home. Many married couples involve both parents who work. However, women are still the one primarily responsible for the children (Demo & Acock, 1993).

As with any other family structure, married couples differ with regard to socioeconomic status, race or ethnicity, family size, religious affiliation, and support from extended family, just to mention a few other salient differences (Lynch & Hanson, 2003).

GENERAL GUIDELINES FOR WORKING WITH MARRIED-COUPLE FAMILIES

1. Do not make assumptions about which parent is the primary caregiver.
2. Understand that married couples may have disparate expectations or goals for their children.
3. Because many mothers are working, find out as much as you can about child care arrangments, including after-school care and extended family responsibilities.

Vignette

John and Martha try to share equal responsibility for their only daughter Sara. They alternate attending parent–teacher conferences. John's parenting style and expectations are easy going or laissez-faire with Sara. He believes she is given too much homework and needs more time to play and enjoy extracurricular activities. Martha is a strict disciplinarian and expects more homework for Sara and more effort from Sara. Both parents' positions are strongly communicated to you during the parent–teacher conference. John insists on less homework. Martha advocates for more. How would you interact with John and Martha, who have differing expectations and meet with you separately?

GRANDPARENTS AS PARENTS

More and more grandparents and great-grandparents are responsible for raising children in the United States (Watts & Tutwiler, 2003). This is particularly true in black families. In most cases of grandparents as parents, grandmothers are responsible for the children. Some grandmothers are responsible for more than one set of grandchildren. With the lifespan increasing, some grandparents or great-grandparents in their 70s and 80s are responsible for children and adolescents.

GENERAL GUIDELINES FOR WORKING WITH GRANDPARENTS AS PARENTS

1. Find out as much as possible about the family structure and responsibilities the grandparents face.
2. Develop or help grandparents (and older parents) find a parenting support group. Issues grandparents face are often different than those of other family structures.
3. Encourage and support grandparent participation in school functions, including the Parent Teacher Organization (PTO) and Parent Teacher Association (PTA). Grandparents often feel marginalized and less welcome than married-couple families.

Vignette

Cora is an 80-year-old grandmother with high blood pressure who is responsible for two sets of grandchildren. She is the guardian of five children ages 4 through 16. The family lives in poverty in a five-room mobile home. The oldest grandchild, LaToya, wants to try out for the dance team at school. Uniforms for the dance team generally run from $1,000 to $1,500 per year. Cora comes to you concerned that LaToya might make the dance team. Although she is pleased that LaToya is interested and could possibly make the team, she is also terrified that she will not be able to support LaToya because she cannot afford the price of uniforms. How would you handle this situation?

GAY- AND LESBIAN-HEADED HOUSEHOLDS

As with all other family types, gay- and lesbian-headed families are an extremely diverse group (Johnson & O'Connor, 2002). In a national study of gay and lesbian parents, the vast majority of those sampled "had been formed within the gay or lesbian relationship" (Johnson & O'Conner, 2002, p. 84). A significantly smaller number had begun with a heterosexual relationship, and these families differed in many ways from families who had children that began with a gay or lesbian relationship.

Many subgroups exist among gay and lesbian families. There are primary gay families, gay stepfamilies, and blended families that include children from both a previous heterosexual relationship and a gay relationship. The same types of structures exist in the lesbian community. Primary lesbian, lesbian stepfamilies, and blended families exist.

Unlike many other family structures, some gay and lesbian parents may choose not to inform the school or teacher of their family structure. Therefore, many teachers may have children of gay and lesbian parents in their classrooms but may be unaware of this.

GENERAL GUIDELINES FOR WORKING WITH GAY AND LESBIAN PARENTS

1. Do not assume heterosexism. In other words, when the family structure is unclear, avoid asking, "What does the father think?" when talking to a mother or "What does the mother think?" when talking to a father.
2. Learn as much as possible about gay and lesbian families and their expectations. A good resource is *The Gay Baby Boom: The Psychology of Gay Parenthood* (Johnson & O'Connor, 2002).
3. Examine your own prejudices. A large number of teachers are uncomfortable with gay and lesbian families. However, all parties, including teacher and parents, are concerned for the child. This should be the major focus of parent–teacher interactions.
4. Be alert with regard to teasing and harassment of children. Teachers are more likely to tolerate negative comments with regard to sexual orientation than other marginalized groups or family structures.
5. Important questions are: Should you have students in your classroom chart "Who are the members of my family?" Many teachers have students develop family trees or discuss their families. Is this always appropriate?

Vignette

You just happen to teach in a very rural, conservative community. You ask the students to bring in their favorite book. Marva brings the book *Heather Has Two Mommies* (Newman, 1991). Knowing your community and also respecting Marva, how would you handle this situation? Why?

BLACK FAMILIES

Once again, black families are as diverse as any other family structure. There are more differences within the black family than there are between the black family and other families. Still, there are things to consider when working with black families, especially when they are not in the majority.

An interesting fact is that 83 percent of teachers in this country are white, middle-class women. A large percentage of white women will teach children of color. There is often a disconnect between the white middle-class teacher and children of color who also live in poverty (Kunjufu, 2002).

GENERAL GUIDELINES FOR WORKING WITH BLACK FAMILIES

1. Have positive, high expectations of black children and their families.
2. Understand that many black families use high-context communication. This means that *how* something is said is often more important than *what* is said.
3. Read and use references that are written within the black community about working with families. A good source to begin with is *Black Students: Middle Class Teachers* (Kunjufu, 2002).

Vignette

Consider the following: A young, white female teacher has just begun her teaching career at a predominantly black school. The first week she notices the discourse (way of talking) used by black teachers is very different from what she is used to. The tone of voice of many of the black teachers is more stern and direct. She further notices that many of the students tend to respect this form of discourse and realize their teacher loves them. However, the white teacher is not comfortable using this form of discourse. She uses what she knows from her white middle-class roots as a softer form of interacting with the students. She begins to have trouble with her class and over time has more and more discipline problems. What recommendations do you have for this teacher? Why?

ASIAN AMERICAN FAMILIES

Although black families are a diverse group, families with Asian roots are an extremely heterogeneous population (Chan, 2003). Once again, differences within the Asian community are often more disparate than differences between Asian families and other groups. For example, a family of Filipino Catholic heritage might have more in common with a family from Venezuela than they would with a Hindu family from India.

Families with Asian roots or Asian American families may also have amazing diversity within the same family. For instance, grandparents may be culturally different or marginal, parents could be bicultural, whereas the children may be predominantly mainstreamers (Hanson, 2003). This will make a difference in how teachers interact with parents and families with Asian roots.

GENERAL GUIDELINES FOR WORKING WITH ASIAN AMERICAN FAMILIES

1. Find out as much about the family's immigration pattern. Some Chinese families in San Francisco are sixth generation Americans, whereas others recently arrived in the United States.
2. Seek out and read reliable and multiple sources concerning the specific Asian heritage from which students in your classroom originated. For example, children of Hmong heritage may have parents or guardians who have specific religious practices that may be unfamiliar to teachers. A good resource concerning this issue is *The Spirit Catches You and You Fall Down: A Hmong Child, Her American Doctors, and the Collision of Two Cultures* (Fadiman, 1997).
3. Because of the importance of the extended family in some Asian cultures, it may be appropriate to ask parents who they want to include in the parent–teacher conference (Chan, 2003).
4. Find out how guardians are greeted in different Asian cultures. For example, in some Chinese cultures, parents are addressed by their surname. Cambodian parents are often referred to by their given names.

Vignette

During the first week of school, both the mother and father of one of your students from Korea come to school and sit in the back of your classroom. You are puzzled because the mother knits and the father sits. They do not appear to be anxious. They have not volunteered to help. Why do you suppose they have come to your classroom and remain all day? What would you do? (Discuss this issue before you read the following note.)

NOTE: Many parents from Korea come to school with their children for the first few days of school. This is to show support and respect for the teacher and the school. There is often no interaction between teachers and the parents. The parents are simply there as a cultural practice.

LATINO FAMILIES

As we have seen in previous chapters, large numbers of Latinos have come to the United States during the past 20 years. Many have settled in states where there were previously no Hispanics and in areas where few people speak Spanish. This is especially true in the Midwest and Southeast. The Latino population is also a heterogeneous group. The cultural and the linguistic heritage of families from Puerto Rico is vastly different from those from Argentina. Even the dialects are quite different.

The history of migration, economic levels, and education backgrounds of Latinos are also diverse. Families who arrived from Cuba in the 1960s were often middle class and well educated. Many families arriving in the 21st century from Mexico are often people of poverty with limited educational backgrounds.

GENERAL GUIDELINES FOR WORKING WITH LATINO FAMILIES

1. Determine language issues before interacting with parents or guardians. If the parents or guardians are Spanish-only speakers and you speak only English, then the need for an appropriate interpreter must be met. It is not appropriate for a child or adolescent to serve as the interpreter for the parent or guardian. Many Latino cultures are patriarchal, and using a child as an interpreter shifts the balance of power within the family structure (Zuniga, 2003).
2. Do not inquire about immigration status. A major goal of interacting with Hispanic families is to establish trust and support for the Latino children we teach. Inquiring about immigration status can undermine this.
3. Read as much as possible about Latino cultures. Zuniga (2003) recommends the *Hispanic Journal of Behavioral Sciences* as an excellent place to start.
4. Understand that independence or autonomy as a goal for children at an early age may not be shared by Latino parents and guardians.

Vignette

Maria is a student in your second grade classroom. Her mother volunteers once a week and goes to lunch with the class. During lunch, Maria's mother feeds her. This practice is not unusual in the home, but it is highly unusual for a parent to feed her second grade child in the school lunchroom. What would you do? Why? How does this lunchroom experience influence Maria's social development in school? Shouldn't we respect the family's goals? Why or why not?

OTHER FAMILY STRUCTURES OR DEFINING CHARACTERISTICS

As mentioned earlier in this chapter there are numerous other ways families can be described. Families may have no religious affiliation or strong spiritual convictions. There are blended families that are seldom like the *Brady Bunch* or like that portrayed in the movie *Yours, Mine, and Ours.* Although we have briefly discussed families from various ethnic groups, some of them are families of recent immigration and others are not. Single-parent families, including those headed by a single-parent father, may be part of our classrooms whereas foster children, homeless families, biracial couples, and families with joint custody may also be a part of our teaching experience at one time or another.

There is even a new group that we call *the hybrid family*. A hybrid family is one that redefines itself and produces something new and different from the origins that created it. Take, for example, Mirta and Hamid. Mirta is from Ecuador and is a fundamentalist Christian. She married Hamid from Pakistan, who is a devout Muslim. They have three children who attend public school in Queens, New York. Their children speak English, but not the original languages of their parents. The children attend church with their mother and the mosque with their father. The culture and familial experience created by this union is distinctly different from a traditional Ecuatorian or Pakistani family.

QUESTIONS

1. What family structures exist in the schools in your community? If you are currently teaching, what family structures are in your classroom? Are you aware of all of them? If you are not teaching, interview a teacher and ask what types of family structures currently exist in her classroom? What issues does she face in working with diverse families?

2. What school practices promote parent involvement? What practices inhibit it? For example, one school has parents' night once a month. Parents are to spend time in their child's classroom during parents' night. This lasts for one hour. Some single parents have three children in the same school. Which classroom should the single parent attend? Other parents are divorced but have joint custody. Both parents want to attend, but one is marginalized on the week he does not have custody of the child. Is this fair? What can be done about this?

3. What are your prejudices concerning families? Are you opposed to gay and lesbian families? Are you turned off by undocumented parents? How can you deal with your own prejudices so that you can work with families to ensure the best possible school experiences for them and their children?

REFERENCES

Chan, S. (2003). Families with Asian roots. In E. Lynch & M. Hanson (Eds.), *Developing cross-cultural competence* (3rd ed., pp. 251–354). Baltimore, MD: Paul H. Brookes.

Demo, D., & Acock, A. (1993). Family diversity and the division of domestic labor: How much have things really changed? *Family Relations, 42,* 323–331.

Fadiman, A. (1997). *The spirit catches you and you fall down: A Hmong child, her American doctors, and the collision of two cultures.* New York: Farrar, Straus and Giroux.

Fuller, M., & Olson, G. (2003). An introduction to families. In G. Olsen & M. Fuller (Eds.), *Home–school relations: Working successfully with parents and families* (2nd ed., pp. 1–11). Boston: Allyn & Bacon.

Hanson, M. (2003). Ethnic, cultural, and language diversity in intervention settings. In E. Lynch & M. Hanson (Eds.), *Developing cross-cultural competence* (3rd ed., pp. 3–22). Baltimore, MD: Paul H. Brookes.

Johnson, S., & O'Connor, E. (2002). *The gay baby boom: The psychology of gay parenthood.* New York: New York University Press.

Kunjufu, J. (2002). *Black students: Middle class teachers.* Chicago: African American Images.

Lynch, E., & Hanson, M. (2003). Children of many songs. In E. Lynch & M. Hanson (Eds.), *Developing cross-cultural competence* (3rd ed., pp. 483–488). Baltimore, MD: Paul H. Brookes.

Newman, L. (1991). *Heather has two mommies.* Los Angeles, CA: Alyson Publications.

Outtz, J. (1993). *Of American families.* Santa Monica, CA: Milken Institute for Job and Capital Formation.

Watts, I., & Tutwiler, S. (2003). Diversity among families. In G. Olsen & M. Fuller (Eds.), *Home–school relations: Working successfully with parents and families* (2nd ed., pp. 44–70). Boston: Allyn & Bacon.

Zuniga, M. (2003). Families with Latino roots. In E. Lynch & M. Hanson (Eds.), *Developing cross-cultural competence* (3rd ed., pp. 209–250). Baltimore, MD: Paul H. Brookes.

CHAPTER 12

DISCIPLINE AND CLASSROOM MANAGEMENT

Discipline and classroom management are two of the most important, if not *the* most, salient topics for which teachers want help. When teachers are surveyed about areas of need, they most often choose discipline and classroom management (Aldridge, 2001; Boynton & Boynton, 2005). There are hundreds of books and articles written on discipline and classroom management. However, the purpose of this chapter is to answer two very important questions. First, what do we expect or want from students? Second, how do we go about getting it? Most discipline and classroom management issues revolve around these two questions.

We know that you must be thinking, "What do you mean by 'what do we want from students?'" This question is at the heart of how we go about the task of discipline and classroom management. Do we want children to obey? Behave? Think? Do we want students to sit a desks? Not talk? Interact with others? Be compliant? Although these questions might seem philosophical, they are, in fact, at the very heart of why we teach in the first place.

All these "subquestions" can be answered by considering two very broad, basic questions:

1. Do we want students to be heteronomous?
2. Do we want students to be autonomous?

These are not new questions. Piaget (1932) believed there were only two stages of moral development—heteronomy and autonomy. Simply put, heteronomy is defined as being governed by others. Autonomy is defined as being governed by one's self. If we want students to be heteronomous and governed by others—namely us, the teachers—then the disipline plan we choose will be much different than if we believe the goal of education is autonomy.

HETERONOMY

If we want students to comply, then we will most likely use as a major part of our discipline and classroom management plan positive reinforcement, negative reinforcement, and punishment (Skinner, 1974). Let's look at each of these briefly.

Positive reinforcement is most similar to "rewards." A positive reinforcer is something that, when applied following a behavior, strengthens the chance the behavior will occur again. Positive reinforcement includes primary reinforcers and secondary reinforcers. Primary reinforcers are things that children naturally need or want. For example, food and water are primary reinforcers. Children naturally want these. If we give children some candy or something good to drink after they have done something we wanted them to do, then we are applying (or giving them) positive reinforcement. Secondary reinforcers are not rewarding at first, but they become rewarding. For example, chips or tokens that can be gathered (like money) to buy a prize are secondary reinforcers. Money is a secondary reinforcer. No one was born wanting a dirty piece of green paper. However, it becomes rewarding because of what we can get with it.

Negative reinforcement is often more difficult to understand because we don't usually recognize its use. A negative reinforcer is something that, when removed, strengthens the chance a behavior will occur again. The seat belt buzzer is a good example of a secondary reinforcer. When you put on your seat belt, the annoying noise goes away.

Punishment is not the same thing as reinforcement. Although reinforcement (or what we usually call *reward*) seeks to increase behaviors, punishment seeks to decrease certain behaviors. Punishment is something that, when applied, decreases certain behaviors. Punishment decreases the chance a behavior will occur again. Unfortunately, punishment does not have a direct connection with the behavior we are trying to discourage. For example, if we want a student to stop hitting other children and we take away his free time, free time has nothing to do with hitting other children.

Extinction can also be used. Extinction is the removal of rewards that encourage or keep a behavior going. For example, if we laugh at the class clown when she does something for attention, this is usually rewarding or reinforcing; but if we ignore the class clown, we are using extinction. We are removing the reward (laughing) that keeps the clown going.

Skinner (1974) defined and explained this. The focus is on the control of behavior by an outside force such as the teacher. If we want students to be compliant, then we will use rewards and punishment. However, many educators believe this supports heteronomy. Children are being governed by others and there is no movement toward being governed by one's self.

Problems with Rewards

In the book *Punished by Rewards*, Alfie Kohn (1993) suggests five reasons rewards are harmful to children. These include (a) "rewards punish" (p. 50), (b) rewards negatively influence relationships, (c) rewards do not consider reasons, (d) rewards discourage "appropriate risk taking" (p. 62), and (e) rewards may make children less interested in what they naturally enjoy.

"Rewards punish" (Kohn, 1993, p. 50). How can rewards possibly punish children, especially when they are designed to do the opposite? For example, for spelling, some teachers give children a star for a perfect spelling paper. One child in the class has a learning disability, another has ADHD, and yet another is a child with mental retardation. These students are punished because of their abilities. Furthermore, rewards are like punishment in that both are used to manipulate people into doing what we want them to do.

Rewards negatively influence relationships. Rewards often foster competition and thus damage or destroy cooperative relationships. If only one person can win in a game, every other child is seen as someone to beat. Is this the message we want to send to children?

Rewards do not consider reasons children do things. If a child is constantly fighting, parents and teachers might give rewards or administer punishment to change the child's behavior. The problem with this is that rewards and punishment do not consider *why* the child is constantly fighting. When we give rewards, we are not addressing the real issue—why children do the things they do.

"Rewards do not encourage appropiate risk taking" (Kohn, 1993, p. 62). The key word here is *appropriate*. What, exactly, is appropriate risk taking? When a child is working for a reward, he may do only what is necessary to get the reward. He won't do any more. For instance, children in some schools are rewarded for reading certain books. However, the student might be interested in harder books or attempt to read more challenging books if rewards are not given. Some children will say, "I will only read a book from the list in which I get rewarded." The focus is on the reward and not the challenge of reading and taking risks with more difficult literature. Children are naturally interested in learning, but if we give rewards, we may be discouraging them from digging deeper for fear they might miss a reward. Rewards work, and they work fast; but in the long term, they may do more harm than good.

Rewards may make children less interested in activities they naturally enjoy. For those children who naturally like to draw or paint, rewards for drawing or painting are discouraging. In an informal study of children and rewards, children (who generally like to play with blocks) were shown two sets of identical blocks in their preschool classroom. The teacher told the children that if they played with one set of blocks they would receive a reward. However, they could play with the other set of blocks, but they would not receive any rewards. What happened? Children immediately flocked to play with the blocks for which they would receive rewards. However, after a couple of weeks, the teacher said,

"You can now play with either set of blocks, but you will not receive any rewards." Then what happened? The children rarely ever played with the blocks for which they had earlier received rewards. They most often went to play with the other set of blocks. When we reward students for things they naturally like to do, we are sending a message: "This is not fun. You must be rewarded for doing this" (Kohn, 1993).

The bottom line is rewards and punishment encourage heteronomy. They encourage students to be dependent on others for rewards. *Is that what we want from students?* Then giving rewards and dishing out punishment is how to get it.

AUTONOMY

Another way of dealing with discipline is more concerned with children's thinking about their actions than simply behaving in appropriate ways. The focus is to get children to think about their actions. Sanctions are used instead of reward or punishment (Piaget, 1932). Sanctions are designed to help children think about their actions so they will act in moral ways. Piaget (1932) recommended six sanctions by reciprocity. Here we discuss four of the most practical sanctions. They include (a) temporary exclusion from the group, (b) calling the child's attention to the consequences of his actions, (c) depriving the student of whatever he has misused, and (d) perhaps the most important—restitution. Restitution means a child must make good that which he has harmed.

Temporary exclusion from the group is not the same thing as a time-out. If a student does something inappropriate during a class meeting, the child is sent to a time-out for five minutes. The adult says, "Go to time-out and don't come back for five minutes." Temporary exclusion from the group is different. A child is asked to leave the group until he can participate and follow the rules of the group. The child makes the decision when he is able and ready to come back and participate. Of course, this will not work with some students. For example, introverts may be pleased to leave the group and choose never to come back. However, children who really enjoy being a part of and participating in the group will be more influenced by temporary exclusion.

Calling a student's attention to the consequences of his actions is another sanction. A child who is breaking crayons can be told, "When you break all the crayons, we will not have any more to use." Of course, anyone who has worked with children will know that some children will defiantly say, "I don't care." In these cases, the third sanction might work.

Depriving the student of whatever he has abused or misused is a sanction a teacher can apply in this instance. When a child is destroying property, a natural consequence is that the child cannot use it. As with all sanctions, the consequences are directly related to the student's actions.

Restitution is perhaps the most important sanction we can use. Restitution means "making good that which you have harmed." Whether a student intentionally commits a transgression or accidentally hurts someone or damages something, restitution can be a powerful tool to help students think about their actions and the consequences of such actions.

Here is a true story about how restitution can be effective. A sixth grader once accidentally spilled blue ink on the white blouse of the girl sitting in front of him. The teacher decided to use restitution. How can the boy make good that which he has damaged? The girl couldn't take off her blouse in class. The teacher thought about it and said to the boy, "I know you didn't mean to spill ink on her blouse, but you must make it right. I've asked the girl to bring her blouse to school tomorrow. It is your job to try to get the ink out. Your mother or father can make suggestions, but it is your job to fix it. I'll call your parents and explain the situation."

The next day the ink-stained white blouse was brought back to school. The boy took it home. His mother showed him how to use bleach and lemon juice, but she left him to make decisions about how to clean the garment. After three tries, the ink came out. The next day the boy brought the blouse back to school, after he had cleaned, dried, and pressed it. This was a powerful lesson.

Sometimes restitution is not possible. For instance, if one child pushes another one and breaks his arm, how can the child make restitution? The child is not a physician. Even so, there are ways the child can make restitution. For example, the child can be responsible for carrying books for the child with the broken arm. She can run errands for the child with the broken limb, such as getting assignments from school. Although exact restitution may not always be possible, the important thing to remember is that if we make a mistake, we must do what we can to correct it.

Having children come up with their own solutions for restitution is often helpful. This is also helpful for disputes. When children have an argument, the most likely solution is to tattle. Adults can discourage this by telling children to work to solve their own disputes and then come back and tell you what they decided and how they solved the problem.

The bottom line is that sanctions by reciprocity encourage autonomy. *Is that what we want from students?* If so, then using sanctions is how we encourage it.

QUESTIONS

1. What do you like about giving rewards?

2. What do you not like about giving rewards?

3. What do children learn when we give them rewards?

4. When should you give rewards?

5. For what should rewards be given?

6. What do you believe about restitution?

7. Can you think of specific examples when restitution worked?

8. Can rewards and punishment be used as well as restitution? If so, how?

9. What messages do rewards send to a student?

10. What message does restitution send to a student?

11. The bottom line is . . . *what do we want from students and how do we get it?*

REFERENCES

Aldridge, J. (2001). *Understanding today's children: Developing tomorrow's leaders today.* Nashville, TN: LifeWay Press.

Boynton, M., & Boynton, C. (2005). *The educator's guide to preventing and solving discipline problems.* Alexandria, VA: Association for Supervision and Curriculum Development.

Kohn, A. (1993). *Punished by rewards: The trouble with gold stars, incentive plans, A's, praise, and other bribes.* Boston: Houghton Mifflin.

Piaget, J. (1932). *The moral judgment of the child.* London: Routledge & Kegan Paul.

Skinner, B. (1974). *On behaviorism.* New York: Knopf.

■ ■ ■ ■ ■

WHAT'S NEXT? FUTURE ISSUES
AND TRENDS IN EDUCATION

When we completed the first edition of *Current Issues and Trends in Education* September 11th was just a month away and No Child Left Behind was on the horizon. Both of these affected the issues and trends we now face in the first decade of the 21st century. As we look toward a possible third edition, we wonder what problems and possibilities, consensus and controversies, and challenges and confrontations we will face.

Even today there are many issues and trends that we were not able to address in the limited pages of one book. The purpose of this epilogue is twofold. First, we want to name a few of the salient topics that we did not address but that are just as important as many of the ones we did. Second, we ponder and speculate what is next in terms of future issues and trends in education.

OTHER CURRENT ISSUES AND TRENDS

As we list some of the other problems and challenges of education, we hope that you will think of others to add to this list. Certainly, types of schooling beyond public education are controversial. Private schools, charter schools, home schooling, and separate-gender classes are worthy of discussion. The whole issues of traditional scheduling versus block scheduling figures into the types of schools and classes that are currently debated. Although there were some research and numerous articles on the pros and cons of homogeneous versus heterogeneous grouping of students during the 1970s and '80s, this debate is emerging again as the push for higher standards increases.

Teacher pay as it relates to student performance is also receiving a lot of attention, as well as the benefits and pitfalls of technology and Web-based learning. Of course the reading wars, although some suggest they have played out, are far from over. And surely the problems of grading, as well as rewards and punishment, continue to plague us.

These are but a few additional issues and trends that are worthy of more research, heated debates, and intense discussions today. What are other problems and possibilities you face? What topics are worthy of more discussion in today's educational arena?

WHAT'S NEXT?

Just as we could not have predicted September 11th or the profound impact No Child Left Behind would have on our current situation, there are several issues and trends we will not be able to predict. However, there are a few for which we believe we do not need a crystal ball.

At no time in our lengthy teaching careers have we seen such a teacher shortage as we have now. We predict this shortage will increase to the point that it becomes a crisis. Many school systems began the school year with hundreds and some thousands of uncertified teachers—not to mention "highly qualified." Until professionalism is restored to the teaching profession, fewer and fewer people will go in to education.

Federal government involvement in public education will also create more and more heated disagreements about what should and should not be the role of government in schools. This will surely happen as 2014 approaches and all students are expected to be on grade level by then. We are anxious to see how this drama plays out.

Very few resources on issues and trends address the topic of dispositions of students or teachers. However, dispositions were added in the not too distant past to accreditation standards, and some educators believe there is already a crisis in this area. We predict more discussions of attitudes and dispositions will take place.

Controversies related to technology are increasing, and by the third edition of this book, we believe we will need to devote an entire section to the many issues surrounding it. Differences in access to information alone would take several volumes to give this problem or possibility justice.

Finally, we believe the bigger questions regarding education must come to the forefront. Although we debate types of schools, federal involvement, dispositions, and technology, we acknowledge that these are just symptoms of the real controversies in education. We hope that the future will bring a return to the big questions, such as

1. What is the purpose of education?
2. What does it mean to be well educated?
3. How do students learn?
4. What is most worth knowing?
5. How should we teach?

These are the issues that are universal and timeless. They have transcended modernism, postmodernism, and now they will continue into our discussions of a modern world in which education can be analyzed and deconstructed in multiple ways.

QUESTIONS

1. Which of the five big questions listed previously do you believe is the most important? Why?

2. Can we ever achieve at least some level of consensus regarding these five questions?

3. What issues and trends do you believe are most current today?

4. What issues and trends do you predict will emerge or increase during the next decade? Why?

INDEX